COMPLETE

PRELIMINARY

Teacher's Book

Second edition

Rod Fricker

For the revised exam from 2020

Cambridge University Press
www.cambridge.org/elt

Cambridge Assessment English
www.cambridgeenglish.org

Information on this title: www.cambridge.org/9781108399586

First published 2010
Second edition 2019

20 19 18 17 16 15 14 13 12 11 10 9 8 7 6 5 4 3 2

Printed in Mexico by Editorial Impresora Apolo, S.A. de C.V.

A catalogue record for this publication is available from the British Library

ISBN 978-1-108-39958-6 Teacher's Book with Downloadable Resource Pack

Contents

DEAR TEACHERS

I'm delighted that you've chosen our official preparation materials to prepare for a Cambridge English Qualification.

We take great pride in the fact that our materials draw on the expertise of a whole team of writers, teachers, assessors and exam experts. These are materials that you can really trust.

Our preparation materials are unique in many ways:

- They combine the skills and knowledge of the teams at Cambridge Assessment English, who create the tests, and the teams at Cambridge University Press, who create the English Language Teaching materials.
- They draw upon the experience of millions of previous exam candidates – where they succeed and where they have difficulties. We target exercises and activities precisely at these areas so that you can actively 'learn' from previous test takers' mistakes.
- Every single task in our materials has been carefully checked to be an accurate reflection of what test takers find in the test.

In addition, we listen to what you tell us at every stage of the development process. This allows us to design the most user-friendly courses, practice tests and supplementary training. We create materials using in-depth knowledge, research and practical understanding. Prepare for Cambridge English Qualifications with confidence in the knowledge that you have the best materials available to support you on your way to success.

We wish you the very best on your journey with us.

With kind regards,

Pamela Baxter
Director
Cambridge Exams Publishing

PS. If you have any feedback at all on our support materials for exams, please write to us at cambridgeexams@cambridge.org

The Complete Exam Journey

The unique exam journey in *Complete Preliminary* allows learners to build their confidence and develop their skills as they progress through each unit, ensuring they are ready on exam day. Along the journey there are …

Full reading, listening, writing and speaking exam tasks in every unit, with step-by-step preparation exercises to ensure students have the skills necessary to understand and do the exam task.

Exam advice boxes with up-to-date tips which are placed before every exam task in every unit, so students can apply the tips as they do the task.

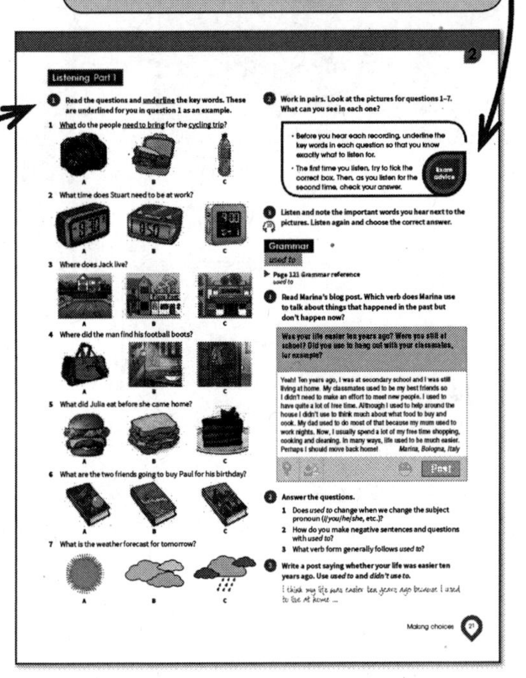

Listening Part 1

1 Read the questions and underline the key words. These are underlined for you in question 1 as an example.

1 What do the people need to bring for the cycling trip?

2 What time does Stuart need to be at work?

3 Where does Jack live?

4 Where did the man find his football boots?

5 What did Julia eat before she came home?

6 What are the two friends going to buy Paul for his birthday?

7 What is the weather forecast for tomorrow?

2 Work in pairs. Look at the pictures for questions 1–7. What can you see in each one?

Exam advice

- Before you hear each recording, underline the key words in each question so that you know exactly what to listen for.
- The first time you listen, try to tick the correct box. Then, as you listen for the second time, check your answer.

3 Listen and note the important words you hear next to the pictures. Listen again and choose the correct answer.

Grammar *used to*

Page 121 Grammar reference *used to*

4 Read Marina's blog post. Which verb does Marina use to talk about things that happened in the past but don't happen now?

Was your life easier ten years ago? Were you still at school? Did you use to hang out with your classmates, for example?

5 Answer the questions.

1 Does *used to* change when we change the subject pronoun (*I/you/he/she*, etc.)?

2 How do you make negative sentences and questions with *used to*?

3 What verb form generally follows *used to*?

6 Write a post saying whether your life was easier ten years ago. Use *used to* and *didn't use to*.

Making choices 21

Opportunities to fine-tune and practise each exam task, confident in the knowledge that the materials are checked by the same team who writes the exams.

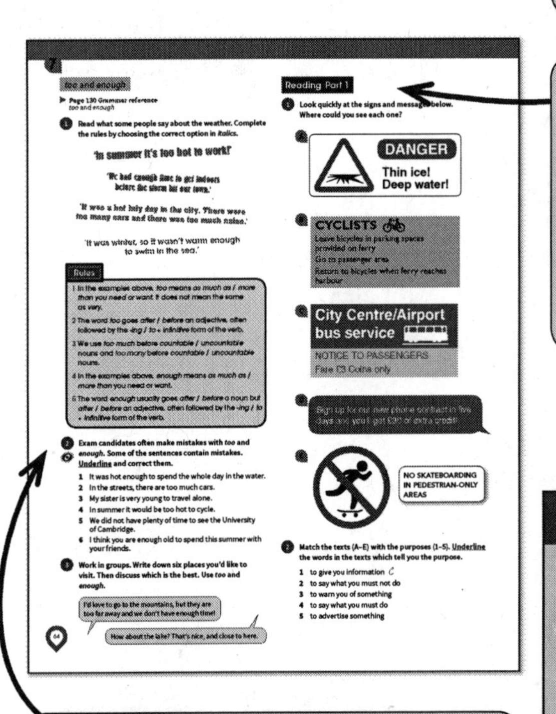

too and *enough*

Page 130 Grammar reference *too* and *enough*

1 Read what some people say about the weather. Complete the rules by choosing the correct option in *italics*.

'In summer it's too hot to work!'

'We had enough time to get indoors before the storm hit our town.'

'It was a hot holy day in the city. There were too many cars and there was too much noise.'

'It was winter, so it wasn't warm enough to swim in the sea.'

Rules

2 Exam candidates often make mistakes with *too* and *enough*. Some of the sentences contain mistakes. Underline and correct them.

1 It was hot enough to spend the whole day in the water.

2 In the streets, there are too much cars.

3 My sister is very young to travel alone.

4 In summer it would be too hot to cycle.

5 We did not have plenty of time to see the University of Cambridge.

6 I think you are enough old to spend this summer with your friends.

3 Work in groups. Write down six places you'd like to visit. Then discuss which is the best. Use *too* and *enough*.

Reading Part 1

1 Look quickly at the signs and messages below. Where could you see each one?

2 Match the texts (A–E) with the purposes (1–5). Underline the words in the texts which tell you the purpose.

1 to give you information

2 to say what you must not do

3 to warn you of something

4 to say what you must do

5 to advertise something

Exercises targeting common B1 Preliminary problem areas, using data from the Cambridge Learner Corpus, so students can overcome language areas of difficulty in time for the exam.

Speaking bank

SPEAKING PART 1

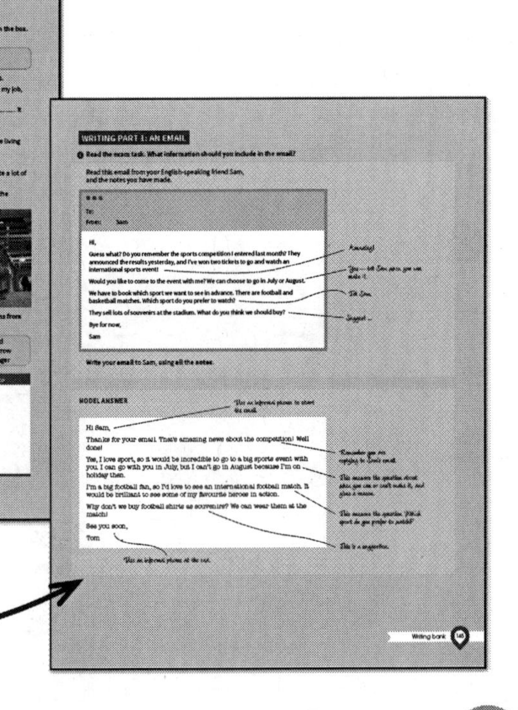

WRITING PART 1: AN EMAIL

1 Read the exam task. What information should you include in the email?

MODEL ANSWER

Writing bank

Extra practice sections for speaking and writing exam tasks at the back of the book, with preparation exercises and model exam tasks for students to follow.

Student's Book overview

Eye-catching images in the *Starting off* section at the beginning of each unit get students interested in the unit topic.

All *Preliminary* full listening, reading, speaking and writing exam tasks have relevant and engaging topics.

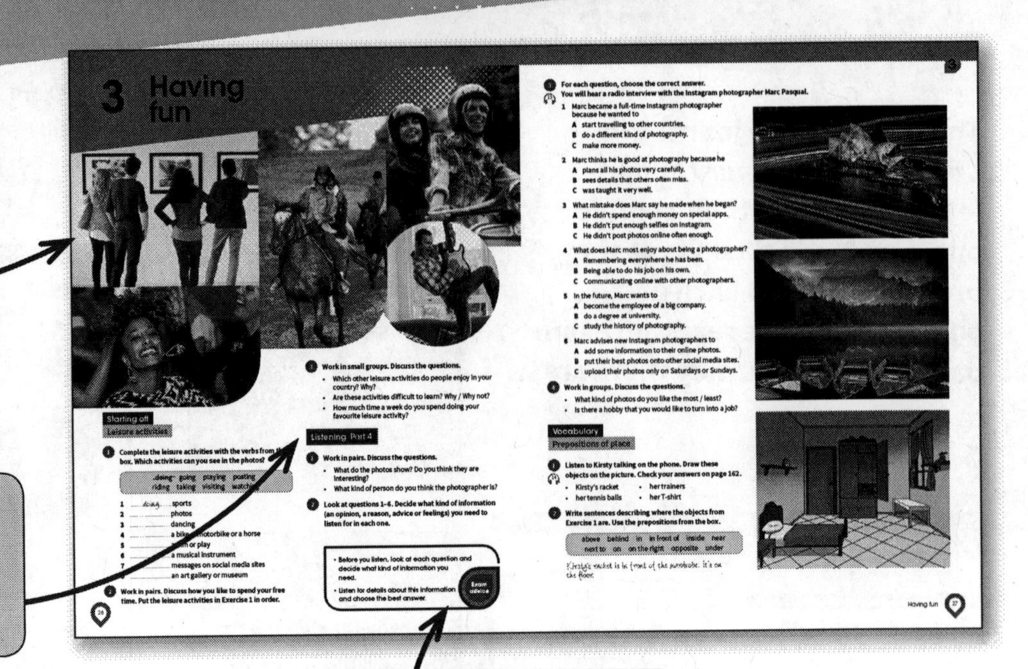

3 Having fun

Starting off
Leisure activities

1 Complete the leisure activities with the verbs from the box. Which activities can you see in the photos?

doing going playing posting riding taking visiting watching

1 ...doing... sports
2 .... photos
3 .... dancing
4 .... a bike / motorbike or a horse
5 .... TV, film or play
6 .... a musical instrument
7 .... messages on social media sites
8 .... an art gallery or museum

2 Work in pairs. Discuss how you like to spend your free time. Put the leisure activities in Exercise 1 in order.

3 Work in small groups. Discuss the questions.
- Which other leisure activities do people enjoy in your country? Why?
- Are these activities difficult to learn? Why / Why not?
- How much time a week do you spend doing your favourite leisure activity?

Listening Part 4

1 Work in pairs. Discuss the questions.
- What do the photos show? Do you think they are interesting?
- What kind of person do you think the photographer is?

2 Look at questions 1–6. Decide what kind of information (an opinion, a reason, advice or feelings) you need to listen for in each one.

- Before you listen, look at each question and decide what kind of information you need.
- Listen for details about this information and choose the best answer.

Exam advice

3 For each question, choose the correct answer.
You will hear a radio interview with the Instagram photographer Marc Pasqual.

1 Marc became a full-time Instagram photographer because he wanted to
A start travelling to other countries.
B do a different kind of photography.
C make more money.

2 Marc thinks he is good at photography because he
A plans all his photos very carefully.
B sees details that others often miss.
C was taught it very well.

3 What mistake does Marc say he made when he began?
A He didn't spend enough money on special apps.
B He didn't put enough selfies on Instagram.
C He didn't post photos online often enough.

4 What does Marc most enjoy about being a photographer?
A Remembering everywhere he has been.
B Being able to do his job on his own.
C Communicating online with other photographers.

5 In the future, Marc wants to
A become the employee of a big company.
B do a degree at university.
C study the history of photography.

6 Marc advises new Instagram photographers to
A add some information to their online photos.
B put their best photos onto other social media sites.
C upload their photos only on Saturdays or Sundays.

4 Work in groups. Discuss the questions.
- What kind of photos do you like the most / least?
- Is there a hobby that you would like to turn into a job?

Vocabulary
Prepositions of place

1 Listen to Kirsty talking on the phone. Draw these objects on the picture. Check your answers on page 162.
- Kirsty's racket
- her tennis balls
- her trainers
- her T-shirt

2 Write sentences describing where the objects from Exercise 1 are. Use the prepositions from the box.

above behind in in front of inside near next to on on the right opposite under

Kirsty's racket is in front of the wardrobe. It's on the floor.

26 Having fun 27

Brightly designed *Exam advice* boxes precede all exam tasks in every unit.

Common mistakes made by students identified and practised in grammar sections.

Relevant pronunciation points clearly link to input language.

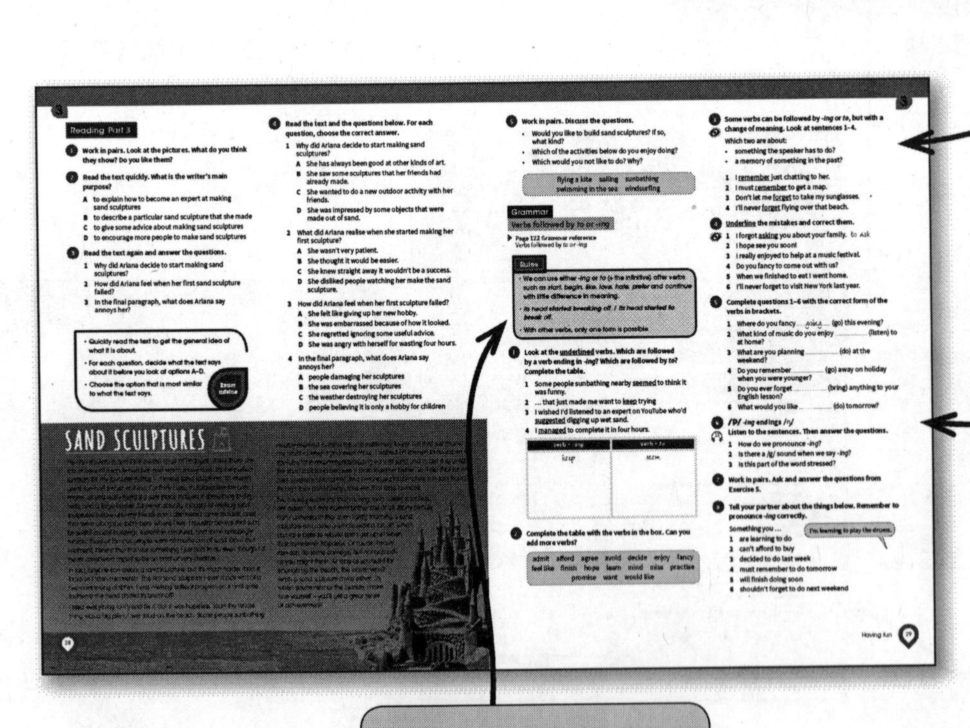

Reading Part 3

1 Work in pairs. Look at the pictures. What do you think they show? Do you like them?

2 Read the text quickly. What is the writer's main purpose?
A to explain how to become an expert at making sand sculptures
B to describe a particular sand sculpture that she made
C to give some advice about making sand sculptures
D to encourage more people to make sand sculptures

3 Read the text again and answer the questions.
1 Why did Ariana decide to start making sand sculptures?
2 How did Ariana feel when her first sand sculpture failed?
3 In the final paragraph, what does Ariana say annoys her?

- Quickly read the text to get the general idea of what it is about.
- For each question, decide what the text says about it before you look at options A–D.
- Choose the option that is most similar to what the text says.

Exam advice

SAND SCULPTURES

4 Read the text and the questions below. For each question, choose the correct answer.
1 Why did Ariana decide to start making sand sculptures?
A She has always been good at other kinds of art.
B She saw some sculptures that her friends had already made.
C She wanted to do a new outdoor activity with her friends.
D She was impressed by some objects that were made out of sand.
2 What did Ariana realise when she started making her first sculpture?
A She wasn't very patient.
B She thought it would be easier.
C She knew straight away it wouldn't be a success.
D She disliked people watching her make the sand sculpture.
3 How did Ariana feel when her first sculpture failed?
A She felt like giving up her new hobby.
B She was embarrassed because of how it looked.
C She regretted ignoring some useful advice.
D She was angry with herself for wasting four hours.
4 In the final paragraph, what does Ariana say annoys her?
A people damaging her sculptures
B the sea covering her sculptures
C the weather destroying her sculptures
D people believing it is only a hobby for children

5 Work in pairs. Discuss the questions.
- Would you like to build sand sculptures? If so, what kind?
- Which of the activities below do you enjoy doing?
- Which would you not like to do? Why?

flying a kite sailing sunbathing swimming in the sea windsurfing

Grammar
Verbs followed by to or -ing

Rules

- With other verbs, only one form is possible.

1 Look at the underlined verbs. Which are followed by a verb ending in -ing? Which are followed by to? Complete the table.
1 Some people sunbathing nearby seemed to think it was funny.
2 ... that just made me want to keep trying.
3 I wished I'd listened to an expert on YouTube who'd suggested digging up wet sand.
4 I managed to complete it in four hours.

verb + -ing	verb + to
keep	seem

2 Complete the table with the verbs in the box. Can you add more verbs?

admit afford agree avoid decide enjoy fancy feel like finish hope learn mind miss practise promise want would like

3 Some verbs can be followed by -ing or to, but with a change of meaning. Look at sentences 1–4. Which two are about:
- something the speaker has to do?
- a memory of something in the past?

1 I remember just chatting to her.
2 I must remember to get a map.
3 Don't let me forget to take my sunglasses.
4 I'll never forget flying over that beach.

4 Underline the mistakes and correct them.
1 I forgot asking you about your family. to ask
2 I hope see you soon!
3 I really enjoyed to help at a music festival.
4 Do you fancy to come out with us?
5 When we finished to eat I went home.
6 I'll never forget to visit New York last year.

5 Complete questions 1–6 with the correct form of the verbs in brackets.
1 Where do you fancy ...going... (go) this evening?
2 What kind of music do you enjoy .... (listen) to at home?
3 What are you planning .... (do) at the weekend?
4 Do you remember .... (go) away on holiday when you were younger?
5 Do you ever forget .... (bring) anything to your English lesson?
6 What would you like .... (do) tomorrow?

6 /ŋ/ -ing endings /ŋ/
Listen to the sentences. Then answer the questions.
1 How do we pronounce -ing?
2 Is there a /g/ sound when we say -ing?
3 Is this part of the word stressed?

7 Work in pairs. Ask and answer the questions from Exercise 5.

8 Tell your partner about the things below. Remember to pronounce -ing correctly.
Something you ...
1 are learning to do
2 can't afford to buy
3 decided to do last week
4 must remember to do tomorrow
5 will finish doing soon
6 shouldn't forget to do next weekend

I'm learning to play the drums.

28 Having fun 29

Clearly flagged, brightly designed grammar rules boxes explain the key grammar points.

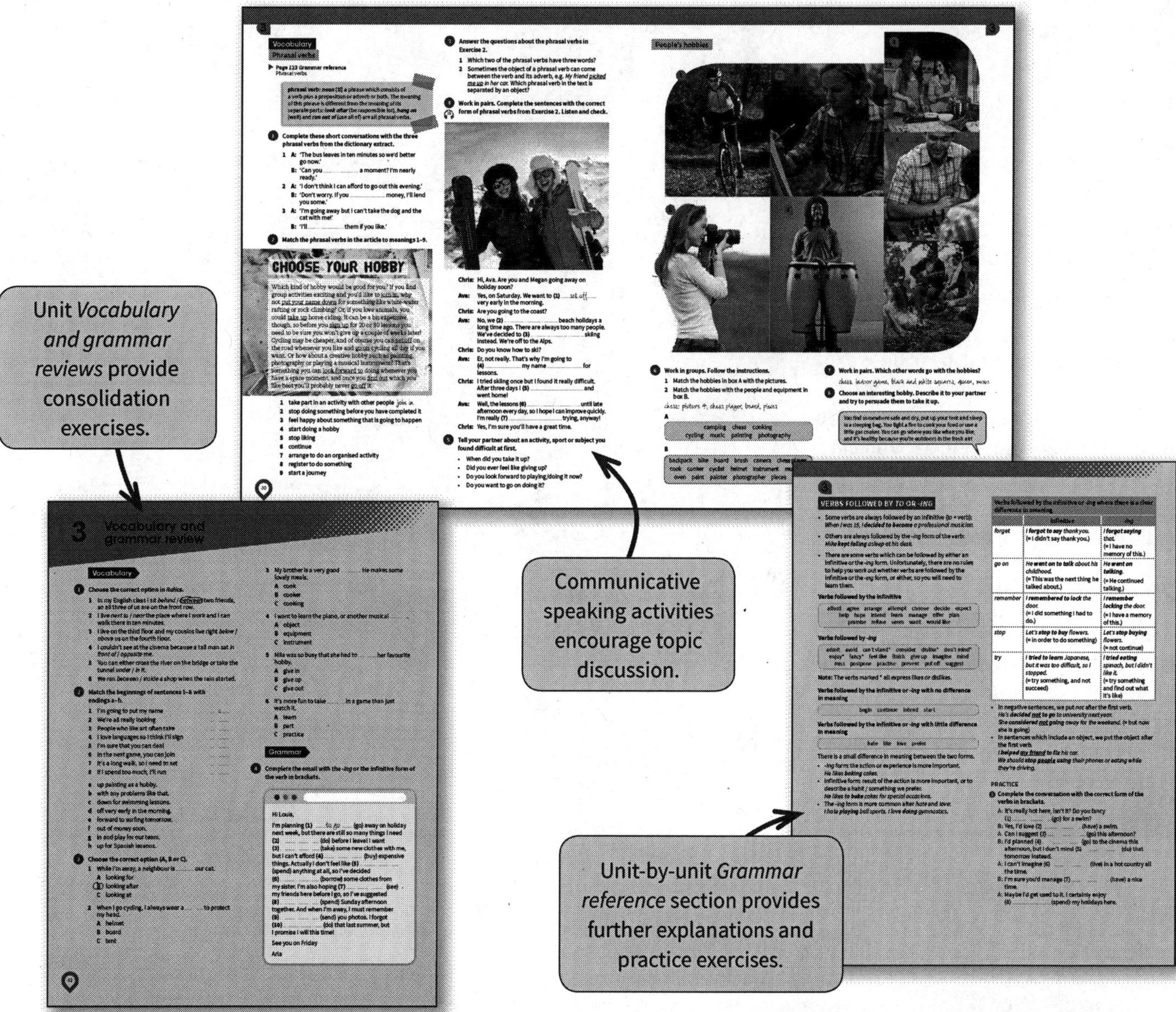

Unit *Vocabulary and grammar reviews* provide consolidation exercises.

Communicative speaking activities encourage topic discussion.

Unit-by-unit *Grammar reference* section provides further explanations and practice exercises.

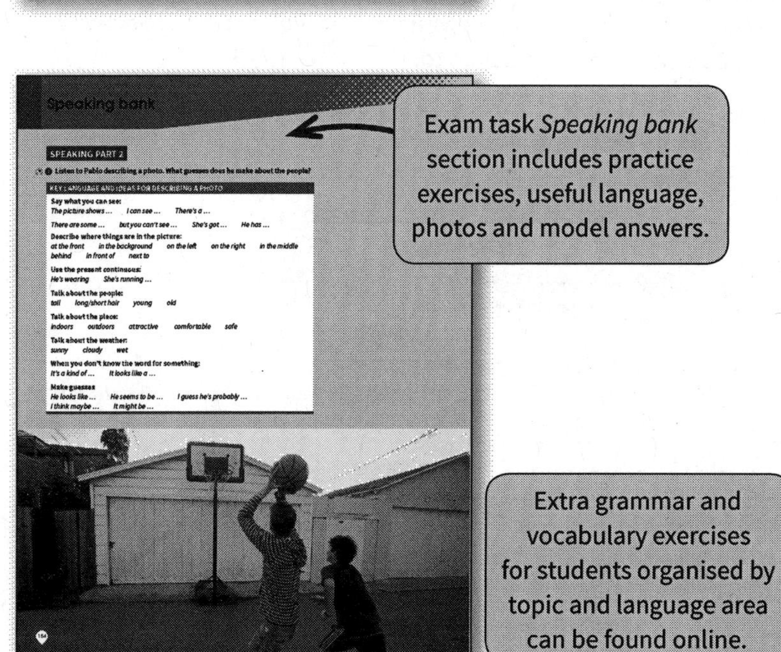

Exam task *Speaking bank* section includes practice exercises, useful language, photos and model answers.

Extra grammar and vocabulary exercises for students organised by topic and language area can be found online.

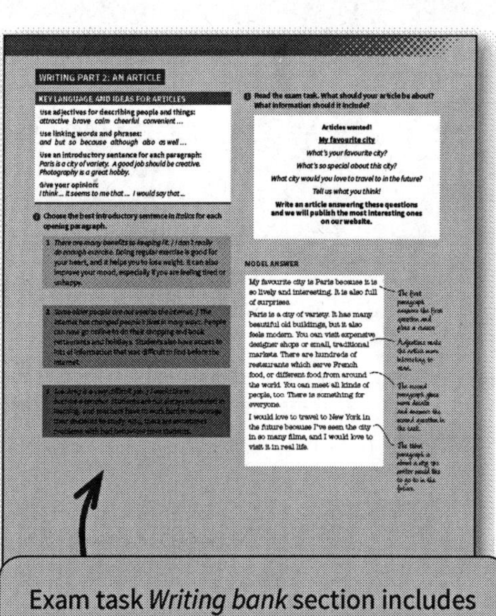

Exam task *Writing bank* section includes useful language, practice exercises and model exam answers.

Component line-up

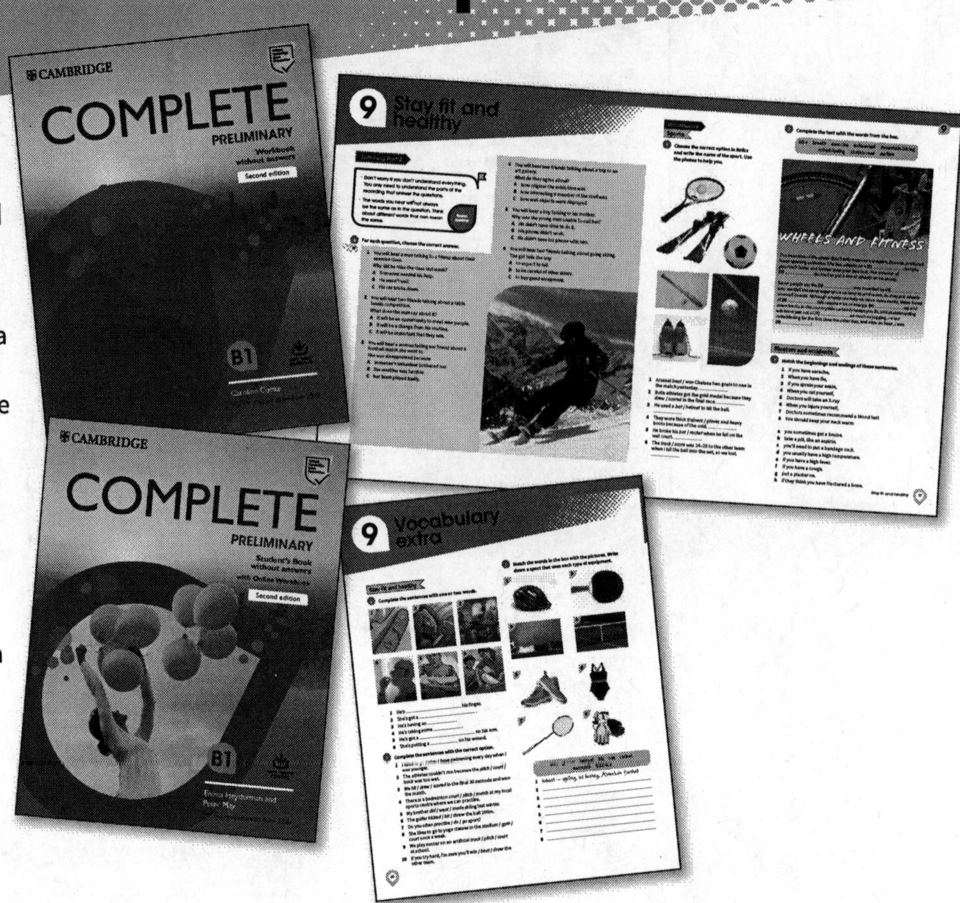

Workbook with and without answers with Audio Download

The activities in the Workbook consolidate the language presented in the Student's Book. It also includes extra exam practice with exam advice boxes. 12 pages of Vocabulary Extra consolidate topic vocabulary taught in each unit in the Student's Book.
Students can access and download the audio files using the code in the book.

Online Workbook

The Online Workbook is a digital version of the print Workbook and allows you to track your students' progress, highlighting areas of strength and weakness for ongoing performance improvement.

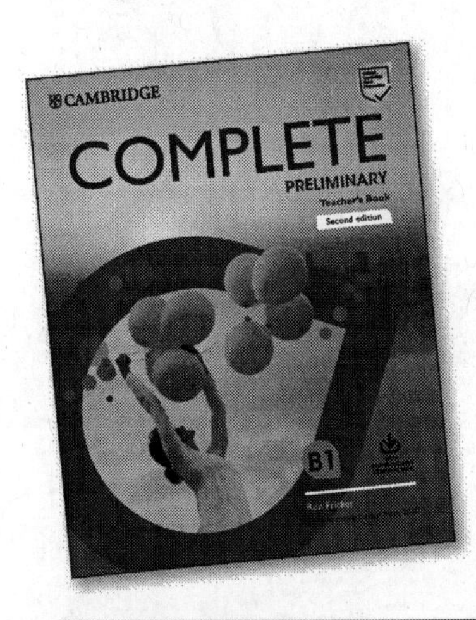

Teacher's Book with Downloadable Resource Pack

The Teacher's Book includes step-by-step activities for each stage of the lesson, with answer keys, background information, extra activities and photocopiable audioscripts. It also includes unit target vocabulary word lists with two vocabulary practice activities per unit. The Teacher's Book also provides access to:

- **The Class Audio**
- **Extra teacher photocopiable resources**
- **Speaking videos**

Test Generators

The test generator allows you to build your own tests for each unit, term and end-of-year assessment. They are available at two levels: standard and plus.

Presentation Plus

Presentation Plus is easy-to-use, interactive classroom presentation software that helps you deliver effective and engaging lessons. It includes the Student's Book and Workbook content and allows you to present and annotate content and link to the online resources.

B1 Preliminary content and overview

Part/Timing	Content	Exam focus
1 **Reading** 45 minutes	**Part 1** Five very short texts: signs and messages, postcards, notes, emails, labels, etc. followed by five three-option multiple-choice questions. **Part 2** Five descriptions of people to match to eight short texts. **Part 3** Longer text with five four-option multiple-choice questions. **Part 4** Gapped text where five sentences have been removed. Candidates must select the five correct sentences from a list of eight. **Part 5** Four-option multiple-choice cloze text with six gaps. Candidates select the word which best fits each gap. **Part 6** An open cloze text consisting of a text with six gaps. Candidates think of a word which best suits each gap.	**Parts 1–4** and **Part 6:** Candidates are expected to read for the main message, global meaning, specific information, detailed comprehension, understanding of attitude, opinion and writer purpose and inference. **Part 5:** Candidates are expected to show understanding of vocabulary and grammar in a short text, and the lexico-structural patterns in the text.
2 **Writing** 45 minutes	**Part 1** An informal email. Candidates write an email of about 100 words in response to a text. **Part 2** An article or story. There is a choice of two questions. Candidates are provided with a clear context and topic. Candidates write about 100 words.	Candidates are mainly assessed on their ability to use and control a range of Preliminary-level language. Coherent organisation, spelling and punctuation are also assessed.
3 **Listening** approximately 30 minutes	**Part 1** Short monologues or dialogues with seven three-option multiple-choice questions with pictures. **Part 2** Six short unrelated dialogues with six three-option multiple-choice questions. **Part 3** Longer monologue. Candidates complete six sentences with information from the recording. **Part 4** Longer interview. Six three-option multiple-choice questions.	Candidates are expected to identify the attitudes and opinions of speakers, and listen to identify gist, key information, specific information and detailed meaning, and to identify, understand and interpret meaning.
4 **Speaking** 12 minutes	**Part 1** A short conversation with the interlocutor. The interlocutor asks the candidates questions in turn, using standardised questions. **Part 2** An individual long turn for each candidate. A colour photograph is given to each candidate in turn and they talk about it for about a minute. Each photo has a different topic. **Part 3** A two-way conversation between candidates (visual stimulus with spoken instructions). The interlocutor sets up the activity. **Part 4** A discussion on topics related to the collaborative task in Part 3. The interlocutor asks the candidates the questions.	Candidates are expected to be able to ask and understand questions and make appropriate responses, and to talk freely on topics of personal interest.

1 My life and home

Unit objectives

Topic: My life and home

Listening Part 2: multiple-choice short dialogues: listening for facts, opinions or feelings

Reading Part 5: multiple-choice cloze: understanding vocabulary

Speaking Part 1: saying your name, where you live ,what you do, and if you like studying English

Writing Part 1: an email; planning a reply

Grammar: prepositions of time; frequency adverbs; present simple and present continuous; state verbs; *a few, a bit of, many, much, a lot of* and *lots of*; prepositions of place

Vocabulary: house and home; countable and uncountable nouns

Pronunciation: -s endings /s/, /z/ and /ɪz/

Starting off SB page 8

Lead-in
Before students open their books, ask them to think of one room in their home: Ask: *What's the room like?* Ask students to write three adjectives, e.g. *bright, small, untidy,* and three objects in that room, e.g. *bed, desk, plants* about their bedrooms. Students then work in pairs and talk for two minutes about their room.

1 Look at the photos with the students. Elicit the rooms and items the students can see and pre-check any unknown vocabulary in the photos, e.g. *armchair, mirror.* Elicit ideas from different pairs after they have discussed the questions in the book.

Answers:
(top left to bottom right) kitchen, sitting room/living room, balcony, bathroom

Listening Part 2 SB page 8

1 Set a time limit of one minute for each topic. Monitor and help with ideas for prompts.

Listening Part 2 (multiple-choice)
Read the advice with the students and also remind them that they will always hear the recording twice and should listen carefully the second time to check their answers.

2 As this is an exam task, set a time limit of 45 seconds for students to look at the questions and identify the key words, and tell them that this is how long they will have in the exam. Elicit that, as well as the information asked for in the questions, the key words which help them to find the answers are *agree, feel, like best, agree, think about, small shop, better if.* Encourage students to underline these words.

Answers
2 a man talking to his friend, changing jobs
3 a woman talking about a trip to the beach
4 two friends, the town where they live
5 two friends, comparing shops
6 two friends, their homes

3 When students have listened once, allow them to compare their answers and reasons in pairs. Tell them not to change their answers until they have listened a second time and then decide who was right.
After the second listening, ask students if they changed any of their answers. Elicit the answers and information from the text which helped them to identify the correct answers.

Answers
1 C **2** B **3** C **4** A **5** B **6** C

Track 2

Narrator: Part 2. For each question, choose the correct answer.

1

Narrator: You will hear two friends talking about the kind of flat they would like to live in.

Man: Wouldn't it be great to live right at the top of that block of flats, with views across the city?

Woman: Nice views are fine but I'm not very keen on lifts. I think I'd rather be on the ground floor. It'd be good to live in a building that's not far from a bus stop, too.

Man: Or an underground station.

Woman: Right. But the most important thing for me would be to have my own room, so it'd have to be a three-bedroom apartment.

Man: I don't mind sharing, so two would be enough for me.

2

Narrator: You will hear a man telling his friend about changing job.

Woman: I haven't seen you for a long time. How do you feel now about your new job?

Man: Well, before I moved at the beginning of January, I thought it'd be difficult to make friends with people in my new office but they've given me a really warm welcome. Of course I'm a bit sad that I don't see anyone from my previous company, but there's nothing I can do about that. My work seem to be going better than I'd expected, too, so making the change hasn't been too hard, really.

3

Narrator: You will hear a woman talking about a trip to the beach.

Man: How was your day out?

Woman: Great! The bus left early on Saturday so I had to get up at 5 a.m. but that meant we got to the beach really early.

Man: Did you go for a swim?

Woman: Yes, I thought I would enjoy that but it was a bit cold so we hired a little boat instead and sailed round the bay. That was fun, too, but not as much as having a game of volleyball. We're going there again in July when it'll be too hot for beach sports, but swimming in the sea will be wonderful!

4

Narrator: You will hear two friends talking about the town where they live.

Woman: It's quite a good place to live, isn't it? Although it would be nice if more people lived here.

Man: Well, it might be livelier, but I think the size is about right, actually. In bigger places there are problems like street crime, especially at night, but here you feel safe anywhere, really.

Woman: That's true, although everywhere you go, the roads are really busy, and it's the same here. All that noise and pollution is horrible early in the morning.

Man: I know. I wish people would walk or go by bike instead.

5

Narrator: You will hear a man talking to a friend about shops.

Woman: I don't really know this part of town. Where's the best place to do a bit of shopping?

Man: The little shop on the corner isn't bad. The range of things there is a bit limited but just about everything is amazingly good value, especially if you compare it to the local supermarket.

Woman: The one opposite the station?

Man: Yes, you can find almost anything you want there but it always seems to be really crowded, with lots of people waiting to pay because it's short of staff.

Woman: Thanks – I'll definitely avoid that one.

6

Narrator: You will hear two friends talking about their homes.

Man: I like my room, though I haven't got much space for my things.

Woman: Mine's about the right size really, but I know what you mean. My cupboards and shelves are far too small.

Man: At least mine's got big windows, so I get plenty of sunshine.

Woman: I do too, though it's a pity I can't turn the central heating up in winter.

Man: Does it get noisy? It can do at my place, especially in the morning rush hour.

Woman: My flatmate complains about traffic noise waking her up too! But I'm on the inside of the building so I hardly notice it.

Extension idea

Photocopy audioscript page 123 so that students can identify why the other two choices were wrong. This will show them that, although all three topics in the choices are mentioned, there is a clear reason why two of them are not correct.

4 Give students a minute to think alone and note down some ideas to share with the group and then about four minutes to discuss them as a group.

Grammar SB page 9
Prepositions of time

5 Ask the students to try to do the exercise alone. Check the answers to the exercise and elicit or point out any problematic areas:
We use 'in' with parts of the day (*in the morning, afternoon, evening*) but we say 'at night'. We say 'in the morning' but 'on Saturday morning'. We say 'in July' but 'on 21 July'. In British English we say 'at the weekend' but in American English we say 'on the weekend'.

Answers
1 in **2** In **3** at **4** In **5** on

6 Allow students to compare their answers in pairs and then work together to add extra expressions.

Students could do Grammar reference: Prepositions of time, page 116, at this point or for homework.

Answers
at: 5 o'clock, bedtime, half past four, night
in: 2020, July, the afternoon, the holidays, winter
on: 25 May, my birthday, Sundays, weekdays

7 Put students into pairs. Set a time limit of two minutes for students to discuss their ideas.

Extension idea
Students write three sentences about themselves using prepositions of time, each of them in two halves on two different slips of paper, e.g. *I often go shopping / at the weekend.* Students work in groups of four. They put all their sentence beginnings in one pile, face down, and all their endings in a second pile. Each student picks one card from each pile, reading the sentence they make together. Some will make logical sentences, some combinations may be amusing. When they have finished, each student takes one other person's cards (using the handwriting to sort them out) and puts them together to form that person's original sentences.

▶ **Grammar reference page 116: Prepositions of time**
▶ **Workbook page 4**

Grammar SB page 10
Frequency adverbs

Lead-in
Put students into pairs. Ask the students to think about three activities that they do and one activity they don't do. Set a time limit of one minute, then ask pairs to discuss, e.g. *I go to the cinema, I do homework, I don't cook.*

1 When students have finished reading, they work in pairs to discuss their ideas.

2 Point out that all the answers can be found in the text in Exercise 1. Elicit the answers and the information in the text which illustrates them.

Answers
1 *be* + frequency adverb **2** before **3** at the end of a sentence

3 Before students do the exercise, check that they understand *occasionally, every two hours, almost every day, hardly ever.* Elicit sentences from different students.

Answers
2 I check my phone for messages every two hours.
3 I'm never late for my English lessons.
4 I sometimes write emails to friends.
5 I don't always have lunch at home.
6 I'm sleepy in the morning almost every day.
7 I hardly ever go out on Monday nights.
8 I stay in bed late most weekends.

Students could do Grammar reference: Frequency adverbs, Exercise 1, page 116, here or for homework.

4 If you think the class need help, make a true sentence about yourself using the information in sentence 1, e.g. *I hardly ever listen to music on the radio.* Elicit sentences from other students, then ask the class to write true sentences about themselves. When students have finished, elicit some of the similarities and differences that the students found.

5 Elicit what activities the photos show. Elicit that to say how often something happens, we say: *once, twice, three, four, five… times a (week/month/year).* Set a time limit of three or four minutes. Elicit sentences from different pairs.

▶ **Grammar reference page 116: Frequency adverbs**
▶ **Workbook page 6**

Reading Part 5 SB page 10

Lead-in
Write the words *flat* and *house* on the board. Elicit what the difference between them is and that both of them can be referred to as *homes.* Have a class survey of how many students live in a flat or a house.

1 Look at the photos on page 11 with the students and elicit or check the words: *(block of) flats, motorhome, yacht.*

2 Elicit why it's a good idea to do this exercise (to get a general idea of the text). Set a strict time limit of two minutes and then elicit the answers.

Answers
1 An article
2 D
3 Emilia does lots of interesting things. Her education takes place on the boat.
Living on a boat has some disadvantages. She sometimes meets her friends.

Reading Part 5 (multiple-choice cloze)
Look at the advice with the students. Elicit why each point is useful, e.g. reading the text quickly helps them to understand what it is about. The words before or after the gap may form collocations or phrases with the missing word, e.g. 2 needs a verb which is followed by *of.* For the third piece of advice, tell them that, if they aren't sure of the correct answer, by reading the whole sentence aloud (or in their heads during an exam) they can often hear which one sounds correct.

Exam advice

3 Remind students about the last piece of advice in the Exam advice box and to try each word in the gap to see which sounds correct if they aren't sure of the answers. The reading paper consists of six exercises in 45 minutes, so allow a time limit of seven minutes to reflect the time they will have in the exam.

Answers
1 D **2** B **3** D **4** C **5** A **6** C

Fast finishers
Tell students who finish early to look at the last paragraph and think about words which could be gapped and what choices examiners might give, e.g. *she…always feels safe on it – nearly, usually, closely, hardly.*

4 Look at the first point with the whole class and elicit good and bad things about going to different places, e.g. *experiencing different cultures, not making close friends,* and what students could say, e.g. *I wouldn't like to go to different places because I wouldn't make close friends.* Allow five minutes for the students to discuss all the points. Have a class discussion of the questions when they have finished.

5 Set a time limit of two minutes for students to discuss ideas about the things she does on a typical day. Elicit ideas and write them on the board, e.g. *makes phone calls, takes photos, writes a diary.* Monitor and help where necessary. The students then make sentences using these ideas, e.g. *She makes phone calls every day. She often takes photos.* Elicit sentences from each pair.

Extension idea
Students work in pairs and use the information in the text and their own imaginations to write a short interview with Emilia about her life. Encourage them to use questions using *How often do you …?* Nominate pairs to act out their interviews in front of the class.

Grammar SB page 12
Present simple and present continuous

Lead-in
Tell students to close their eyes and imagine they are on holiday looking at a view. Give the students 30 seconds to think and then put them in pairs to describe where they are and what they can see. Elicit some ideas from the class.

1 Look at the example with the class and then ask them to complete the exercise alone, or in pairs if you think some need more help. When students have finished the exercise, ask them to make sentences about their own lives for each of the uses (a–e).

Answers
2 d **3** a **4** b **5** c

2 Look at the first sentence and elicit why Molly has used the present continuous (she is writing at the present moment – now). Check answers and for each answer, ask students to identify which use in Exercise 1 it corresponds to.

Answers
2 am/'m sitting **3** has **4** am/'m looking **5** love **6** stay
7 go **8** is getting/'s getting **9** leave **10** is blowing
11 are/'re having **12** don't want

3 Monitor and help the students where necessary. If students have problems with question 3, point out that when *who* is the subject of a present simple question, we don't need to use the auxiliary verb *do* in the question.

Answers
1 What does 'habit' mean?
2 Do any buses stop in your street?
3 Who watches the most TV in your house?
4 Do you prefer to get up early or late?
5 Is everyone talking to their partners at the moment?
6 What colour clothes are you wearing today?
7 Is anyone sitting behind us in class right now?
8 What do you sometimes forget to do?

Fast finishers
Students imagine that their friend is on holiday and they are going to phone them. They should think of some questions they could ask using the present simple and present continuous and then, in pairs, act out their conversations.

4 When students have asked and answered in pairs, elicit questions and answers from the class to check that they have formed the questions and answers correctly.

5 Encourage students to write alternate questions in the present simple and present continuous so that, even if some students don't finish the activity, they have got at least some questions in both the present simple and present continuous. Monitor and correct where necessary.

/P/ /s/, /z/ and /ɪz/

6 When students have repeated the words, tell students to put their hands on their throats and say the words *likes* and *does*. When their throat vibrates, we say that the verb is voiced. Voiced endings are followed by the /z/ sound. Unvoiced endings are followed by the /s/ sound. When students have finished the exercise, drill all the words with the class to make sure they say them correctly.

Answers
/s/: forgets, likes, speaks, thinks, walks, wants, works
/z/: does, goes, lives, loves, plays, prefers, sees, studies, wears
/ɪz/: changes, chooses, finishes, passes, practises, uses, washes

7 Set a time limit of one minute per student, then elicit sentences and check the pronunciation of the third person *-s* ending.

8 Look at the two example questions with the class before they work in pairs and then monitor and prompt students with ideas if necessary. Elicit questions and answers from different pairs.

Students could do Grammar reference: Present simple and present continuous, Exercise 1, page 117, either before or after exercise 8 or for homework.

▶ **Grammar reference page 117: Present simple and present continuous**
▶ **Grammar reference page 118: State verbs**
▶ **Workbook page 6**

Vocabulary SB page 13
House and home; Countable and uncountable nouns

Lead-in
Put students into groups of four. Tell students you are going to give them a letter of the alphabet and they have to write five things beginning with that letter that may be found in a house. Give an example: B – *book, bed, bedroom, bottle, baby.* As soon as they have five things, they put their hand up and read them out. If all the words are correct, they get a point. Use: C, M, P, S.

1 Elicit the meanings of each word and then put students in pairs to discuss what their homes have and haven't got.

2 Ask students to work in pairs. Ask students to match as many of the words as they can but, if they don't know any of the words, to leave them. Point out that more than one answer may be possible as some items can be found in more than one room. Elicit the answers and check the meanings of each word.

Suggested answers
Living room: armchair, cushions, rug, sofa
Bathroom: bath, cupboards, mirror, taps, toilet, towels
Kitchen: cooker, cupboards, dishwasher, fridge, microwave, sink, taps, washing machine
Bedroom: blankets, chest of drawers, cupboards, duvet, mirror, pillow, wardrobe

Extension idea
Draw one of the words from Exercise 2 on the board and elicit what it is. Tell the students to close their books so they can't look at the list of words. Invite students to take turns to draw a different item on the board. The other students have to guess what it is. Either allow the student who guessed to draw the next item or invite different students who volunteer.

3 Discuss any words which are uncountable in English, e.g. *information, advice*, but countable in the students' L1 (native language).
Point out that the pronunciation of the plural *-s* of countable nouns follows the same rules as the third person *-s* that the students looked at earlier in the unit. Drill *taps* /s/, *sofas* /z/ and *fridges* /ɪz/ to illustrate the difference.

Answer
furniture

4 Elicit the answers and point out that some words can be both countable and uncountable, e.g. *glass* (U) the material – *glass* (C) the thing you drink out of; *hair* (U) all the hair on your head – *hair* (C) individual hairs.

Answers
[U] tells you the noun is uncountable.
[C] tells you the noun is countable.

Students could do Grammar reference: Countable and uncountable nouns, Exercise 1, page 118, at this point or for homework.

5 Elicit items from Exercise 2 that students said could be found in the kitchen (*cooker, cupboards, dishwasher, fridge, microwave, sink, taps, washing machine*). Elicit that these are all countable items. Set a time limit of two minutes and then elicit ideas.

Grammar SB page 13
a few, a bit of, many, much, a lot of and *lots of*

1 Look at rule 1 with the class and ask them to find the phrase *a few* in the speech bubble (*I like to invite a few friends…*). Ask whether *friends* is countable or uncountable and elicit that the correct choice is countable.

Fast finishers
Tell students to think of one more example for each quantity expression and write a sentence to illustrate it, e.g. *My parents are on holiday for a few days.*

Answers
1 countable **2** uncountable **3** uncountable **4** countable

2 Look at the first sentence with students and elicit the correct answer. Ask why *a bit of* is correct (*make up* is uncountable) and why *much* is correct (*make-up* is uncountable and this is a negative).

Answers
1 a bit of, much **2** much, a few **3** a few, a lot of
4 a lot of, lots of **5** much, a bit, a lot **6** much, many

Students could do Grammar reference: *a few, a bit of, many, much, a lot of* and *lots of*, Exercise 2, page 119, at this point or for homework.

3 Write *Watch TV* on the board. Elicit possible questions to ask, e.g. *Do you watch much TV? How much TV do you watch? Do you watch many TV programmes?* Monitor and help where necessary. Elicit surprising things students learned about their partners.

Extension idea
Tell students they are going to play a memory game. Start by saying: In my room there is an armchair. Now say: In my room, there is an armchair and there are some books. Ask for a volunteer to repeat what you have said and add another item beginning with C. Continue with other letters of the alphabet. Allow students to prompt each other if they can't remember what has been said or think of a new idea.

▶ **Grammar reference pages 118–119:** *A few, a bit of, many, much, a lot of* and *lots of*
▶ **Workbook page 6**

Speaking Part 1 SB page 14
Prepositions of place

Lead-in
Write in the middle of the board: *Personal Information*. Around it, write *family* and *studying*. Students work in pairs and copy what you have written and try to think of as many other topics as they can. Set a time limit of one minute and elicit ideas. Now under the word *family* on the board write: *Have you got any brothers or sisters?* Under *studying* write: *What subjects are you studying?* Give students two more minutes to think of one question for each of their topics. Students now ask and answer the questions in pairs.

1 When students have finished the exercise, elicit more sentences about the room they are in, e.g. *There is a desk on the left of the board.*

Answers
1 at **2** in **3** at **4** on **5** at **6** on

2 Encourage student A to speak at a natural speed and tell student B to note key words only. Allow three minutes for student A to describe their home. When student B has described the home from their notes, the students could swap roles. Monitor and help where necessary.

3 Elicit the answers and point out that we also don't use an article with *at home / school.*

Answers
at (college, etc.), in (a city, etc.), on (the coast, etc.)

4 When students have finished, they can work in pairs and take it in turns to ask and answer the questions as if they were Rafael.

Answers
2 b Where do you live? **3** d What do you do in Recife?
4 e Do you like having English lessons?
5 a Will you use English in the future?

Students could do Grammar reference: Prepositions of place, Exercise 1, page 119, at this point or for homework.

5 Depending on where the students' town is located, elicit or check how they would give its location, e.g. *in the middle of; in the mountains; in the southwest of …; on the River (Thames).*

6 When students have finished the dialogue, elicit the answers one line at a time and then play the recording of that line for students to check.

Answers
2 in **3** in **4** on **5** are you **6** at **7** do you get **8** in **9** in **10** do you like **11** in **12** at

Fast finishers
Students look at the words in Exercise 4 and ask their partner where different things are. For each place or object their partner has to give two answers, e.g. *Where's Barcelona? It's in Spain. It's on the coast.* Put some ideas on the board to help students with ideas if they need them, e.g. Buckingham Palace, The Trevi Fountain, Tokyo.

Track 3
Hugo: Where do you come from, Sara?
Sara: I live in Vigo, a city in Galicia. That's in north-west Spain, on the Atlantic coast.
Hugo: Do you work or are you a student?
Sara: I'm a second-year student at the University of Vigo. I'm studying Economics.
Hugo: How do you get there in the mornings?
Sara: The University isn't in the city so I usually take the bus, but in summer I often ride there on my bike.
Hugo: And where do you like to go in the evenings?
Sara: Sometimes I go out with my friends, but most evenings I stay at home studying. I've got exams soon!

Speaking Part 1 (individual questions)
Go through the exam advice with the students. Ask why these things are important: 1 Make a good impression at the start. 2 If they can't hear you, they can't assess you properly. 3 If you add more information, it shows the examiner that you have more knowledge of English. Point out that students won't gain extra marks for any information that doesn't answer the question.

Exam advice

7 Tell the class that only the student asking the questions should have their books open while doing the activity. The other student should answer the questions as fully as possible while also being friendly, polite and speaking clearly. They then swap roles and repeat the activity and give each other feedback on how well they followed the exam advice.

Extension idea
Students work with a different partner and ask each other the questions from the lead-in activity so that the students answering don't know in advance what the questions will be. If students didn't do the lead-in, elicit some ideas for new questions, e.g. *Have you got any brothers or sisters? What subjects are you studying?* Students think of questions in pairs then change pairs and ask and answer their new questions.

▶ **Speaking bank page 152: Speaking Part 1**
▶ **Workbook page 4**

Writing Part 1 SB page 15

Lead-in
Ask students to think about an email they wrote recently. They should think about who it was to and what it was about. If they never write emails, ask about the last text they wrote. Students then work in small groups to tell each other their information.

1 When students have found all the information, elicit the style of writing they will use in an email to a friend (informal, friendly).

Answers
2 an email plus four notes that you have made
3 an email in reply
4 Alex's boss said he/she could have some time off work; very pleased.
5 which would be the best month for her/him to visit; when he/she can come and why that would be the best month
6 what your home is like
7 which things he/she should bring

Writing Part 1 (an email)
Go through the exam advice with the students and point out why the first piece of advice is important (because in the second task, students will have a choice of two writing tasks). Re-elicit that one paragraph for each point makes the email clear to read.

2 Elicit the answers and ask students why paragraphs are useful (to organise information and make it easier to read).

Answers
1 four
2 Brilliant!: first, Say when and why: second, Describe: third, Suggest: fourth
3 two
4 *at* my place, *in* a three-bedroom flat, *on* the fifth floor, *in* a quiet neighbourhood, *in* August, *at* weekends, *in* the summer; *usually* away in August, *sometimes* have barbecues, *hardly* ever rains in July

3 Before students complete the table with their own ideas, elicit phrases that Frankie used: Brilliant – I'm so happy; I'm really looking forward to it; Say when and why – Summer is lovely; July would be the perfect time; Describe – three-bedroom flat; on the fifth floor; in a quiet neighbourhood; with modern furniture; a larger balcony; Suggest – I'd recommend bringing ... .

4 Set a 15-minute time limit for the email. Explain that they get 45 minutes to write two texts in the exam but that includes planning time so fifteen minutes is only a little less than they will have in reality. Students write on a piece of paper without writing their name at the end. This is so the extension activity is anonymous.

Model answer
Hi Alex,
That's brilliant you can come to stay with us. I'm really excited!
You should definitely come in July as there are a lot of things happening then. There's a big music festival during the first week of July. Would you like to come when that's on?
We live in a house about 5 km from the town centre. It isn't huge but it's comfortable. We have a small garden where we often have barbecues in the summer.
Don't forget to pack shorts and a sun hat. It'll be hot in the day but it gets cool in the evenings, so bring a light jacket too.
See you soon!
Luis

5 Tell students to also check that they have followed the instructions in Exercise 4. Encourage them to give positive and negative feedback to their partner if possible, e.g. *You included all the information and organised it well in paragraphs but we say 'in August' not 'on August'.*

Extension idea
Collect in the emails and redistribute so that everyone has an email written by someone else. Tell students that, this time, they should read the email not for mistakes but to find interesting words and phrases the other person used. Elicit some of these and write them on the board.

▶ **Writing bank pages 145-148: Writing Part 1: an email**
▶ **Workbook page 7**
▶ **Complete Preliminary new edition Test Generator Unit 1**

Vocabulary

Parts of the house

balcony
bathroom
bedroom
dining room
garage
garden
hall
kitchen
living room
stairs

At home

armchair
bath
blankets
chest of drawers
cooker
cupboards
cushions
dishwasher
duvet
fridge
furniture
microwave
mirror
pillow
rug
sink
sofa
taps
toilet
towels
wardrobe
washing machine

Countable and uncountable quantifiers

a few (C)
many (C)
a bit (of) (U)
much (U)
a lot (of) (C/U)
lots (of) (C/U)

Vocabulary activity 1

Students choose one of the words from the list and write this on a small piece of paper. They then write a definition (weaker students can use a dictionary to help them). The students then mingle and read each other their definitions. If the other student guesses the word, the first student keeps the card. If the other student can't think of the word, they take the card. The aim is not to have any cards when the activity finishes.

Vocabulary activity 2

Divide the class into two teams. Invite one student from each half to come to the front of the class and sit facing the other students. Write a word on the board. The students who can see the word have to take turns to define or describe it to their team member until one of the two students in front says the word. *The students can't say, spell or translate the word on the board. The students at the front cannot look at the word on the board.* The student who guesses the word first wins a point for their team. After each word, repeat the process with a new word and two different students.

2 Making choices

Unit objectives

Topic: Life choices, work

Listening Part 1: picture multiple choice; listening to find key information

Reading Part 6: open cloze: understanding grammar in a short text

Speaking Part 3: collaborative task: agreeing and disagreeing; making a decision

Writing Part 2: an article: using a mind map to plan an answer

Grammar: past simple; past simple and past continuous; *used to*; *So do I* and *Nor/Neither do I*

Vocabulary: *fail, pass, take, lose, miss, study* and *teach*; *do, earn, make, spend, take* and *win*

Pronunciation: *-ed* endings /d/, /t/ and /ɪd/

Starting off SB page 16
Life choices

1 Set a time limit of one minute for students to match the words to the photos. Elicit what is happening in each and what each phrase means. Students then discuss the best order. Elicit or point out that some things may happen more than once, e.g. applying for a job. Elicit ideas and add the events to a line on the board.

Suggested answers
A get some work experience **B** take a gap year **C** retire early **D** quit your job **E** apply for a job
1 take a gap year **2** get some work experience **3** apply for a job **4** quit your job **5** retire early

2 Set a time limit of two minutes for students to discuss the questions then discuss them with the whole class.

Reading Part 6 SB page 16

1 Remind students not to write anything in the gaps. Set a time limit of two minutes for students to read the text and discuss the question.

2 Look at gap number 1 with the students. Ask them what kind of word is needed (a relative pronoun). Monitor and help where necessary.

Suggested answers
1 relative pronoun **2** preposition **3** verb **4** preposition **5** pronoun **6** linker

3 Students work alone and check their answers in pairs. Discuss why these words are used if students have problems, e.g. **1** We use *who/that* when the relative pronoun refers to a person. **2** we use the verb *have to* to talk about rules and things we must do. **3** This is the plural form of the verb *to be* used as part of the present continuous.

Answers
1 who / that **2** to **3** are **4** with **5** their **6** and

4 Ask the students to describe the photos in pairs and discuss how they may relate to the title. Elicit ideas from different pairs.

Suggested answer
Some unusual university courses

5 Tell the students to read the text quickly without writing anything. Set a time limit of one minute and elicit how close their ideas were to the actual information in the article.

Reading Part 6 (open cloze)
Read the advice and ask how it will help students in the exam. (They will understand what the text is about before thinking about the gaps; they have an idea of what kind of word is needed.)

6 Set a time limit of six minutes. Allow students to compare answers in pairs then elicit the answers and look at any problematic areas.

Answers
1 about **2** are **3** an **4** as **5** their **6** from

7 Look at the first idea with the class and elicit one or two ideas from students, e.g. *modern, comfortable, computers*. Allow weaker students to work in pairs. Monitor and help with ideas where necessary.

8 When students have discussed their ideas, invite one student from each group to share their most interesting idea with the class.

Vocabulary SB page 18
fail, pass, take, lose, miss, study and *teach*

Lead-in
Write *exam* on the board. Elicit words related to *exam* and write these around the word, e.g. *pen, nervous, questions*. Put the students into small groups and give them one minute to think of more words. Add these to the board.

1 Allow students to discuss the vocabulary in pairs if they are unsure. Elicit the answers and then elicit more examples of similar collocations, e.g. *pass/fail a driving test, miss a flight, lose money.*

Answers
2 pass **3** fail **4** miss **5** lose **6** learn **7** teach **8** study

2 Students work alone and refer to Exercise 1 if necessary. Check answers, then ask the questions to the class. Don't ask for more details at this stage as the students will do this in Exercise 3.

Answers
2 lose **3** teach **4** learn **5** miss **6** study **7** teach **8** fail

3 Students take turns to ask the questions from Exercise 2 and try to remember the answers. Elicit the most interesting things the students found out.

Extension idea
Put students into small groups to make a group presentation. Give the students a choice of three topics: *how to pass exams; how to learn a new language; how to stop losing things.*

▶ **Workbook page 8**

Grammar SB page 18
Past simple

1 Elicit some heading ideas for possible differences that Emily found before students start, e.g. *weather, food, language, things to do.*

Suggested answers
Life in St. Andrews is very quiet – it is a very small town and there isn't much to do, while Mexico City is an enormous city with many people and there is a lot to see and do.

2 Encourage students to write one or two words for each topic only, so that they don't miss the next answer. Allow students to discuss their ideas in pairs and elicit the differences that they remember.

Answers
The city: Mexico City – a very large city;
Shops and entertainment: shopping centres, museums, large cinemas with a choice of films; restaurants with food from all over the world.

Track 4

Interviewer: Emily Cale's finishing her degree in chemistry right now. She's here with us today to talk about the nine months she spent abroad when she left school. Hello, Emily.

Emily: Hi!

Interviewer: So, where did you go?

Emily: I went to Mexico for nine months and I worked in a laboratory.

Interviewer: Young people often go straight to university in their own country when they leave school. Why did you decide to work abroad?

Emily: When I left school, I wanted to get some work experience to be sure that I really wanted to study chemistry. I wanted to improve my Spanish and Mexico City's the capital, of course, and it's also the largest Spanish-speaking city in the world!

Interviewer: How did you find a place in the laboratory?

Emily: My dad contacted an agency and they found me a place to do work experience in a research centre.

Interviewer: Where did you stay?

Emily: I stayed with Alicia and her family in Mexico City. Alicia's around my age and we got on really well.

Interviewer: Did you speak Spanish before you went?

Emily: Yes, I did. I studied French and Spanish at school and I thought I was good at languages. But when I got to Mexico I couldn't say anything. It was awful.

Interviewer: How did you feel when you first arrived?

Emily: To tell you the truth, when I arrived, I was scared. Mexico City is so different from my home town. It's enormous! And of course, I didn't know anyone.

Interviewer: Did you like the city?

Emily: I liked it a lot. You see, there's so much to see and do unlike Saint Andrews, my home town. There are shopping centres, museums, large cinemas with a choice of films and then there are restaurants with food from all over the world.

Interviewer: Did you enjoy the experience?

Emily: Oh yes, I did. I loved working in the laboratory. My Spanish also got better and I even began to dream in Spanish. I made so many really good friends and Alicia is coming to stay with me very soon.

Interviewer: Thank you, Emily … and if you'd like to know more about getting work experience abroad, contact …

3 Elicit how we form questions in the past simple and write the structure on the board: (question word) + *did* + noun/pronoun + base form of the verb. Check the students' questions before they listen to the recording again.

> **Answers**
> **2** Why did you decide to work abroad?
> **3** How did you find a place in the laboratory?
> **4** Where did you stay?
> **5** Did you speak Spanish before you went?
> **6** How did you feel when you first arrived?
> **7** Did you like the city?
> **8** Did you enjoy the experience?

4 Encourage students to read the answers before they listen again and to discuss in pairs what they think the missing verbs might be.

> **Answers**
> **2** wanted **3** contacted; found **4** stayed **5** studied
> **6** arrived; was **7** liked **8** loved

5 Check: *regular* and *irregular*. Elicit that, in the past simple, regular verb forms are formed by adding *-ed* to the base form of the verb, e.g. *stayed, finished.* Irregular verbs have different forms. Elicit the verbs Emily used and the base forms of the irregular verbs *went – go, was – be, left – leave, found – find.*

> **Answers**
> **Regular verbs:** wanted, contacted, stayed, studied, arrived, liked, loved
> **Irregular verbs:** went, found, was

/P/ /d/ /t/ and /ɪd/

6 Remind students of the pronunciation of the third person *-s* in the present simple. Model and drill the verbs in the examples, emphasising the sound of the *-ed* endings.

> **Answers**
> **1** /ɪd/ **2** /d/ **3** /t/

> **Track 5**
> **1**
> **Emily:** I wanted to improve my Spanish.
> **2**
> **Emily:** I stayed with Alicia and her family.
> **3**
> **Emily:** I liked the city a lot.

7 Ask students to say the verbs aloud in pairs. If they aren't sure which sound to use, they should try saying the verbs with different sounds and try to hear which one sounds correct. Elicit the answers.

> **Answers**
> /d/: arrived, enjoyed, loved, studied
> /t/: helped, liked, watched, worked
> /ɪd/: contacted, decided, invited, needed, wanted

> **Track 6**
> /d/: arrived, enjoyed, loved, stayed, studied
> /t/:, helped, liked, watched, worked
> /ɪd/: contacted, decided, invited, needed, wanted

8 When students have practised in pairs, ask pairs to act out the dialogues. Check the pronunciation of the verb endings.

9 When students have finished, point out what problems the errors illustrate.

> **Answers**
> **1** My friends and I ~~plaied~~ **played** football yesterday.
> **2** In our first English lesson our teacher ~~teached~~ **taught** us some new words for sports.
> **3** When I went to university, I ~~studyed~~ **studied** very hard.
> **4** Last weekend, I ~~founded~~ **found** a very good restaurant in my town.
> **5** When I ~~arribed~~ **arrived** at work, my colleagues weren't there.
> **6** My friend Sara ~~bringed~~ **brought** her dog to class one day.
> **7** I'm reading a book that my English teacher ~~recommend~~ **recommended** to me.
> **8** We ~~puted~~ **put** all our things in the car and we set off on holiday.

10 Remind students that they should quickly read the text to see what it is about before they try to complete the verb forms. Elicit the answers and make sure students pronounce the regular *-ed* endings and any new irregular verbs properly.

> **Answers**
> **2** spent **3** chose **4** wanted **5** left **6** was **7** felt **8** said
> **9** looked after **10** ate **11** saw **12** made

11 Elicit possible answers to the questions, e.g. *I went to … I wanted to …* . When students have finished, elicit any interesting information that students found out.

▶ **Grammar reference page 120: Past simple**
▶ **Workbook page 9**

Grammar SB page 20

Past simple and past continuous

1. Elicit what the students can see in the picture. Set a time limit for the discussion and help with vocabulary where necessary.

2. When students have listened, elicit what happened and how the story ended. Elicit ideas about what might happen next.

Answer
She saw a group of dogs.

Track 7

Emily: It was in my second week. The sun was shining and I was feeling good. I was walking to work with Alicia when we saw a group of dogs. We were frightened and we didn't know what to do.

3. After students have listened, ask them what really happened and which ending they prefer; their own or the one in the listening.

Possible answer
They started shouting for help.

Track 8

Emily: Suddenly a woman appeared from nowhere and she started screaming at the dogs. The dogs ran off. We said 'Gracias!' and went to work.

4. Elicit the answers and point out that in 1 the verbs describe short, single actions. In 2, the verbs are setting the scene for the story. This is a useful way of starting their own story-writing. In 3 there is a longer activity in progress when a single action happens.

Answers
1 No, they were three separate actions which happened one after the other. The dogs ran off last.
2 We don't know when the sun started shining or if it stopped shining.
3 No, they didn't. They saw the dogs during their walk to work.

5. Go through the rules with the students and point out that we can reverse the order of the sentences when we use past continuous and past simple together: *I saw a group of dogs as/while/when I was walking to work.*

Answers
2 past continuous **3** past simple
4 past continuous (or 3 past continuous / 4 past simple)
5 past simple **6** past continuous

6. Look at the example and ask why it is in the past simple (it is a single action, not a longer activity). Students compare answers in pairs and try to justify their answer, using the rules in Exercise 5. After the listening, elicit why each verb form has been used.

Answers
2 went **3** was talking **4** stopped **5** said **6** was feeling **7** didn't know **8** helped **9** were setting off **10** shouted **11** took off **12** started

Students could do Grammar reference: Past simple and Past continuous Exercises 1 and 2, page 121, at this point or for homework.

Fast finishers
Students tell the story from Alicia's point of view: *One morning, I woke up early … .*

Track 9

Emily: One morning, Alicia woke up early and she went to the kitchen where I was talking loudly to my flatmate. We stopped talking and I said, 'Look outside! There's 20 centimetres of snow on the ground. We'll have to ski to the town centre.' Alicia was feeling excited and nervous at the same time. Snow in Mexico City is very rare and she didn't know how to ski. I helped her to put on the skis. As we were setting off, one of the neighbours shouted at us, 'Everything is closed, even the shops!' We took off our skis and we started throwing snowballs.

7. Encourage students to start by setting the scene, e.g. *It was raining and I was sitting in the café next to the park.* Allow five minutes for students to plan their stories. Monitor and help students where necessary.

8. Monitor and note down any mistakes with verb forms. When students have swapped stories, write some mistakes on the board and elicit correct sentences.

Extension idea
In small groups, students choose a title from Exercise 8 that they didn't write about. Students work alone to write a sentence containing the past simple and past continuous that could appear in that story. Students share sentences and work together to make a story which can naturally include them all.

▶ **Grammar reference pages 120–121: Past simple and Past continuous**
▶ **Workbook page 9**

Listening Part 1 SB page 21

Lead-in
In pairs, students think of a question to ask their partner, e.g. *What's your favourite sport?* Students swap questions, then have one minute to draw three simple pictures, one of which shows the correct answer. Students show each other their pictures and ask the question, and their partner has to guess which picture is correct.

1 Elicit the key words and synonyms, e.g. *bring – make sure you've got, don't forget.* This will help students to identify the information they need in the recording.

Answers
2 What time does Stuart need to get to work?
3 Where does Jack live?
4 Where did the man find his football boots?
5 What did Julia eat before she came home?
6 What are the two friends going to buy Paul for his birthday?
7 What is the weather forecast for tomorrow?

2 Point out that this stage will help them to predict the words they will hear. For question 2 elicit two ways of saying each time, e.g. *8.30, half past eight.*

Suggested answers
1 A a large camera, B a packed lunch for a trip, C a water bottle
2 A it's eight thirty or half past eight, B it's eight fifty or ten to nine, C it's nine or nine o'clock.
3 A a house next to the swimming pool, B a house next to a pizza restaurant, C a house next to a cinema
4 A a sports bag, B a kitchen C a cupboard
5 A a burger, B a sandwich, C a chocolate cake
6 A a thriller, B a book about surfing C a book about music / a pop group or band.
7 A rain B sun C clouds

Listening Part 1 (multiple-choice with pictures)
Go through the box with the students. Remind students that they should always listen carefully the second time even if they think their answer is correct.

3 Tell students that they should write only one or two words for each picture or they may miss the next part of the answer. When students have listened once, they share ideas with a partner before listening again to complete the task.

Suggested answers of important words
1 A don't bring any large items, like cameras B lunch provided and C don't forget a water bottle
2 A next bus, B Stuart should be at work and C Stuart arrives
3 A swimming pool later, B a great pizza place next door to us and C the cinema where I used to live
4 A in the bag over there, B to dry and C not there
5 A burgers tonight, B boy having sandwich and C someone's birthday cake
6 A getting a new spy thriller for Fred, B he got a book about surfing and C a book about his favourite band
7 A all day today, B doesn't like playing when hot and C cloudy but dry

Answers
1 C 2 B 3 B 4 A 5 C 6 A 7 B

Track 10

Narrator: Part 1. For each question, choose the correct answer.

1

Narrator: What do the people need to bring for the cycling trip?

Woman: Just before you leave. Ssh! Listen carefully. Don't forget it's our annual day out tomorrow and the office will be closed. For those of you on the cycling trip, we're meeting outside the train station. Lunch will be provided so you don't have to bring any food but don't forget a water bottle. It may be hot. Please don't bring any large items like heavy bags or cameras as you won't be able to carry them.

2

Narrator: What time does Stuart need to be at work?

Woman: Stuart! It's ten past nine.

Stuart: I know, I'm late again. You see, I left my mobile at home so I went back for it. Then I missed the bus and the next one was at half past eight. There was a terrible traffic jam so I got off the bus and ran the rest of the way.

Woman: Yes but the shop opens at nine. I can't manage everything on my own. You should really be here by ten to nine.

Stuart: I'm sorry.

3

Narrator: Where does Jack live?

Jack: Hi, it's Jack. Do you still fancy going to the swimming pool later? George lives near the pool so he might want to come too. Shall we meet outside the cinema? You know, the one where I used to live. And if you like we can get a take-away afterwards and have it at my house. They've opened a great pizza place next door to us. Let me know what you think. Bye!

4

Narrator: Where did the man find his football boots?

Man: Have you seen my football boots anywhere? I brought them home from training yesterday. They were wet so I left them in the kitchen to dry and now I can't find them.

Katie: We were tidying up this morning. Have you looked in the cupboard in the hall?

Man: Yes, but they weren't there. Wait a minute. What's in that bag over there? Oh, they must be my boots.

5

Narrator: What did Julia eat before she came home?

Man: Hi Julia. How was your day? I'm just having a cheese sandwich. Would you like one?

Julia: No thanks. I'm not hungry. You know Nigel at work, don't you? It was his birthday today and he brought in a homemade chocolate cake. It was delicious.

Man: I guess you don't want dinner then.

Julia: Oh yes, I do! What are you making?

Man: It's my special burgers tonight. They should be ready by about eight.

6

Narrator: What are the two friends going to buy Paul for his birthday?

Man: It's Paul's birthday next weekend. We should get him something. We got him a book about his favourite band last year.

Woman: Oh yeah, that's right but his sister had bought him the same one so he took it back to the shop. He got a book about surfing instead, didn't he?

Man: Yes, that's right. I know! My brother's reading a new spy thriller. It's set in Italy and he says it's really exciting. Let's get him that.

Woman: OK.

7

Narrator: What is the weather forecast for tomorrow?

Joe: Best of luck with the tennis competition, Vicki! It's tomorrow, isn't it?

Vicki: Thanks, Joe! They might have to cancel it. It hasn't stopped raining all day today and we're playing outdoors.

Joe: Have you looked it up on the internet? It says on this page that it's going to be cloudy but dry. It won't be sunny though.

Vicki: That's OK – I don't like playing when it's hot but I'll take my sun cream just in case.

Extension idea

Put the students into seven groups. Photocopy the audioscript on page 123 and give each group one part of the listening task. Ask students to say why the other two options were wrong.

Grammar SB page 21
used to

Lead-in

In small groups, students think of three good things about their school days and three bad things. Elicit ideas and reasons why.

1 When students have identified the form, point out that *used to* has a similar meaning to using the past simple with adverbs of frequency.

Answers
used to, didn't use to

2 Go through the rules and point out the similarities between *used to* in questions and negatives to regular past forms (we use *did/didn't* + the base form of the verb).

Answers
1 No **2** We write *didn't use to* (NOT *didn't used to*) and *did you use to* (NOT *did you used to ….?*) **3** the infinitive

3 Remind students not to use *used to* for actions that only happened once. Tell students to use some of the ideas from the lead-in. When they have finished, put students in pairs to read their texts to each other.

Model answer
I think my life was easier ten years ago because I used to live at home and I didn't use to do any housework. I was still at school so I used to see my friends at school every day and we used to make plans for the weekend. I didn't use to have to phone them to meet them. However, I used to do a lot of homework and we used to do lots of exams, which I didn't enjoy.

Students could do the Grammar reference: *used to*, Exercise 1, page 121, at this point or for homework.

▶ **Workbook page 9**

Vocabulary SB page 22
do, earn, make, spend, take and *win*

Lead-in

With books closed, put students into small groups. Give them a minute to brainstorm what makes a good job. Stop the activity and elicit ideas from each group.

1 Ask the students if the verb collocations are the same in their language. When students have finished, point out or elicit other useful collocations with the same verbs, e.g. *spend money, make an effort, do experiments.*

Answers
2 earn **3** take **4** spend **5** take **6** take/do **7** do **8** win

2 Set a time limit of two to three minutes for students to discuss the question. Elicit ideas from each group.

Speaking Part 3 SB page 22

Lead-in
Put students into small groups and ask them to think about social activities that companies organise for their employees. Set a time limit of two minutes and elicit ideas.

1 If students didn't mention any of the activities in the lead-in, elicit what happens on them and which the students think are a good idea. Elicit guesses about which activity Gareth and Tanya will choose before they listen.

Answers
1 quiz night, weekend trips, cooking classes
2 a team meal, a running group, yoga and relaxation
3 a team meal

Track 11

Tanya: Have you got a moment, Gareth?
Gareth: Yeah, go on!
Tanya: Well, you know our boss wants us to vote on a new social activity at work. Can we talk about the choices first?
Gareth: Sure!
Tanya: Shall we start with the quiz night?
Gareth: OK, go on.
Tanya: Don't you think it would be a great idea? Quizzes are such fun and I love competitions, you know.
Gareth: Um… I don't think many of our colleagues would agree with you. How about a team meal? In my sister's company, each department has lunch together once a month so that they can get to know each other better.
Tanya: Good point. Let's talk about another one. Then we can decide. Perhaps we could go on a weekend trip and try new sports or activities together.
Gareth: Do you really think that's a good idea? Some of our colleagues have families and they can't go away at the weekend.
Tanya: That's a good point. I often go round to my grandma's house on Saturdays anyway.
Gareth: I think it'd be better to start something like a running group where we meet at lunchtime twice a week and go for a run together for about forty minutes.
Tanya: I don't agree. Some of us hate running. What's left on the list? Let's see … What about cooking classes? Did you see *MasterChef* on TV last night?
Gareth: I'm not sure about that one.
Tanya: Nor am I.
Gareth: Yeah! I'd prefer to do yoga and relaxation, to be quite honest. Then we would all feel less stressed.
Tanya: That's true but I still think a team meal is the best option.
Gareth: So do I. Let's go for that.

2 Elicit the answers and ask what Tanya means when she says *Nor am I* (she isn't sure either) and what Gareth means when he says *So do I* (he thinks a team meal is the best option).

Answers
Nor am I; So do I
We use 'so' to agree with positive sentences and 'nor' to agree with negative sentences.

Students could do the Grammar reference: *So (do) I and nor/neither (do) I,* Exercise 1, page 121, at this point or for homework.

3 Point out that, when making suggestions or decisions, we use: *shall* + *we* + base form of the verb, *Let's* + base form of the verb, *How about* + *-ing* form of the verb.

Answers
1 start **2** about **3** point **4** agree **5** sure **6** Let's

Track 12

1
Tanya: Shall we start with the quiz night?
2
Gareth: How about a team meal?
3
Tanya: Good point. Let's talk about another one.
4
Tanya: I don't agree. Some of us hate running.
5
Gareth: I'm not sure about that one.
6
Gareth: Let's go for that.

4 Go through the headings with the class and elicit what they mean e.g. *suggesting – saying an idea, agreeing – saying 'yes', disagreeing – saying 'no', deciding – saying what the final choice is.* Students then work in pairs to complete the table.

> **Answers**
> **Suggesting:** How about, Shall we
> **Agreeing:** Good point
> **Disagreeing:** I don't agree, I'm not sure
> **Deciding:** Let's go for that

Speaking Part 3 (discussion)
Go through the advice with the students. Ask if it is a good idea to make a quick decision straight away (*No, because they wouldn't discuss all the activities and wouldn't speak for long enough*). Ask why it is a good idea to start the conversation by suggesting which activity to talk about (*it shows you have confidence in using English and you can choose an activity you find easy to talk about*).

Exam advice

5 When students have read the instructions, ask questions about what they have to do, e.g. *Will students talk alone?* (no, they will talk together); *How long will they talk for?* (two minutes); *What do they have to decide?* (which activity would be the most popular). Put students into pairs. When students have finished, ask what they decided and how they felt during the talk

▶ **Speaking bank pages 159–160: Speaking Part 3**
▶ **Grammar reference page 121** *So (do) I* and *nor/neither (do) I*

Writing Part 2 SB page 23

Lead-in
Ask students to think about an article they read recently: where it was, what it was about. Put them in small groups to share their information, then elicit ideas from each group.

1 Elicit the answers and then ask students what makes them want to read an article, e.g. a topic they are interested in.

> **Answers**
> **1** an article **2** What makes a great place to work? Is it the people, the facilities or something else? What kinds of social activities should a great place to work offer?

2 Set a time limit of one minute and elicit ideas from different pairs so that students can use each other's ideas in Exercise 3.

> **Suggested answer**
> staff; facilities (office space, furniture, kitchen, canteen etc.); working day, location and views; technology; career opportunities etc.

3 Set a time limit of three minutes. When students have finished, point out that they won't use all of their ideas in their article but should choose the most important or interesting.

> **Suggested answer**
> A great place to work
> **Staff:** a fair boss who encourages us, interesting colleagues, easy to get on with
> **Facilities:** a large bright office with space is more pleasant to work in
> **Working day:** workers can choose their hours, one afternoon off a week, lots of holidays
> **Social activities:** a place to work should offer different activities so we can get to know each other

4 Elicit the answers and ask students their opinions about the ideas in the article. Ask students who work whether their work place is similar to Charlotte's or not.

5 When students have finished, elicit that the answers are all 'Yes' and then discuss what they are.

> **Answers**
> **1** Yes; information – people who work there (staff, boss), facilities (large, bright office, space), something else (start times); social activities (sports competitions, camping trips)
> **2** Yes; paragraphs (two)
> **3** Yes; connecting words (because, and, but, also, while)

Exam advice: Writing Part 2 (an article)
Tell students to underline the important parts of the advice. Look at the first point and elicit that they could underline: *Read, instructions* and *text, Decide, information, need to include.* Students do the same for the other two points in pairs. Elicit their ideas. Students have about 22 minutes for each task. This gives them about three minutes to read the instructions, note useful vocabulary and plan their ideas, 16 minutes to write and three minutes to check their work.

Exam advice

6 Before students start writing, elicit that *In my opinion* is a good way to start the article. Set a time limit of fifteen minutes for the writing, similar to the time they will have for writing in the exam.

> **Model answer**
> In my opinion, people make a great work place. You need friendly, helpful colleagues who share ideas and help out when necessary. You also need a boss who is organised and fair and isn't more friendly with some workers than others. Facilities can help, too. My work place has a good canteen with healthy food. There are also lots of plants in the building which make it look nice.
>
> It's good to have a variety of social activities such as weekend trips and parties but it is important that workers don't think they have to join in all the time, especially if they have families. Free time is also important.

▶ **Writing bank pages 148–149: Writing Part 2: an article**
▶ **Workbook page 11**
▶ **Complete Preliminary new edition Test Generator Unit 2**

Vocabulary

Life choices

apply for a job
get some work experience
quit your job
retire early
take a gap year

Verb and noun combinations

do a course / (your) best
earn a salary
fail / pass / take (an exam)
learn (how to do something)
lose (something)
make friends
miss (a lesson)
spend time
study (a subject) / a degree
take a long time / breaks
teach (someone how to do something)
win a match

Jobs

architect
hairdresser
journalist
lawyer
police officer
research assistant
teacher
volunteer

College or university

accommodation
classrooms and facilities
fees and other costs
journey and location
teachers and courses
timetable and exams

Social activities

a cooking class
a quiz night
a running group
a team meal
a weekend trip
yoga and relaxation

Vocabulary activity 1

Put students into groups of three. Each group thinks of one or two sentences containing a verb–noun combination from the word list. They then rewrite the sentences, this time with a gap in place of the verb. When they have finished, the groups close their books and swap their sentences with another group. They try to guess the other group's missing word. Groups then tell each other their guesses and see if they were correct.

Vocabulary activity 2

In pairs, students choose one of the words from the list and think of a short dialogue about the word but they cannot say the actual word they have chosen, e.g. if the word is *accommodation,* they can act out a dialogue about accommodation but they can't say the word *accommodation*. Set a time limit and then invite pairs to act out their dialogues in front of the class. Other students have to guess what their word is.

Vocabulary and grammar review Unit 1

1 **2** in **3** on **4** in **5** in **6** at **7** In **8** at/on **9** in **10** at **11** in **12** on

2 **2** a bit of **3** a lot **4** much **5** time **6** much **7** a bit of **8** a few

3 **2** Hello, ~~I call~~ **I'm calling** to ask if you want to go out somewhere tonight.
3 Why ~~do you stand~~ **are you standing** here in the rain at this time of night?
4 I'm ~~tired usually~~ **usually tired** in the morning.
5 ~~I'm never believing~~ **I never believe** anything that newspaper says.
6 I ~~every day water the plants on the balcony~~ **water the plants on the balcony every day.**
7 How ~~do you often~~ **often do you** have a bath?
8 I ~~get normally~~ **normally get** home at about half past five.

4 **2** sofa **3** fridge **4** cooker **5** dishwasher **6** microwave **7** duvet **8** chest of drawers **9** wardrobe **10** washing machine

Vocabulary and grammar review Unit 2

1 **2** do **3** learned **4** pass **5** earning **6** made **7** taking **8** did

2 **2** I think I ~~lefted~~ **left** my bag at your house last night.
3 Our teacher was kind. She ~~teached~~ **taught** us very well.
4 I woke up very early because I was ~~planing~~ **planning** to go to the lake.
5 My dad only ~~payed~~ **paid** €75 for his mobile phone.
6 While my sister was riding her bike, she ~~felt~~ **fell** and injured her leg.
7 When I was younger, I ~~prefered~~ **preferred** to take the bus everywhere.
8 I met Holly a very long time ago. We were ~~studing~~ **studying** at the same university.

3 **2** were chatting, was writing **3** were having, rang **4** was buying, saw **5** thought, was **6** began, was walking **7** sat (*or* was sitting), broke **8** watched, understood **9** went, enjoyed **10** was feeling, went

4 **2** use **3** give **4** used **5** didn't

3 Having fun

Unit objectives

Topic: Hobbies and free-time activities

Listening Part 4: multiple-choice: listening for detailed meaning

Reading Part 3: multiple-choice: reading to understand gist and detailed comprehension of a text

Speaking Part 2: describing a picture

Writing Part 2: story: planning paragraphs

Grammar: verbs followed by *to* or *-ing*

Vocabulary: leisure activities; prepositions of place; phrasal verbs; people's hobbies

Pronunciation: *-ing* endings /ŋ/

Starting off SB page 26

Leisure activities

Lead-in

Put students into pairs. Ask them when they have free time, e.g. lunch breaks at work, in the evening after they have finished work, at the weekend. Students ask each other questions about what they do or what they did at a specific time, using adverbs of frequency for present simple questions and past time expressions with the past simple. Elicit examples of each and questions that could be formed with them, e.g. *usually – What do you usually do during your lunch breaks? last night – What did you do last night?* Set a time limit of two minutes and elicit some of the activities mentioned.

1 Tell students to open their books and cover everything except the photos. Students work in pairs to discuss what the people are doing. Elicit the answers and point out that when we use the *-ing* form of the verb, we follow it with a singular verb form, e.g. *dancing / riding horses is fun*. Elicit similar sentences about other activities in the list.

Answers
2 taking **3** going **4** riding **5** watching **6** playing **7** posting **8** visiting
Activities in the photos: (From top left) visiting an art gallery or museum, riding a horse, playing a musical instrument, riding a bike, going dancing.

2 Elicit phrases which the students could use for this activity and write them on the board, e.g. *Which activity do you think is the best? What about…? Where shall we put…?* Monitor and help students where necessary. Elicit the best and worst activities from different pairs.

3 Elicit one or two ideas to start with e.g. walking, cycling. Tell students to think of one activity each and then discuss the three questions together. Set a time limit of three minutes and then elicit ideas from each group.

Extension idea

Put students into groups of three. They have two minutes to list as many other free time activities ending in *-ing* as they can, e.g. *reading*. Find out how many ideas each group have got and elicit these, starting with the group who have the least.

Listening Part 4 SB page 26

1 Tell students to also give their opinions about the photos, saying which they like best and why.

2 Tell students they don't need to look at the options yet. Elicit the information and some possible answers, e.g. *Why did he become a full-time Instagram photographer? Because he likes meeting famous people.*

Answers
1 a reason **2** an opinion **3** an opinion **4** feelings **5** an opinion **6** advice

Listening Part 4 (multiple-choice)

Discuss the advice with the students. Tell them that they should quickly underline key words in the questions and options to help them decide what information they need to listen for. Point out that this form of multiple-choice is very similar to the multiple-choice activity with three pictures. In both cases, there are references to the information in all three options, but only one will be correct, so the students have to listen carefully to what the speaker says about them.

Exam advice

3 When students have chosen the correct answers, allow them to discuss their choices in pairs and try to justify their answers if they disagree with each other. Play the recording again. Elicit the answers and information from the text which helped students to decide which was the correct answer. If necessary, make a photocopy of the audioscript on page 124 for students to also see why the other two answers are incorrect.

Answers
1 B **2** B **3** C **4** A **5** C **6** A

Track 13

Narrator: Part 4. For each question, choose the correct answer. You will hear a radio interview with the Instagram photographer, Marc Pasqual.

Interviewer: Today I'm talking to photographer Marc Pasqual, who posts all his pictures on Instagram. Marc, what made you want to do that full-time?

Marc: I was an international tour guide, visiting some amazing countries. I was also doing wedding photos as a hobby, but I was finding that pretty boring and was keen to try something more creative, even though I felt it unlikely I'd earn much money from it. I noticed my favourite people on Instagram, like the chef Lauren Bath, had given up interesting careers to concentrate on photography, so I decided to make the change, too.

Interviewer: How did you become such a good photographer? With a good teacher?

Marc: I did have some lessons with an experienced photographer. He encouraged me to think about how I wanted my photographs to look before I actually took them. That works for some people but not others, and personally, whenever I arrive somewhere new I start taking photos, such as drops of rain on a flower, or the sun shining through a small window. Not everyone notices these little things and it can really improve your pictures.

Interviewer: Did you make any mistakes?

Marc: Well, some beginners can't help posting lots of selfies on Instagram, but I avoided doing that. However, only uploading weekly, as I did at first, means people soon forget you. I saw those ads for expensive apps that promise to make you an Instagram star in a week, but fortunately I ignored them.

Interviewer: What's the best thing about your work?

Marc: I love getting messages on Instagram and replying to them, or working with other photographers because I get lonely if I'm by myself. But nothing gives me quite as much pleasure as having the memories of all the fantastic places I've travelled to. Taking photos means I'll never forget them.

Interviewer: What do you most want to do next?

Marc: I've thought of studying photography at university and that would be great, but it'd probably be more useful for someone aiming to start a career in a large organisation. I'd rather read lots about it since its invention in the nineteenth century, and still be able to work on my own.

Interviewer: What would you say to new Instagram photographers?

Marc: Make sure people on Instagram notice your work. Research shows that it doesn't really matter whether you post on weekdays or weekends, so do so whenever you like. Some photographers say you shouldn't add any text, but I disagree. I tell the story of each picture, saying why and how I took it, and people like that. Also add a link to your blog or Facebook page and upload some of your photos there – though keep your best ones for Instagram.

4 Set a time limit of two minutes and then elicit ideas. Continue the discussion by asking students about photos they have seen on the Internet or social media.

Extension idea
Students work in groups of four and choose one hobby which they could turn into a job. When they have agreed, they discuss how they could do this and think of advice they could give to someone who was interested in such a career, e.g. *riding a bike – bike courier. You have to keep your bike in good condition. You have to get fit so that you can ride fast,* etc.

▶ **Workbook page 14**

Vocabulary SB page 27
Prepositions of place

Lead-in
Write *What is it?* on the board. Look around the room and make a sentence using a preposition of place, e.g. *It is on my desk next to my books.* or: *It is on the floor between the door and the board.* The students have to identify the object. You could make this a competitive activity by putting the students into groups and giving a point for the first group to give a correct answer.

1 Before students start the activity, elicit: *racket, wardrobe, floor, shelf* so that they can concentrate on the prepositions of place without being worried about unknown vocabulary. Ask students to compare their pictures before they check on page 162.

Answers
Kirsty's raquet: on the floor in front of the wardrobe
her tennis balls: on the shelf opposite the window, behind the clock
her trainers: under the small table next to the bed
her T-shirt: inside the wardrobe on the right, on the shelf above the shelf where her jeans are

Track 14

Kirsty: Hi Jack, I forgot I'm playing tennis later and I've left all my things at home! Can you find them for me? And could you bring them with you later?

Jack: Sure, I'll go and look for them in your room now. Where's your racket?

Kirsty: You'll see that as soon as you walk in. It's lying on the floor just in front of the wardrobe.

Jack: Right, I'm just opening the door ... yes, there it is.

Kirsty: Great. Now there should also be some tennis balls, four I think, on the shelf that's opposite the window. Can you see that?

Jack: Yes, I can.

Kirsty: They're actually behind the clock there.

Jack: Yes, all four are there. I'll bring those too. What else?

Kirsty: My trainers. Do you see the small table next to my bed? Well, they're under that.

Jack: I've got them. Is that everything?

Kirsty: Just one more thing. Could you get my T-shirt?

Jack: Sure. Where is it?

Kirsty: If you look inside the wardrobe, on the right, you'll see it on the shelf above the one where my jeans are. And that's all.

Jack: OK, if I can find a big enough bag, I think I can carry everything!

Kirsty: Thanks, Jack.

Jack: No problem, see you later.

2 Tell students that more than one answer may be possible. Look at the example sentence and compare it to what was said in the recording (*It's lying on the floor just in front of the wardrobe*). Students can then make their sentences, knowing which prepositions of place to use for each object. Elicit sentences to make sure they are correct.

Suggested answers
2 Her tennis balls are on the shelf opposite the window, behind the clock
3 Her trainers are under the small table, next to the bed.
4 Her T-shirt is inside the wardrobe on the right, on the shelf above her jeans.

Extension idea
Ask students to quickly draw the room in the picture twice without the added objects. Set a time limit of two minutes so they don't try to draw it too carefully. Then ask them to add five objects of their own wherever they like in the picture. Students now join together in pairs and, without showing their pictures to each other, describe where their five objects are. Their partner draws these in their second picture. When they have both described and drawn, they compare pictures with each other to see if the objects are in the same places.

Reading Part 3 SB page 28

Background information
There are several sand sculpture world championships. The world's tallest sand castle was built on Myrtle Beach in South Carolina in 2007. It was 15.1 metres high and took 10 days to build and used 300 truck-loads of sand.

1 Set a time limit of one minute and then ask students if they have ever seen anything like this before and, if so, where.

Answer
Sand sculptures; students' own answers.

2 Ask the students what the writer's main purpose means (it is the overall reason for writing, what the writer wants to do). Set a two-minute time limit. Check the answer and students' reasons for choosing the answer: the first paragraph talks about how enjoyable they are to make and the last one encourages readers to make one themselves.

Answer
D

3 Set a time limit of two minutes for the students to find the answers and discuss them in pairs. Pair stronger students with weaker to find the information.

Answers
1 Because she saw some on the beach near where she lives.
2 She felt determined to try harder to build it.
3 That people don't realise that even lightly touching a sand sculpture can damage it.

Reading Part 3 (multiple-choice)
Discuss the exam advice with the students. Point out that as well as deciding which answer is correct, they can also check that they are right by understanding why the other options are wrong.

4 The students now look at the options and choose the ones most like their answers to Exercise 3. If none of them are similar, they have to read that section of the text again to find the correct answer. Tell them they should also read the parts of the text where the answers are written and check that the other two choices are definitely wrong.

Answers
1 D **2** B **3** C **4** A

Fast finishers
Students look at the wrong choices and find evidence for why they are wrong. When you elicit the correct answers, if anyone has chosen wrongly, the fast finishers can then explain why it is the incorrect answer.

5 Elicit what the activities are in the box. Set a time limit of three minutes for the discussion and then elicit ideas from the class.

▶ **Workbook page 12**

Grammar: SB page 29

Verbs followed by *to* or *-ing*

Lead-in
Elicit a verb from the class, something that they do every day, e.g. *eat, sleep*. Elicit a sentence containing the *-ing* form and *to* + verb for both verbs, e.g. *I enjoy sleeping. I want to eat now.* Put students into groups of four and ask them to think of four more verbs and do the same. Write two columns on the board headed: *X* and *Y*. Write *enjoy* in one and *want* in the other. Elicit sentences from the students and, if they have used a verb + *-ing* or a *to* + verb combination, write the verbs on the board below either *enjoy* or *want*. If the verbs can be used with *to* or *-ing*, e.g. *like*, write these between the two columns. When students have finished, elicit what the difference between the two groups of verbs is.

1 Elicit the answers and then ask students to think of different sentences using the same underlined verbs, e.g. *Dan seems to be worried about something.*

Answers
-ing: 2, 3; *to*: 1, 4

2 Allow students to work in pairs to discuss the verbs. Elicit the answers and any other verbs the students can think of. Write these on the board for students to add to their tables.

Answers

verb + *-ing*	verb + *to*
avoid, enjoy, fancy, feel like, finish, keep, mind, miss, practise, suggest	agree, decide, hope, learn, manage, promise, seem, want, would like

Extension idea
Put students into groups of three or four. Tell them to write four sentences, two using verbs which take *-ing* and two with verbs which take *to*. When they have finished, elicit sentences from different groups.

3 Look at the instructions with the students. Elicit some verbs which can be used with *-ing* or *to* without any change in meaning, e.g. *start*, *like*, then ask them to look at the sentences in the exercise. Elicit the answers.

Answers
something you have to do: 2, 3
a memory of something in the past: 1, 4

4 Ask students to read the instructions. Monitor and help the students. When students have finished, elicit the answers.

Answers
2 I hope ~~see~~ **to see** you soon!
3 I really enjoyed ~~to help~~ **helping** at a music festival.
4 Do you fancy ~~to come~~ **coming** out with us?
5 When we finished ~~to eat~~ **eating** I went home.
6 I'll never forget ~~to visit~~ **visiting** New York last year.

5 Elicit that most of the correct verb forms can be found by looking at Exercises 2 and 3. Check their answers when they have finished.

Answers
2 listening **3** to do **4** going **5** to bring **6** to do

Students could do Grammar reference: Verbs followed by *to* or *-ing*, Exercises 1 and 2, pages 122–123, at this point or for homework.

/P/ *-ing* endings /ŋ/

6 When students have listened to the sentences, drill the /ŋ/ sound on its own and then the words in which it appears alone (*going, listening, planning, going, bring*). Model the different sounds by saying the words with no /ŋ/ (*doin'*) and with a pronounced /g/.

Answers
1 /ŋ/ **2** no **3** no

Track 15
1 Where do you fancy going this evening?
2 What kind of music do you enjoy listening to at home?
3 What are you planning to do at the weekend?
4 Do you remember going away on holiday when you were younger?
5 Do you ever forget to bring anything to your English lesson?
6 What would you like to do tomorrow?

7 To ensure students get the most practice possible of the verb forms, make sure they use them in both questions and answers, e.g. *1 I fancy going to the cinema* – not just '*the cinema*'. Monitor and check pronunciation and then elicit questions and answers from different students.

Fast finishers
Students think of questions they could ask other people in the class using different verbs in Exercise 2, e.g. *When did you last promise to help someone?* When everyone has finished Exercise 7, these students can ask other students in the class their questions.

8 Encourage students to make the task more communicative by asking follow-up questions. Elicit interesting information that the students found out from each other during the activity.

▶ **Grammar reference pages 122–123: Verbs followed by *to* or *-ing***
▶ **Workbook pages 14-15**

Vocabulary SB page 30
Phrasal verbs

Lead-in
Write the verbs: *take, get, put* in one column on the board and prepositions: *on, off, up, down, away, out, in, back* in another. Give examples of phrasal verbs which can be made from the words on the board, e.g. *take off (clothes), get up (in the morning)*. Put the students into small groups and ask them to write as many phrasal verbs as they know, using the words on the board. Elicit ideas and definitions.

Grammar box
Look at the definition of phrasal verbs with the students. Point out that it can sometimes be difficult to decide whether the second part of a phrasal verb is an adverb or a preposition but that they don't need to know when they are adverbs and when they are prepositions at this stage.

1 Elicit the answers and then point out that there are three different types of phrasal verb here: *hang on* doesn't have an object. You don't hang on something; *Look after* has an object, e.g. *my phone/your brother*, etc. It is inseparable, i.e. the object always comes after the complete phrasal verb; *Run out of* is a three-part phrasal verb. Again the object comes after the complete phrasal verb, e.g. *run out of money/time/petrol*.

Answers
1 hang on **2** run out of **3** look after

2 Tell students to identify the nine phrasal verbs first. With a weaker group, this can be done as a class. With stronger students, as soon as most of the class have found them, elicit what they are and where in the text they can be found. This will enable all students to spend more time on deducing the meaning of the verbs.

Answers
2 look forward to **3** put (your) name down **4** go on
5 sign up for **6** go off **7** set off **8** take up **9** give up

3 Remind students that with the phrasal verb *look after*, we say *look after someone*, not *look someone after*. In this exercise, there is a phrasal verb where the person or thing is written in the middle of the phrasal verb. Elicit the answers and encourage the students to note down what kind of phrasal verb it is by writing *sth/sb* with the verb when noting new vocabulary. If there is no object, the students just write the phrasal verb, e.g. *put sth down, give up sth, set off*.
Tell students that with separable phrasal verbs the noun can go between the verb and adverb/preposition or afterwards: *put your name down / put down your name*. However, pronouns always go between the noun and the particle: *put it down*, NOT *put down it*.

Answers
1 sign up for, look forward to
2 put (your name) down

4 When students have listened, elicit the correct answers and then ask students to explain what the speakers are saying without using the phrasal verbs, e.g. *They want to start their journey very early in the morning*.

Answers
2 went off **3** take up **4** put … down **5** gave up **6** go on
7 looking forward to

Fast finishers
Students look at the phrasal verbs used in the text and dialogue and think of different situations in which they could be used, e.g. *set off for work.*

Track 16

Chris: Hi, Ava. Are you and Megan going away on holiday soon?
Ava: Yes, on Saturday. We want to set off very early in the morning.
Chris: Are you going to the coast?
Ava: No, we went off beach holidays a long time ago. There are always too many people. We've decided to take up skiing instead. We're off to the Alps.
Chris: Do you know how to ski?
Ava: Er, not really. That's why I'm going to put my name down for lessons.
Chris: I tried skiing once but I found it really difficult. After three days I gave up and went home!
Ava: Well, the lessons go on until late afternoon every day, so I hope I can improve quickly. I'm really looking forward to trying, anyway!
Chris: Yes, I'm sure you'll have a great time.

Students could do Grammar reference: Phrasal verbs, Exercises 1 and 2, page 123, at this point or for homework.

5 Remind students of the advice to give longer answers by adding details such as places and times. Tell students that when they answer the questions they should practise this part of the exam and extend their answers. Elicit some of the interesting information students found out about their partner.

▶ **Grammar reference page 123: Phrasal verbs**
▶ **Workbook page 13**

Vocabulary SB page 31
People's hobbies

6 Look at the example with the students and ask what a *board* is and what the *pieces* are. Check other vocabulary when they have finished the activity, especially *cook/cooker* as *cooker* is often mistaken for a job.

Answers

hobby	Person	equipment
1 cycling	cyclist	bike, helmet
2 painting	painter	brush, paint
3 cooking	cook	cooker, oven
4 chess	chess player	board, pieces
5 photography	photographer	camera
6 music	musician	instrument
7 camping		tent, backpack

7 Look at the example. Elicit the meaning of the words, e.g. *indoor game* – refers to where you play it, usually in a building; *black and white squares* – this refers to the design of the board; *queen* – this is one of the pieces; *move* – an action you do when you play. Set a time limit of two minutes for students to brainstorm their vocabulary.

Suggested answers
cycling: wheels, seat, chain, lock, ride
painting: landscape, frame, picture, oils
cooking: recipe, saucepans, frying pan, boil, roast, bake
photography: digital, zoom, close-up
music: practise, performance, notes, keys
camping: sleeping bag, fire, campsite

Extension idea
Divide the class into six groups, splitting up pairs from Exercise 7. Allocate one of the activities from Box A, not including chess, to each group. The students share all the vocabulary they wrote down for that one activity and explain any words that other group members don't know. Each group then presents its vocabulary to the rest of the class.

8 Allow students a few moments to think of ideas alone before they work with a partner. Monitor and note interesting descriptions and ask those students to describe their hobby to the class for other students to guess the hobbies.

▶ **Workbook page 13**

Speaking Part 2 SB page 32

Lead-in
Tell students they are going to describe a photo for their partner and see if their partner can recognise it from the description. Students work alone to find a photo in the Student's Book from Units 1 or 2 and think of how to describe it. Set a time limit of one minute. They then close their books and work in pairs, describing their photo to their partner. When they have both finished, they race to find their partner's photo first.

1 When students have discussed the questions, find out who does or has done any of the activities. Elicit details of where, when, with whom, etc. and whether or not the students would recommend them to other people.

Answers
A acting **B** sightseeing **C** camping

2 Allow students to compare which things they heard in pairs. Elicit their answers and any details they can remember.

Answers
He is talking about photo C. He describes all of them.

Track 17

Eduardo: In this picture I can see two people in the countryside and they're camping there. The woman on the left is wearing a green jacket, grey trousers and walking boots, and the other is wearing a red jacket and hat, blue trousers and boots. It looks like they're cooking some vegetables in a, er, frying pan on a small gas cooker, perhaps in the evening. Behind them is their yellow tent, where they're going to spend the night. It seems they are backpackers because there is a big bag for carrying things on the left of the photo, and another one on the right. In the background there's a high mountain and a forest, with some trees quite close to their tent. It appears to be winter because there's some snow on the mountain, and although the weather looks dry, I think it's probably very cold there.

3 Ask students to read through the questions in pairs and ask them to discuss what the missing words could be. Stronger students or classes could write the words and check if they are correct. Weaker classes or students shouldn't write anything yet or, if they do, they should use a pencil. After listening, elicit the answers.

Answers
2 is wearing **3** looks like **4** It seems **5** In the background
6 appears to be **7** looks

4 It may be worth pointing out that there is a third phrase '*looks as if*'. This is commonly used with verb phrases and could replace *looks like* in the phrase *looks like they are in a skateboarding park*. Where there is only a noun and no verb, students can only use *look like*, e.g. *She looks like my mum. He looks like a teacher.* When looking at the prepositions, emphasise that we always say 'in the photo', not 'on the photo'.

Answers
1 We use *look like* with a noun (it *looks like* they're cooking) and *look* (without *like*) with an adjective to give a physical description (the weather *looks dry*).
2 He uses *In, on, behind, on*

Speaking Part 2 (describing a picture)

Discuss the advice with the students. Ask why it is important to listen carefully to the instructions (the examiner generally asks students to describe the photo without any other task but students should listen just to be sure that this is what they are asked).

Exam advice

5 Tell students that while one is talking, the other should act as an examiner. Read the information in Exercise 6 with the class so that students know what the 'examiner' is listening out for. Time the activity and tell students when one minute has passed.

6 Encourage students to say what their partner did well and what they can improve on.

Extension idea

Once students have given each other their feedback, they could repeat Exercises 5 and 6, this time describing the other photo and trying to improve their performance.

7 Look at the instructions with the class. Give an example using something you can see in the classroom. Use prepositions of place and the phrases: *It looks / It looks like* in your description and elicit what the thing is. Monitor and help students where necessary. Elicit descriptions from different students for the rest of the class to guess.

▶ **Speaking bank pages 154–158: Speaking Part 2**
▶ **Workbook page 13**

Writing Part 2 SB page 33

Lead-in

Ask students to close their eyes and think about a great day out that they will never forget. Give them 30 seconds to think about the day and then put them in pairs to talk about their day. Elicit some of the places and activities mentioned during the activity.

1. Discuss the instructions with the students and ask them what kind of day it could and couldn't be, e.g. It could be a day trip to a city or the countryside. It couldn't be a day spent at home. It must be a positive experience.

Answers
1 Yes, you are. **2** first person

2. Before students read the story, ask them to describe the photo in pairs. Elicit what they can see and check their use of prepositions of place and *look / look like*. Students then read the story quickly to understand what it is about before doing the matching.

Answers
b 1 **c** 3 **d** 2 **e** 1

3. Point out that the first three ideas give students a choice either to use their imaginations or to write about a real event or about something based on a film or TV programme. Allow students two minutes to work alone, one minute to share ideas and two minutes to plan their story.

Writing Part 2 (a story)
Discuss the advice with the students. Ask students whether they think it is easier to write a story or an article and what each one requires, e.g. a story needs past forms and adjectives. Also the writer needs to use their imagination. An article is often written using present forms and requires some topic vocabulary. In the story, the student will use linking words such as *at first, later, suddenly, finally* to show the order of activities. In both stories and articles they can use linking words to connect ideas, e.g. *because, but, and.*

Exam advice

4. Set a time limit of fifteen minutes. In the exam they have 22.5 minutes but need some time for planning and checking their work. When students have finished, ask them to swap stories with a partner and give feedback on the ideas and the language used.

Model answer
I had a really great day out. It started badly. My parents decided to go walking in the mountains and I'm not keen on walking.

It was warm and sunny as we got out of the car and there was a ski lift to get to the top of the mountain. That was fun and very easy! We then walked for about four hours. The views were incredible.

We didn't go down the same way. There were special bikes which don't have pedals. You can only use them to go downhill. You just sit on them and go down the mountain path as fast as you want. It was brilliant.

Extension idea
Students work in groups of three or four. Look at the story in the book and ask comprehension questions, e.g. *What was the weather like? Who was the writer with?* Elicit the answer (good; his/her brother). Tell the groups to write the first line of a story and five comprehension questions. You can write question words on the board: *Who, What, Where, When, Why, How, How long.* Monitor and help groups with ideas.

Groups now swap papers with a different group. They look at the first line and the questions and use their imaginations to answer the questions logically.

▶ **Speaking Bank pages 154–158: Speaking Part 2**
▶ **Writing Bank pages 150–151: a story**
▶ **Workbook page 15**
▶ **Complete Preliminary new edition Test Generator Unit 3**

Vocabulary

Leisure activities

doing sports
going dancing
playing a musical instrument
posting messages on social media sites
riding a bike, a motorbike or a horse
taking photos
visiting an art gallery or museum
watching a film or play

Prepositions of place

above
behind
below
between
in
in front of
inside
near
next to
on
on the right
opposite
under

Phrasal verbs

give up
go off
go on
find out
hang on
join in
look after
look forward to
put (your name) down
run out of
set off
sign up for
take up

People's hobbies

backpack
bike
board
brush
camera
camping
chess, chess player
cook, cooker, cooking
cycling, cyclist
helmet
instrument
music, musician
oven
paint, painter, painting
photographer, photography
pieces
tent

Vocabulary activity 1

Gapped word points. Divide the class into two teams. Tell the class they are going to guess the missing letters to find the word. Their team gets a point for every time a letter they guess appears in a word. They can't say the word, only individual letters. However, the team which recognises the word first can gain more points by knowing which letters to say. Start by writing: _ _ _ _ _ _ _ _ _ _ _ (*photography*) on the board. For example, If a team guesses 'e', write the letter on the board and give them 0 points. If a team guesses 'o', write the two 'o's in the gaps and award two points. The team with the most points at the end of the activity is the winner.

Vocabulary activity 2

Students work in groups of four. They write down two words each from the leisure activities and people's hobbies sections of the list which can be shown in a mime, e.g. cooking. One student starts by miming one of their words. The other students have their books closed so they can't look at the word lists and try to guess the word. The first to guess the word wins a point. Students continue until everyone has mimed two words.

4 On holiday

Unit objectives

Topic: holidays and places

Listening Part 3: information completion: listening for specific information

Reading Part 1: short texts, multiple choice: reading notices and other short texts to identify the main message

Speaking Part 3: collaborative task: making suggestions and giving reasons

Writing Part 1: email: writing an email

Grammar: comparative and superlative adjectives; *a bit, a little, slightly, much, far, a lot, (not) as ... as; big* and *enormous* (gradable and non-gradable adjectives)

Vocabulary: holiday activities; *travel, journey* and *trip*; buildings and places

Pronunciation: weak forms in comparative structures

Starting off SB page 34
Holiday activities

Lead-in
Look at the photos with the students. Ask them where they think each place is and to describe what is happening. Put the students into pairs and allow two minutes. Elicit ideas from different pairs.

1 Encourage students to talk about activities that could be done and also give their opinions about the places.

Suggested answers
1 look around a market / buy gifts / souvenirs **2** go snowboarding **3** hire a bike **4** take photos / go sightseeing **5** hang out with friends/relax on a beach **6** go snorkelling

2 Tell students to listen out for four activities that she mentions. Elicit the answers and ask what Joe's idea of a good holiday is (hanging out on a beach and relaxing).

Answers
Marrakesh: go sightseeing, take photos, look around markets, buy gifts

Track 18

Joe: Where did you go on holiday, Sonia?
Sonia: Well, I went to Marrakesh with my cousin Nicky.
Joe: Marrakesh? Where's that?
Sonia: It's a city in Morocco, North Africa.
Joe: What did you do there?
Sonia: Well, you know my cousin. She loves to see everything so we went sightseeing almost every day.
Joe: Did you see a lot of things?
Sonia: Yeah! We looked around so many palaces, mosques and museums and of course I took lots of photos. You've seen them, haven't you?
Joe: I think so. Do you like visiting museums?
Sonia: It's OK but I prefer going shopping and wow, in Marrakesh the *souks* are amazing.
Joe: What's a *souk*?
Sonia: It's an open-air marketplace where you can buy almost everything.
Joe: So, did you buy anything?
Sonia: Oh yes! I bought some little gifts for my friends and I got a couple of scarves.
Joe: I'm not sure I'd enjoy that kind of holiday.
Sonia: What do you mean?
Joe: When I go on holiday, I prefer hanging out on the beach. It's much more relaxing.

3 Set a time limit of two minutes for each question. Give each student in the group a number (1–4). Students have to start the discussion of the question with the same number as theirs. Encourage students to give reasons and talk about their own experiences to explain them.

Reading Part 1 SB page 35

Lead-in
Ask students if they have ever been on a boat trip? Ask: *What are the advantages and disadvantages of going on a boat trip?*

1 Look at the first question with the students and elicit which part is the text (the part with the heading *Boat trip*) and what the instructions say (choose the correct letter).

Suggested answer
Read the text, decide what it says and then choose the correct option.

2 Students now cover the options so they can concentrate on the text. Give a twenty-second time limit and elicit the answers.

> **Suggested answers**
> It's a sign. The weather is bad, the time is the same, the day is 'tomorrow' and the food is still lunch.

3 Elicit the key words and then tell the students to uncover the options. Tell the students that some of their key words may not have a matching word in the options. That doesn't mean they were wrong to choose those words, just that the question isn't about them, e.g. *bad weather.*

> **Answers**
> lunch – refreshments
> same time tomorrow – time / day

4 When you have elicited the correct answer, elicit why the other two choices are wrong (*A – lunch still provided B – same time*).

> **Answer**
> C

Reading Part 1 (multiple-choice)
Go through the advice with students and ask them why the stages are important. First they need to know what they have to do, then they have to understand the text, what kind of text it is and what its purpose is. They then need to look at specific key words and matching words in the options. They will then be able to find the answer to the question and understand why the other two choices are wrong.

Exam advice

5 Give students no more than eight minutes to do the same for the remaining four questions. It may take less time, in which case you can stop the activity and elicit the answers.

> **Answers**
> **2** C **3** A **4** A **5** B

Fast finishers
Students think of a notice they might see at work or in the town. They write one notice about 25 words long.

6 Ask the students to discuss which option to choose and why. Set a strict time limit so that they don't spend too much time trying to agree on one place. Allow another five minutes for them to discuss the questions in the book. Elicit useful expressions to use in the discussion, e.g. *What about ... Let's ... Shall we ...* . Monitor and see how well they are working together. Encourage quieter students to contribute ideas.

7 Encourage students to start by explaining their choice of place and making it sound as attractive as possible. They then present the other information with reasons for their choices.

Extension idea
Students create an advert for their holiday from Exercises 6 and 7, containing factual information as well as language to persuade people to book this holiday.

▶ **Workbook page 17**

Vocabulary SB page 36
travel, journey and *trip*

Lead-in
Students work in pairs and think about a holiday they would like to go on: the activities, the weather, the nightlife etc. Set a time limit of two minutes. Students join up with a second pair and act out roleplays as travel agents and customers.

1 Tell students to cover Exercise 2. Allow students to discuss their ideas in pairs. Don't elicit the correct answers yet.

2 When students have finished, elicit the correct answers and why they are correct: 1 a journey is just the travelling from one place to another; 2 a journey wouldn't include the hotel; 3 the verb *trip* has a different meaning. It means 'to almost fall'; 4 *travel* isn't a countable noun so can't come after 'a' and an adjective; 5 this is just talking about the time on the plane which is the *journey.*

> **Answers**
> **1** trips **2** trip **3** travelled **4** trip **5** journey

3 To ensure that students get practice speaking even if their answer is 'No', encourage follow-up questions as in the example, e.g. for the first bullet: *Why not?* Elicit interesting ideas from each group.

Grammar SB page 36

Comparative and superlative adjectives

Lead-in

Write the places: *Rome, Canada, Tokyo, Brazil* on the board. Put the students into pairs and give them one minute to think of any adjectives that they can to describe the places.

Background information

Canada population 36.6 million (2017); Tokyo city centre 9.2 million but Greater Tokyo Area 38.2 million; Brazil is 4395 km from north to south. Canada and Chile are both officially longer but only when including islands; Rome has fewer rainy days but more rain altogether (800 mm compared to Paris 637 mm).

1 Allow students to discuss the facts for one minute before eliciting ideas. Share the background information with them during feedback.

Answers
a true **b** false **c** true

2 Elicit the answers and ask which two things are being compared in a and c (*Canada and Tokyo, Rome and Paris*) and which group is being looked at in b (*all the countries in the world*).

Answers
1 c **2** b

3 Allow students to work in pairs. Elicit the answers and make sure students have corrected any spelling mistakes but don't elicit or give the rules yet.

Answers
1 deeper **2** safer **3** noisier **4** bigger **5** worse **6** noisiest **7** biggest **8** most beautiful **9** best **10** worst **11** most **12** least

4 Allow students to work in pairs and encourage them to refer to the table to find the same or similar types of adjectives. Elicit the answers but do not explain the rules at this stage.

Answers
1 more safe = safer **2** worse = worst **3** bigest = biggest **4** hotest = hottest **5** more quiet = quieter **6** taler = taller

5 Allow two minutes for students to try to identify the rules and elicit their ideas, correcting or adding to the rules where necessary. Write the rules on the board for students to copy into their notebooks.

Suggested answers
For short adjectives, add *-er* or *-est*
For short adjectives ending in a vowel + a consonant, double the last letter and add *-er* or *-est*
For short adjectives ending in *-e*, add *-r* or *-st*
For two-syllable adjectives ending in *-y*, change the *y* to *i* and add *-er* or *-est*
For longer adjectives, or most two-syllable adjectives not ending in *-y*, put *more* (*less*), *most* (*least*) in front of the adjective. (some two-syllable adjectives form comparatives by adding *-er* / *-est* such as *quieter* / *the quietest*.)

Students could do Grammar reference: Comparative and superlative adjectives, Exercises 1 and 2, page 124, at this point or for homework.

Extension idea

Look at the places and adjectives on the board from the lead-in and elicit a comparative sentence and a superlative sentence. Students then make more sentences using the adjectives on the board.

6 Point out that the important task for students is to write the correct form of the adjectives so they should do this first and then guess the answers to the questions. Elicit the answers to the comparative and superlative forms and check that they are spelt correctly. Don't elicit answers to the quiz yet.

7 To make the activity more competitive, you could elicit the answer to the first question and then play that section of the recording until: *it's bigger than South America*. Repeat for the other questions, eliciting answers then playing the part of the text they appear in.

Answers
1 C **2** A **3** the most dangerous, B **4** lighter, A **5** noisier, C **6** the slowest, A **7** faster, C **8** the busiest, C **9** the deepest, A **10** drier, C

Track 19

Lucas: And here are the answers to the quiz. We all know that Asia is the biggest continent in the world, followed by Africa, but did you know that North America is the third largest continent in the world? This means that it's bigger than South America.

Nora: And of course, at seventeen million square kilometres, Russia is the largest country in the world. That's twice the size of Canada, which is the second largest country.

Lucas: And now for the animal facts. The most dangerous animal on the planet is not the snake or the shark but the tiny mosquito because it carries diseases. The African elephant can weigh up to eight thousand kilos so it is the largest and heaviest land animal, but the blue whale is the heaviest living animal. It can weigh around 150 tonnes – that's

150,000 kilos. I wouldn't like to share my home with a howler monkey. They are much louder than parrots or lions, in fact they are the noisiest animals on Earth – you can hear them from up to five kilometres away. The slowest-moving fish is the sea horse. It would take this fish about an hour to move 15 metres. As for the fastest fish, tunas are one of the fastest fish. Some tunas can swim at eighty kilometres per hour while the Killer Whales can swim at fifty-five kilometres per hour. Great White Sharks can swim at forty kilometres per hour, so they are faster than dolphins, which can swim at thirty kilometres per hour. You've got some answers about places, haven't you, Nora?

Nora: Yes, I have. Did you know that the busiest train stations in the world are in Tokyo, Japan? Around one million people travel through Shinjuku station every day. And, if you like diving then you should go to Y40 Deep Joy in Italy. Its deepest point is nearly 40 metres which makes it the deepest diving pool in the world.

Lucas: And finally, Antarctica is the coldest, driest and windiest continent. On 21 July 1983, the temperature was minus eighty-nine degrees centigrade. That's the lowest temperature ever! And it only rains or snows two hundred millimetres a year there. The second driest continent is Australia where it rains six hundred millimetres a year. That's all for now.

/P/ Weak forms in comparative structures

8 When students have listened to the recording, model and drill the words with the class, first chorally then individually.

Answer
They aren't stressed in conversation and they are pronounced /ə/ ('schwa').

Track 20

1: I wouldn't like to share my home with a howler monkey. They're much louder than parrots or lions.

2: Great white sharks can swim at forty kilometres per hour, so they're faster than dolphins, which can swim at thirty kilometres per hour.

9 When students have practised the two sentences, invite students to read other sentences from Exercise 6 which have comparative forms (1, 4, 10).

▶ **Grammar reference page 124: Comparative and superlative adjectives**

▶ **Workbook page 16**

Grammar SB page 38

a bit, a little, slightly, much, far, a lot

10 Students do the exercise in pairs or alone. Monitor and help where necessary.

Answers

2 An African elephant's brain is much / far / a lot heavier than a human's brain.
3 Arica is much / far / a lot drier (or dryer) than Death Valley.
4 Atlanta International Airport is much / far / a lot busier than Heathrow Airport.
5 Cherrapunji is a bit / a little / slightly wetter than Tutendo.
6 Cheetahs can run much / far / a lot faster than elephants.

Fast finishers
Students write two similar sentences about people or places they know. If appropriate, allow students to research sizes on their phones.

(not) as ... as

11 Before students look at the text, elicit anything they know about China. Check the meaning of *polluted* and *international*. When students have answered the questions, ask for another phrase which means the same as: *not as ... as* (*less* + adjective + *than*: *Shanghai is less polluted than Beijing*).

Answers
1 *as ... as* **2** *not* **3** no

Students could do Grammar reference: *a bit, a little, slightly, (not) much, far, (not) a lot; (not) as ... as,* Exercise 3, page 125, at this point or for homework.

12 Set a strict time limit so students don't worry too much about their choices. Monitor and help where necessary.

13 Look at the example with the students and ask how B might respond using comparatives or *as ... as*, e.g. *Art museums are more relaxing. You can see the Mona Lisa at the Louvre – the most famous painting in the world.* Set a time limit for the activity and discuss some of the students' ideas with the class.

▶ **Grammar reference page 125: *a bit, a little, slightly, (not) much, far, (not) a lot***

▶ **Grammar reference page 125: *(not) as ... as***

Vocabulary SB page 39
Buildings and places

Lead-in
Tell students to cover everything except the four photos. Students work in groups of four and have one minute to write as many adjectives as possible to describe one of the photos. Elicit adjectives from each group and ask the other students to guess which photo is being described.

1. Elicit the answers and the names of the places if the students know them (Camp Nou Stadium, Barcelona, The Statue of Liberty, New York, The Mall of the Emirates, Dubai, The Trevi Fountain, Rome).

Suggested answers
A stadium - Camp Nou football stadium in Barcelona
B monument - The Statue of Liberty in New York
C shopping centre – The Mall of the Emirates in Dubai
D fountain – The Trevi Fountain in Rome

2. When students have discussed the question, ask: *What can you do or see in each place?* and ask them about the ones in their town or famous examples in their country.

3. When students have matched all the vocabulary, elicit the meaning of the adjectives and examples of places the words could describe, e.g. *crowded* means full of people: *a football stadium during an important match.*

Answers
2 wide **3** low **4** old **5** clean **6** ugly **7** dull (accept quiet)
8 interesting **9** dangerous **10** cheap **11** quiet **12** near

Extension idea
Students work in small groups. Each group makes sentences about their town using comparative or superlative forms of some of the words from the exercise.

4. Look at the example sentence and the use of *too* + negative adjective to talk about a problem. Elicit another example for one of the other activities, e.g. *We don't go to the gym because it is too expensive.* Set a time limit for the group discussion and elicit some ideas from each group.

▶ **Workbook page 17**

Grammar SB page 39
big and *enormous*

1. Students discuss the questions in pairs. Elicit the answers and point out that *very, extremely, totally* and *absolutely* make the adjective stronger whereas *quite* makes it less strong.

Answers
1 B **2** C **2** A
very, extremely and quite: tall and large;
absolutely and totally: enormous

2. Look at the example with the students and elicit another gradable adjective with the same meaning in the text (*large*).

Suggested answers
2 small **3** hot **4** cold **5** bad **6** tiring **7** interesting **8** good

3. When students have finished, elicit alternative sentences using the wrong option, e.g. 1 *It's a very nice place.*

Answers
1 absolutely **2** extremely **3** absolutely **4** quite **5** very

Students could do Grammar reference: Gradable and non-gradable adjectives, Exercises 1 and 2, page 125, at this point or for homework.

4. After the students have found the answers, play the recording again and ask them to list the gradable and non-gradable adjectives they hear. Elicit these (*G – nice, crowded, small, boring NG – tiny, amazing*) and point out that a useful non-gradable equivalent of *crowded* is *packed*.

Answers
1 Katikati, New Zealand
2 it's an open-air gallery, it never gets crowded, it's safe, easy to get into the countryside
3 quite boring, I'd like to live somewhere bigger with nightlife, cinemas, shopping centres and sports centres.

Track 21
Ani: Er, I come from New Zealand, I live in Katikati which is a town about 6 hours away from the capital, Wellington. There are only about 4,000 people there – it's tiny. My town is amazing because it's also an open-air gallery. There are paintings on the walls, sculptures everywhere and other artwork. Katikati is a very nice place to live because it never gets too crowded and because it's a small town, it's extremely safe. It's also very easy to get into the countryside to go walking, fishing or even hunting. Sometimes, I find living here quite boring. I'd like to live somewhere bigger with a more lively nightlife and with more cinemas, shopping centres and sports centres.

5 Tell students to try to talk for one minute each. Monitor and help students where necessary. Elicit ideas from different pairs and ask other student if they agree or disagree and why.

▶ **Grammar reference page 125: Gradable and non-gradable adjectives**

▶ **Workbook page 16**

Listening Part 3 SB page 40

Lead-in
Write the word *bushcraft* on the board. Students work in small groups to try to guess what it means. Set a time limit and then elicit ideas.

1 Students stay in the same groups as they were in for the lead-in. Tell the students to spend one minute describing each photo using phrases such as *on the left/right, in the foreground/background, look(s) / look(s) like* and then two minutes giving their opinions about doing a course.

2 Discuss the first gap with the students and elicit that it is a place (*bus station*). Elicit ideas and point out that with a gap such as gap 5 where there is a name or real noun, this will be spelt out by the speaker.

Answers
1 place **2** noun (something you can sleep in)
3 noun (type of food) **4** countable noun (something you use to predict the weather) **5** email address or name **6** number

Listening Part 3 (information completion)
Discuss the exam advice with the students. Point out that the words before and after the missing word won't necessarily be the same as what they hear. For example, it may say:
Age: _____ and students may hear:
He is 15 years old.

Exam advice

3 Point out that, in the exam, students will transfer their answers to a separate answer sheet at the end of the listening exam. The important thing is that they can read what they've written.
When students have listened a second time, elicit the answers including the spelling of Justyna. Also elicit how the speaker said the telephone number using *zero* for 0 and *double-7, double-4* and *double-2*. Point out that English speakers sometimes say '*oh*' like the letter 'O' for the number '0' in phone numbers.

Answers
1 station **2** hut **3** rabbit **4** clouds **5** justyna / Justyna / JUSTYNA **6** 01773442256

Track 22

Narrator: Part three. For each question, write the correct answer in the gap. Write one or two words or a number or a date or time. You will hear a woman talking to a group of people about the bushcraft courses she organises.

Justyna: I'm here to tell you about our bushcraft courses. Since 2007, we've been teaching people the necessary skills to stay alive in the wild by using the things around them.

So what are weekend courses like? On Saturday morning, your guide will pick you up for your adventure in front of the station and drive you to our main office. There, you'll need to repack your backpack with just the essential equipment and then it's time to walk to the forest camp.

The first lesson is how to use the equipment, for example you'll learn how to use a knife properly so that you don't hurt yourself or others. The next job is building your own hut. It doesn't need to be beautiful but it will be your place to spend the night as it will get cold. But don't worry, your guide will have an emergency tent for the group to sleep in if necessary.

You'll learn how to catch a rabbit, although I can't promise you'll be lucky enough to get one. If you do, I'll show you how to prepare it and we'll have it for lunch. We'll also go fishing in the river but whatever we catch there, we will have to put back into the water. Those are the rules in this area.

Over the rest of the weekend you'll learn how to make drinking water, use the stars and moon to find your way and check the clouds for rain or a change in temperature.

Please visit our website for more details but if you have any questions, please email me on Justyna at bushcraftskills dot com, that's J-U-S-T-Y-N-A. Or if you prefer, you can telephone us. Our number is zero one, double seven, three, double four, double two, five, six. There's someone in our office from Monday to Friday from ten to five.

4 Re-elicit what the skills are. Elicit some ideas for how using a knife might be useful in everyday life, e.g. for chopping vegetables, and then set a time limit of five minutes for students to discuss the other skills and the second question.

▶ **Workbook page 18**

Writing Part 1 SB page 40

1 Elicit the answers and point out to the students that the writing task always gives the student information to respond, to either as notes like here or questions within an email that students have to reply to.

Answers
1 an email **2** the notes – a reaction to your friend's news, describe the city, say the most popular time of the year, and recommend other places to visit

2 Ask students to read the reply on page 41 quickly to find the answer.

Answer
Johannesburg, South Africa

3 Point out that the students should also find the information which helped them to answer the questions. Elicit that they are all 'Yes' and why. Ask students what they found out about Johannesburg from the email.

Answer
The answer is 'yes' to all the questions.

4 Set a time limit of twenty minutes. Elicit that they have to write about their hometown even if they don't think it is very interesting. Later they will recommend other places to visit.

Fast finishers
Tell students to think of questions they would like to ask Bandile about Johannesburg, e.g. *What kind of food can you buy in the food market?*

5 As well as checking that students have included all the information, encourage them to check for grammar and spelling errors and to give feedback about these if they notice them.

Writing Part 1 (an email)
Discuss the exam advice and elicit why it is useful, e.g. if students make notes for all the information they need to find, they are less likely to forget to answer or respond to each of the four prompts related to the email. It will also help them organise their text and to think of useful vocabulary and structures to use.

Exam advice

6 This task could be done in class or for homework. You may want to look at the exam advice before they write. They should use their original text and the feedback they received in Exercise 5 to help them. Set a shorter time limit as they are correcting and improving an already-written email.

▶ **Writing bank pages 145-147: Writing Part 1: an email**
▶ **Workbook page 19**

Speaking Part 3 SB page 41

Lead-in
Ask students to think for one minute about a type of holiday they would love to go on and one they would hate to go on.

1 Ask students to note all the ideas the speakers mention and then decide which one they chose.

Answer
a cruise

Track 23

Martyn: Someone from work has just got back from an absolutely fantastic holiday in Paris. They stayed in an apartment in the city centre and they did loads of sightseeing. He said the art museums were amazing, better than the museums here. Why don't we all go to Paris for our next holiday?

Nathan: Martyn! Not more museums! And don't you think Paris will be really crowded? I'd like to go somewhere quieter. We could hire a campervan and go camping. My friend Dan went to a park in the USA and he says it's one of the most beautiful places in the world.

Pete: Not camping again, please! We got really wet last time. That was the worst holiday of my life! What about trying a new sport like surfing or snorkelling? It would be so much fun. Yeah! Let's do that! Please!

Charlie: Um... But snorkelling is as dangerous as surfing. I'm not sure I fancy doing either of those two sports.

Martyn: OK. What do you suggest, Charlie?

Charlie: Well, how about a cruise?

Martyn: Why do you think we should choose that?

Charlie: Because there's so much to do and we don't need to plan where we're going to stay or what we're going to do. It's all done for you.

Martyn: What can you do on a cruise? I really think a city break would be more interesting than a cruise.

Charlie: No, no at all! There are loads of different things to do – there are swimming pools and gyms, cinemas and organised entertainment. And then when you wake up in the morning, you're in a new place! I think that's a lot more exciting than other types of holiday.

Pete: That sounds perfect!

Nathan: I agree!

Martyn: OK.

2 Look at the questions with the students and ask them to think together what kinds of holiday the friends suggested and why and also the other people's reasons for disagreeing.

Answers
1 yes **2** yes

3 Tell the students that they only need one word in each gap. Tell students to ignore the spaces after the sentences for now. Elicit the answers and remind students that *really* can be used with gradable and ungradable adjectives.

Answers
2 like **3** most **4** really **5** about **6** do **7** much

4 Elicit the answers and check the different ways of making suggestions:
– *Why don't* + subject + base form of the verb without *to*
– *Let's* + base form of the verb without *to*
– *What/How about* + *-ing* form of the verb

Answers
2 R **3** R **4** R **5** S **6** S **7** R

5 Tell students that, when they are given photos or pictures to talk about, the examiners will expect them to look at them quickly before starting to talk. However, they shouldn't pause too long. One idea is for students to start by asking their partner a question which gets the conversation underway.

Speaking Part 3 (collaborative task)
Go through the exam advice with the students and ask why these are important to remember. Elicit that Part 3 also tests the students' ability to make suggestions, ask for opinions, agree and disagree. If they don't let their partner speak, they can't do these things. Giving reasons allows them to show more of a range of vocabulary and grammar and also shows that they understand the task.

Exam advice

▶ **Speaking bank pages 159–160: Speaking Part 3**
▶ **Complete Preliminary new edition Test Generator Unit 4**
▶ **Complete Preliminary new edition Test Generator Term Test Units 1–4**

Vocabulary

Holiday activities

buy gifts/souvenirs
go sightseeing
go snorkelling
go snowboarding
hang out with friends
hire a bike
look around a market
take photos

Travel, journey and trip

journey
travel
trip

Buildings and places

art gallery
bookshop
bridge
cinema
department store
factory
fountain
library
market
monument
shopping centre
sports centre
stadium
town hall
youth club

Adjectives to describe places

beautiful
boring
cheap
clean
crowded
dangerous
dirty
dull
empty
expensive
far
high
interesting
lively
low
modern
narrow
near
noisy
old
quiet
safe
ugly
wide

Non-gradable adjectives

boiling
enormous
exhausting
fantastic
fascinating
freezing
terrible
tiny

Vocabulary activity 1

Tell the students to choose a word from one of the word lists and to write it backwards. It should be something easy to pronounce even when written this way round, e.g. fountain – *niatnuof*. Students work in pairs and tell each other the section their word is in, e.g. buildings and places, and say the word backwards. The other student has to find the word and say what it means. Or, to make the activity easier, the student could show the words written backwards. Elicit words from different students for others to guess.

Vocabulary activity 2

Students work in pairs and choose three words to make into anagrams. The anagrams can use all the letters in one block or split them up into smaller chunks, e.g. *forbidden* could be *difnebrdo* or *ford in bed*. When students have written their anagrams, they swap them with a second pair and try to work out what the words are and what they mean.

Vocabulary and grammar review Unit 3

1 **2** near **3** above **4** in front of **5** under **6** inside

2 **2** e **3** a **4** h **5** b **6** g **7** d **8** f

3 **2** A **3** A **4** C **5** B **6** B

4 **2** to do **3** to take **4** to buy **5** spending **6** to borrow **7** to see **8** spending **9** to send **10** to do

Vocabulary and grammar review Unit 4

1 **2** great **3** wettest **4** coldest **5** freezing **6** lively **7** huge **8** boring

2 **2** than **3** very **4** far **5** travel **6** library

3 **2** It is more ~~easy~~ **easier** for you to walk to my house.
3 That's the ~~worse~~ **worst** restaurant we've ever been to.
4 I like living in the city much more ~~that~~ **than** the countryside.
5 Those days on holiday were the ~~happier~~ **happiest** days of my life.
6 Hotels are more ~~cheaper~~ **cheaper** here than the hotels in the city.

4 **2** than **3** most **4** best/most **5** as **6** in

5 Different feelings

Unit objectives

Topic: feelings

Listening Part 2: identifying the situation and what you need to listen for

Reading Part 4: text insertion: understanding text structure for cohesion and coherence; identifying linking words (*this, then, do, also, however,* etc.)

Speaking Part 4: general discussion; describing personal experiences; asking people what they think

Writing Part 2: story: using adjectives to describe a feeling

Grammar: *can, could, might* and *may* (ability and possibility); *should, shouldn't, ought to, must, mustn't, have to* and *don't have to* (advice, obligation and prohibition)

Vocabulary: feelings; adjectives and prepositions; adjectives with *-ed* and *-ing*; adjectives and their opposites

Pronunciation: modal verbs: weak and strong forms

Starting off
Feelings

Lead-in
Write *feelings* on the board and elicit words to describe someone's feelings, e.g. *happy, sad, tired.* Students work in groups of four. Elicit adjectives from the groups but don't ask who they referred to.

1 Elicit a definition of *jealous* (unhappy and angry because you want something that someone else has). Point out that different pictures will elicit different feelings from different people. Ask students to explain why they feel the emotions they do, e.g. *The photo of the climber makes me feel afraid because I'm scared of high places.*

Answers
Someone rock climbing, a happy family, someone throwing rubbish (a banana skin) out of a car window, a rich young man in an expensive sports car, a flood in a rural area.
Students' own answers.

2 To help students, you could say that the nouns for the other four words end in *-er*, *-ess* and *-y*. Elicit the answers and check how students could use both adjectives and nouns in sentences, e.g. *I am afraid of spiders. / I have a fear of spiders.*

Answers
angry – anger; happy – happiness; jealous – jealousy; sad – sadness

3 Elicit from students that they are only completing the missing noun at this stage, not what they would do in this situation. Students should work alone.

Answers
2 anger **3** fear **4** happiness **5** jealousy

4 Look at the example and elicit what other people may do, e.g. *someone might forget about it very quickly.* Set a time limit of two minutes for students to complete their responses alone.

Suggested answers
2 say nothing to them / tell them it's OK / shout at them
3 a bit nervous / absolutely terrified / completely relaxed
4 you laugh and jump around / you smile a little / do nothing because you knew you would pass
5 you say they're very lucky / you say they don't deserve it / you take no notice and say nothing

5 Before students work in groups, check *emotional–unemotional.* Elicit how an emotional person differs from an unemotional one.

Listening Part 2 SB page 45

1 Allow students to work in pairs to do the matching. Elicit the answers and ask students for examples of feeling these emotions.

Answers
2 disappointed **3** nervous **4** confident **5** embarrassed **6** bored

2 Look at question 1 with the class and elicit who is talking (a woman), what she is talking about (a singing competition) and what we need to know (how she felt after singing). Students do the same with 2–6 in pairs. Elicit the key words in each of the other questions and what information they have to listen for.

Answers
1 how a woman felt after a singing contest
2 the advice that the man gives the woman
3 how the student feels
4 who a woman had most fun with
5 the reason a man decided to go to work by bike
6 who annoyed the woman yesterday

Listening Part 2 (multiple-choice)
Discuss the advice with the students and ask them why they think it is useful (*they now have a clear idea of what they are listening out for*).
Re-elicit the advice from previous units that students hand in a separate answer sheet so their corrections won't be seen by the examiners.

3 Tell students to work alone and not to compare answers between listening so they should get used to working under exam conditions. When students have listened a second time, allow them to compare their answers in pairs and try to remember what was said on the recording to help them choose the answers. If there is time, photocopy the audioscript so that students can find the part of the text with the correct answer and why the other two options are wrong.

Answers
1 B **2** B **3** C **4** B **5** B **6** A

Track 24

Narrator: Part 2. For each question, choose the correct answer.

1

Narrator: You will hear a woman talking about taking part in a singing contest.

Man: What did you think of the judges' scores?

Woman: Well, I thought I'd sung pretty well, certainly nothing to be ashamed of, but I must admit they were lower than I'd expected. I knew then that I had little chance of beating the others, but at least I'd done my best. For me that's the most important thing.

Man: Yes, definitely. So do you think you'll try again in next year's contest?

Woman: Yes, if I can. I might not win but I think I could do better than this year.

2

Narrator: You will hear two friends talking about camping.

Woman: I'm going camping in the mountains on Friday.

Man: That'll be great fun, especially with the hot weather we're having right now, but the temperatures there can really drop at night, even in summer. You'd better put a jacket and a thick sweater in your backpack instead of lots of things to eat. You can always get a tasty meal in one of the local villages. Where exactly will you be going?

Woman: Up by the lake.

Man: It's beautiful there, isn't it? But perhaps it'd be best to put your tent up somewhere else. At this time of year the mosquitoes there are awful. They never stop biting!

3

Narrator: You will hear a student talking to his friend about a literature exam.

Woman: You've got that literature exam next week, haven't you? How's the revision going?

Man: I thought I'd be getting tired of it by now, but your suggestion that I should watch films of the books we have to study has made it more interesting and I understand the stories better. Usually just before an important exam like this one I feel really worried about what could go wrong on the day, but this time's quite different.

Woman: That's great to hear. I'm sure you'll do really well on Monday morning. Good luck!

4

Narrator: You will hear a young woman telling a friend about studying abroad.

Man: Did you enjoy your month abroad?

Woman: Yes, I was in a small town in the countryside. The lessons were good even though the rest of the class were younger than me and we didn't have much in common. I had a lovely room in the house where I was staying with a couple. They were kind to me but they had a busy social life and I hardly saw them. So I went to the main square where all the shops and cafés are and made friends there. We had a great time hanging out and chatting.

5

Narrator: You will hear a man telling his friend about how he travels to work.

Woman: I see you're using your bike every day now, instead of coming to work in your friend's car.

Man: Yes, I've been doing that for a couple of months. Actually he still goes right past our office on his way to work, so it's not about protecting the environment, spending less on petrol or anything like that. It's just that I realised I was spending nearly all my time sitting down, in the office and at home, and I thought I'd better do something about it.

Woman: That's a good idea. Maybe I should do the same.

6

Narrator: You will hear a woman talking to a friend about going shopping.

Man: So how was your shopping trip yesterday? I imagine the city centre's pretty crowded on a Saturday morning at this time of the year.

Woman: Yes, there were lots of people walking in the streets and the department store was full of customers, too. I don't mind that, but I wasn't happy about having shop assistants trying to sell me stuff when all I wanted to do was look at things. I noticed they were bothering other customers, too. If they carry on like that, their shop won't be full much longer.

▶ **Workbook page 22**

Grammar SB page 45
can, could, might and *may*

Lead-in
Put students into groups of four and ask them to write two questions: one about ability starting: *Can you …?* and one about a possibility starting: *Could there it / be …?* They ask each other the questions. Elicit ideas from each group.

1 Allow students to work in pairs. When they have finished, give them more rules about modal verbs: modals always have the same form; there is no third person *-s*; we form questions by reversing the order of the modal and the subject *I can – Can I?* Abbreviated forms: *will not – won't, shall not – shan't, may not* and *might not* rarely have a shortened form.

Answers
1 *might not* **2** *not* goes after the modal verb
3 *can't* and *couldn't* **4** the infinitive without *to*

2 Allow students to work in pairs. When they have completed the sentences, elicit which rules they illustrate: 1, 2, 5, 7 – they are followed by the base form without *to*; 3 – *not* comes after the modal verb in negatives; 4 we reverse the word order in questions; 6 we don't use the verb *to be* before a modal.

Answers
1 We can to **go** to the cinema next weekend.
2 I know it may ~~seems~~ **seem** strange.
3 Sorry but tomorrow ~~I'm not can~~ **can't** go.
4 What ~~we could~~ **could we** do?
5 Here we can ~~doing~~ **do** a lot of sports here.
6 ~~It's~~ **It** could be quite boring for you.
7 We could ~~met~~ **meet** at 8 o'clock near the cinema.

3 Allow students to work in pairs. Elicit the answers point out that we can use *could* for a future possibility (*it could be good* ✓) but not for a future ability (*I don't think I could go out on Thursday* ✗)

Answers
1 can, could **2** may, might, could

4 Look at the example with students and ask why *couldn't* is the correct choice (it is about a negative past ability not a negative present possibility). Students work alone and then compare their answers in pairs.

Answers
2 can **3** might **4** can't **5** can **6** could

Students could do Grammar reference: Modal verbs: *can, could, might, may* (ability and possibility), Exercises 1 and 2, page 126, for homework.

5 Look at the example and point out that eating ice cream is popular in British cinemas and theatres. Set a time limit of two minutes for each activity and then elicit ideas from the class.

Extension idea
Point out that we often use the modal of ability from this lesson when chatting with friends, e.g. *Do you want to meet later? I can't, sorry, but I can go out tomorrow.*
Students work in pairs to think of two similar dialogues with one question and one response in each.

▶ **Grammar reference page 126: *can, could, might* and *may* (ability and possibility)**
▶ **Workbook page 22**

Speaking Part 4 SB page 46

Lead-in
Tell the students to imagine they have some amazing news which they want to share with their friends. Ask: *How do you tell your friends this news? When?*, e.g. *text everyone immediately*. Students discuss their ideas in small groups.

1 Students stay in the same groups to discuss the questions. Set a three-minute time limit and elicit ideas from each group.

2 Look at the questions with the students before they listen and ask what the missing words could be, e.g. *1 Who do you most enjoy chatting to? Who / What do you most enjoy chatting about?*

Answers
1 Who, to **2** How, usually **3** When, to **4** What, about

Track 25

Daniel: Who do you most enjoy chatting to?

Wen: To my friends. Especially my best friend An, who lives in another city now. We always have so much to say to each other! How about you?

Daniel: Yes, to friends too. And also to my cousin Ricardo. He's about the same age as me and we get on really well so we spend a lot of time talking to each other. How do you usually chat? By phone?

Wen: Quite often, but sometimes we text. Especially when it's difficult to talk aloud, for instance if I'm at work. And you?

Daniel: Mostly on Instagram, if I've got an internet connection of course. And it doesn't cost anything to post messages, which is great. I can't do that at work, though. When can you chat to people?

Wen: In the evenings, mainly. After I get home from work and I can relax. I think that's the best time. What about you?

Daniel: Oh I can't wait that long. I check my messages and reply as soon as I get out of the office! It's usually to make plans for the evening, or just to catch up with what's going on. What do you most like chatting about?

Wen: Sorry, could you say that again?

Daniel: Sure. What do you most like chatting about?

Wen: Well, An and I often give each other advice. For example, if I'm worried about something, I ask her what I should or shouldn't do and she might tell me what I could do. I think that's very important. Do you agree?

Daniel: Yes I do. That's what friends are for. But other times they tell me about something funny that's happened and we laugh and I think that's good too. What do you think?

Wen: Oh yes, definitely. It's not good to be serious all the time!

3 Again, encourage the students to read the expressions before they listen and remind them that they should always read through questions before they start listening to the recording.

Answers
1 about **2** And **3** about **4** agree **5** think

Speaking Part 4 (general discussion)
Discuss the advice with the students and ask why it's important: 1 Speaking for the right length of time is fair and shows that you are interested in what the other person has to say. 2 This helps both students. The one asking the questions shows that they have good English skills and the one being asked has the chance to reply and show off their own ability.

Exam advice

4 Once students have practised in pairs, put them in groups of three and ask one student to act as the examiner.

▶ **Speaking bank page 161: Part 4**

Grammar SB page 47
Modals for advice, obligation and prohibition

Lead-in
Tell students you are going to ask three questions and that, for each one, they should write the first person they think of. Ask: *Who do you ask if you need help deciding what to wear, do or buy? Who often tells you what you must do? Who often tells you what you mustn't do?*

When students have written their three answers, put them in groups of four to tell each other what they wrote and give examples.

1 Elicit the modal verbs they learned before and some of the rules for using them. When students have finished, point out that *ought to* is also followed by the bare infinitive. Elicit the negative form of *ought to* (*ought not to*).

Answers
ought to, shouldn't

2 When students have finished the activity, give an example of the difference between *must* and *have to*, e.g. *I must get my hair cut* (it looks a mess). *I have to get my hair cut* (my boss told me to). Elicit that the negative form of *have to* is *don't have to* / *doesn't have to*.

Answers
2 B **3** A **4** C

3 Students work alone and compare their answers in pairs. Elicit why each answer is correct (1, 2, 4 are rules; 3 it isn't necessary; 5 is a rule but the use of *shouldn't* rather than *mustn't* shows that the speaker thinks it is a rule which is sometimes broken).

Answers
2 have to **3** don't have to **4** must **5** shouldn't

4 Students work alone and compare their answers in pairs. Point out that in sentences such as 2, we could use *must* or *should* with little difference in meaning. Sometimes, this is called strong advice. Elicit some examples: *You must go to see the new superheroes film at the cinema. It's amazing.*

Answers
2 must **3** mustn't **4** don't have to **5** have to/must

Fast finishers
Tell students that for each initial sentence in Exercise 4, they should try to make a different, logical follow-up sentence using a different modal verb.

Students could do the Grammar reference: Modal verbs: *should, shouldn't, ought to, must, mustn't, have to, don't have to* (obligation and prohibition), Exercises 1 and 2, page 127, at this point for homework.

5 Set a time limit of two minutes for students to discuss the sentences. Elicit their ideas and, if any are different from their place of work or study, ask which they think is better, the place in the exercise or their own.

6 Look at the two example questions with the class. Elicit answers for the two questions. You could allow students to work in pairs to think of more questions together and then change their partners to ask the questions to someone new.

Extension idea
Put students into groups of four. Set a time limit of two minutes for each person to make sentences about their own life using: *I don't have to …* Students then share their ideas and try to find things that only they in their group don't have to do.

/P/ Modal verbs: weak and strong forms

7 When students have repeated the full sentences, model and drill the individual modals as well. Model and drill the *schwa* sound.

Answers
1 names **2** nouns **3** main **4** articles **5** prepositions **6** modal

8 When students have listened to the sentences and repeated them, ask why negative modals are said more clearly than positive ones (in a positive sentence, the important information is in the main verb but in a negative one, the important information is that you *can't/mustn't/shouldn't do* the action of the main verb).

Answers
1 b, d, f; yes **2** *n't*; no **3** a, c, e; no

Track 27
a I can buy another one.
b I can't afford that one.
c I could meet you at 5.30.
d I couldn't live without my phone!
e I should get up earlier on Sundays.
f I shouldn't go to bed so late.

9 Before the students start, ask them to look at sentences 1 and 4 and elicit what the difference between them is (*1 is a rule from someone else; 4 is something the student themselves think is a necessity*). When students have finished, ask them what the most interesting fact they found out from their partner was.

▶ **Grammar reference pages 126–127: Modal verbs: *should, shouldn't, ought to, must, mustn't, have to* and *don't have to* (obligation and prohibition)**
▶ **Workbook page 22**

Vocabulary SB page 48
Adjectives and prepositions

Lead-in
Elicit one or two adjectives of feeling from the class, e.g. *happy, tired*. Put students into groups of four and set a time limit of one minute for each group to think of as many adjectives of feeling as they can. Tell the groups they are going to take turns to say one of their adjectives and the group that can continue for the longest wins. Start by saying: *I'm happy*. Another group continues with a different adjective, etc.

1 Tell students to think of their reactions to different people, e.g. a parent, a boss, a friend, a work colleague as they might feel differently for each. Set a time limit of two minutes and then elicit ideas.

2 When the students have finished, elicit how these prepositions can be tested in the exam, e.g. students' writing, multiple-choice gap fill, open cloze gap fill.

Answers
1 with **2** of **3** about

3 Set a time limit of two minutes, then elicit ideas and write them on the board for all students to make a written record of.

Answers
1 of **2** with **3** about

4 Before students look at the questions, look at the photos with the class and elicit what they can see and which adjective they think best matches each, e.g. *spider – afraid*. Set a time limit of three minutes for students to ask and answer the questions. Encourage students to make notes of their partner's answers. When students have finished, elicit the most interesting things they found out.

Answers
1 about **2** with **3** of **4** of/with **5** of/about

Extension idea
For homework, students write a short description of their partner using the information they found out in Exercise 4.

▶ **Workbook page 20**

Adjectives with *-ed* and *-ing* SB page 49

Lead-in
Ask the students to think about the adjectives of feelings they looked at during the last section and give them one minute in pairs to write down as many adjectives as they can remember ending in *-ed*.

1 Put students into pairs and give them one minute to use their imaginations to think of what the story could be about. Elicit ideas from the class and then give them one minute to quickly read the text to find out the answers to both questions.

Answers
1 He wanted to contact the woman he met (and needed her details / phone number).
2 They met again and got married.

2 Discuss the question with the whole class and elicit some more verbs ending in *-e* that can be changed to *-ing* adjectives with the same spelling rule, e.g. *tire*.

Answer
boring: it drops the final *-e* and adds *-ing*

3 Either discuss the question with the whole class or allow students to work in pairs to explain the rule. Point out that, if an adjective ends in a consonant + *y*, we change the *-y* to an *-i* for *-ed* adjectives but not *-ing* adjectives (*satisfy–satisfied–satisfying*).

Answer
bored; we use *-ing* to describe something; *-ed* to describe how someone feels about it.

4 Students work alone. Monitor and help where necessary. Elicit the answers and spelling.

Answers
2 relaxed **3** surprising **4** embarrassing **5** amused **6** annoyed **7** disappointed **8** interested **9** amazed **10** excited

Fast finishers
Ask students to think about a journey they have been on and to describe it and their feelings with *-ed* and *-ing* adjectives.

5 Set a time limit of three minutes for students to discuss the situations. When they have finished, ask students to describe a situation without mentioning the adjective. The other students have to guess the correct adjective.

6 Look at the example sentences and elicit that the *-ing* form describes the activity of listening to music and the *-ed* form describes the person's feeling. Look at the other two adjectives, *interested* and *excited*, and elicit situations that these could be used in. Students then write their sentences alone or in pairs. Monitor and help where necessary.

Students could do Grammar reference: Adjectives with *-ed* and *-ing* endings, Exercise 1, page 127, at this point or for homework.

Extension idea
Students work in pairs and think of three *-ed* or *-ing* adjectives. They then join up with a second pair and swap their adjectives. Each pair now has to think of a situation in which they can use all three of the other pair's adjectives. Set a time limit of three minutes for this and then the pairs tell each other how they used the adjectives, e.g. *tired, excited*.

▶ **Grammar reference page 127: Adjectives with *-ed* and *-ing* endings**
▶ **Workbook page 21**

Reading Part 4 SB page 50

Lead-in
Talk to students about advice you can find on the internet, e.g. *How to pack a suitcase*. This can be articles or videos. Put students into groups of four and set a time limit of three minutes for them to discuss advice they have found.

Background information
Mindfulness is about concentrating on what is happening at the present moment. This can be done by meditation or other training. Mindfulness aims to reduce our worries and make us more positive.

1 Check: *stress* (n), *stressful* (adj), *stressed* (adj), e.g. *stress* – a feeling of worry, about work or your personal life, for example, which means you can't relax. Set a time limit of three minutes and elicit ideas and reasons from different pairs.

2 Set a time limit of two minutes for students to think of the topic for the other four paragraphs and elicit ideas. They can discuss their ideas in pairs first.

Possible answers
paragraph **2:** lifestyle changes
paragraph **3:** changing work habits
paragraph **4:** using technology to reduce stress
paragraph **5:** amusing things

Reading Part 4 (sentence insertion)
Discuss the advice with the students and ask why it is useful: 1 So that the students have an overall understanding of the text. 2 and 3: Students should check that the ideas in the sentences and in the text go together and that they also make sense grammatically. Encourage students to read the section of the text to themselves after they have chosen the missing sentence to make sure it sounds logical.

Exam advice

3 Before students start, look at the example with the whole class. Look at the words *That made me realise …* in sentence C. Ask *What made the writer realise that he/she couldn't go on feeling so stressed?* Elicit the answer (the fact that everyone thought he/she was always in a bad mood). Remind students that, in the exam, they have 7.5 minutes for each task in the reading paper but allow ten minutes for this if necessary as it is the first time the students have looked at this type of activity.

Fast finishers
Before students start reading, tell them that if they finish early, they should think of a question to check that the inserted sentence is correct as with the example above.

Answers
2 F **3** H **4** A **5** E

4 Set a time limit of three minutes and encourage students to try to discuss all three questions in that time. Elicit ideas from different pairs.

Extension idea
Students work in small groups to discuss something they have read about or seen in a video which made them change their life in some way. Give students a few seconds to think alone and then one minute each to tell the group what it was and answer any questions the group may have. Elicit one or two ideas from each group.

▶ **Workbook page 21**

Vocabulary SB page 51
Adjectives and their opposites

Lead-in
Choose two students – the tallest and the shortest – and ask them to come to the front of the class. Ask the class to make a sentence about each student using superlatives. Elicit: *[Name] is the tallest student in the class* and *[Name] is the shortest student in the class*. Write *tall–short* on the board and elicit that they are opposites.

Students now work in small groups. Set a time limit of one minute for the groups to write as many pairs of opposites as they can. Elicit their ideas.

1 Students work in pairs to match the adjectives. Elicit the answers and definitions for the adjectives. Ask students what the pairs could describe, e.g. *awful–fantastic – a holiday*, and elaborate on their answers.

Answers
funny/serious; generous/mean; miserable/cheerful; negative/positive; nervous/relaxed; simple/complicated; strange/ordinary

2 Set a time limit of four minutes, one minute for each anecdote.

▶ **Workbook page 20**

Writing Part 2 SB page 51

Lead-in
Write the words *thick fog* on the board. Elicit the meaning and then put students into groups to use their imaginations to think how thick fog could affect someone.

1 When students have discussed the questions, elicit the answers and ask who their story will be about (*Olivia and her friend*) and how the key words will affect their story (*we know that Olivia's friend has written her a message and we know it must be good news because of Olivia's reaction*). The students' stories will explain the message and then tell us what happened next.

Answers
1 the first line
2 third person – it is about Olivia and her friend, not the students
3 read, message, friend, smiled

2 Set a time limit of three minutes for students to read the example and another minute to answer the questions together.

Answers
1 in an airport / in two airports, a Friday evening
2 Olivia and Ellie; friends
3 They live in different countries and Ellie intends to visit Olivia.
4 Fog is preventing Ellie's flight from taking off.
5 The sky eventually clears.
6 At last they meet, and are very happy to see each other.

Fast finishers
Ask students to find useful expressions in the text. When everyone has finished, elicit these and ask students to note them down.

3 When students have found the words, ask them to cover the story. Ask: *Why was she surprised?* (her friend was coming to visit her from abroad) *Why was she excited?*, etc.

Answers
excited, disappointed, miserable, delighted

4 Elicit the answers and ask for ideas about why Matthew is excited, e.g. *Someone is arriving on the train; He is going somewhere exciting.*

Answers
1 the first line **2** third person **3** excited, waited, train

5 Allow the students to discuss their ideas in pairs or small groups. Set a time limit of three minutes and elicit some ideas so that all the students have got more ideas they can use when they write their own stories.

Writing Part 2 (a story)
Discuss the exam advice with the students. Tell students they have 22.5 minutes for each writing task in the exam so they can spend five minutes planning their writing before they start. This will ensure that they don't run out of ideas in the middle of the story and that they have noted down some useful vocabulary to use before they start.

Exam advice

6 This can be done in the class or for homework. If it is done in the classroom, set a time limit of fifteen minutes as they have already spent time planning the story and make sure the students write under exam conditions. Allow the students to share their stories, either by reading them aloud in groups or by displaying them around the class so that students can see each other's work.

Model answer
Matthew felt excited as he waited for the train. He was there to welcome his friend, Simon, who was coming to stay with him.
Matthew looked at his watch while he waited on the platform. Then he noticed an old school friend who he hadn't seen in a long time. Matthew went over to him and they chatted about school.
Suddenly Matthew noticed a crowd of people walking towards the exit. The train was there! He ran towards the crowd, then he saw a young man carrying a large suitcase. 'Simon!' he called, and his friend turned round and smiled.

▶ **Writing bank pages 150–151: Writing Part 2: a story**
▶ **Workbook page 23**
▶ **Complete Preliminary new edition Test Generator Unit 5**

Vocabulary

Feelings

afraid–fear
angry–anger
confident
grateful
happy–happiness
jealous–jealousy
(bad) mood
sad–sadness

Adjectives and prepositions

afraid of
angry with/about
ashamed of
bored of/with
crazy about
depressed about
disappointed with/about
fond of
jealous of
nervous about
pleased with/about
sad about
satisfied with/about
sure of/about

Adjectives with *-ed* and *-ing*

amazed–amazing
amused–amusing
annoyed–annoying
disappointed–disappointing
embarrassed–embarrassing
excited–exciting
interested–interesting
relaxed–relaxing
surprised–surprising
tired–tiring

Adjectives of emotion and surprise

ashamed–proud
awful–fantastic
dull–spectacular
funny–serious
generous–mean
miserable–cheerful
nervous–relaxed
strange–ordinary

Vocabulary activity 1

Students describe an adjective from the vocabulary list using one word or sound. Give an example by saying *Aaaah* in a long, relaxed sigh as if you had just sat down on the sofa after a hard day at work. Elicit *relaxed*. Put students into small groups to think of ideas for three words, then elicit words from each group for other groups to guess.

Vocabulary activity 2

Put students into small groups. Each student thinks of an adjective from the vocabulary list of opposite adjectives, e.g. *awful*, and a situation which the adjective could describe (*failing an exam*). The students take turns to say the situation (*I failed my exam*) and the others have to respond using the adjective, e.g. *Oh, that's awful.*

6 That's entertainment!

Unit objectives

Topic: entertainment

Listening Part 1: multiple-choice (pictures): listening to find key information

Reading Part 2: matching people to activities/things; finding specific information and detailed comprehension

Speaking Part 3: discussion: making and responding to suggestions; discussing alternatives; making recommendations; negotiating agreement

Writing Part 2: an article: using the correct style for an article

Grammar: present perfect; *just, already* and *yet; since* and *for*; present perfect or past simple

Vocabulary: television programmes; going out; *been/gone, meet, get to know, know* and *find out*

Pronunciation: contrastive stress

Starting off SB page 52
Television programmes

1 When the students have matched the words, elicit what each word in the box means and ask for examples from the students' own country.

Answers
A sports **B** wildlife documentary **C** cooking show
D cartoon

2 Ask students to read the instructions and elicit possible answers to the two questions, e.g. *an hour a day / four hours a week; chat shows.*

Answers
Nick watches quite a lot of TV. His favourite types of programme are comedy series, wildlife documentaries and cooking shows.

Track 28

Nick: Did you see that new comedy series on TV last night?
Clare: No, I didn't. I don't watch TV very often. How much TV do you watch?
Nick: Quite a lot actually. When I get up, I often watch a bit of a series on while I'm having breakfast and then I also watch something when I get home.
Clare: Really? Have you got more than one TV in your house?
Nick: No, I don't but I don't need more than one. I mainly watch TV on my mobile or on my tablet.
Clare: Do you usually watch TV on your own?
Nick: No, not always. I watch sports programmes on the TV in the living room with my flatmates or at my dad's because the screen is much bigger there but for everything else, I watch it online and often alone.
Clare: What sorts of things do you watch?
Nick: A little bit of everything but I really like comedy series, wildlife documentaries, cooking shows, that sort of thing. I'm not very keen on films or drama.
Clare: No? Do you ever go out? You know, to the theatre or to the cinema?
Nick: Not really. To be honest, I find plays and films a bit dull.
Clare: You're joking! I love seeing plays and films, much more than staying in and watching TV in fact.

3 Encourage students to make notes of key words, e.g. *How much/watch?* and complete the questions after listening. Elicit the correct questions before the students do Exercise 4.

Answers
How much TV do you watch?
Have you got more than one TV in your house?
Do you usually watch TV on your own?
What sorts of things do you watch?
Do you ever go out to the theatre or to the cinema?

Reading Part 2 SB page 52

1 Point out that, as well as likes and dislikes, the students should also identify things that the people can't do or don't have.

Suggested answers
Tom and Ian have a <u>free afternoon</u> but <u>neither</u> of them <u>like crowds</u>.
They're <u>interested</u> in <u>theatre</u> and <u>exhibitions</u>, but they <u>don't have much money</u>.

2 Tell the students to first identify all the paragraphs which involve theatre or exhibitions (B, D, E, possibly G, H). Students then answer questions 1 and 2 in pairs and decide which of the other options is best (*B is free, a museum is unlikely to be crowded, E requires tickets and might be crowded, H might be crowded and the price might be too much for them*).

Answers
B
1 D is a musical but you have to pay for a ticket.
2 G has long queues for everything and neither of them like crowds.

Reading Part 2 (matching people to things)
Go through the exam advice with the students and ask why it is important to underline all the key words in the descriptions of people (there are three requirements for each person and all three must match the correct answer).

Exam advice

3 Students have 7.5 minutes for each reading task in the exam. Encourage them to underline key words in the descriptions of people and events before they attempt to answer the questions. When students have finished, they compare answers in pairs. If they have different answers from their partner, they look at the texts again to find the correct answer.

Answers
2 E (First performances this week, family discounts at our restaurant, two-minute walk from the underground)
3 G (comic market celebrates Japanese animation, fans can meet other fans, buy rare comics)
4 H (he uses traditional words from his own country, snacks will be available)
5 F (Marco Morelli has fallen in love with a rich young woman. However, one of the family's servants is also in love with her, Italian opera with amazing singing and real classical music)

4 Allow students one minute to choose an event alone and think of reasons why they would choose that one. They then discuss their ideas together. Elicit different choices and reasons for them and have a class vote to find the most popular event.

Extension idea
Students brainstorm entertainment in their own town. Students work alone for one minute to think of the type of entertainment they like best and reasons why, then work in small groups to discuss their ideas.

▶ **Workbook page 25**

Vocabulary SB page 54
Going out

1 Look at the example words and elicit what they mean and why they are in those places (screens are usually associated with films; intervals are associated with plays and concerts but not films). Draw the diagram from the book on the board. When students have finished, elicit the meaning of each word and where they should go in the diagram on the board.

Suggested answers
Films: screen, subtitles **Plays:** None **Concerts:** live music
Films and plays: acting
Plays and concerts: interval, stage
All three: book early, perform, reviews, refreshments, ticket

Fast finishers
Students add their own words to the diagram.

2 Students work alone and then compare their answers in pairs. Check that all the students have got the correct answers before they go on to Exercise 3.

Answers
2 subtitles **3** book early **4** refreshments **5** live music
6 ticket **7** stage **8** acting

3 Look at question 1 in Exercise 2 with the class. Ask how students could answer the question, e.g. *Yes, I always read reviews on the Internet. My favourite review website is …* Encourage students to keep talking for as long as possible when answering questions. Elicit ideas from different groups when they have finished.

Extension idea
Put the students into pairs to think of a film that they have both seen and both like or dislike. They write a short review together, giving their opinions and reasons for them. When the students have finished, ask pairs to read out their reviews.

▶ **Workbook page 24**

Grammar SB page 54
Present perfect

Lead-in
Tell the students that you are going to ask three questions and they should write the answers. Ask: *When did you first meet your best friend? When did you start at this school? What time did you get to school this morning?* Students compare their answers in pairs.

1 When students have listened to the recording, elicit the different things they talked about (*Lion King musical, Robin Hood film, Carmen opera, film and pizza at home*). Ask students which they would choose.

Answers
Go to Bella's house, watch a film and have pizza.

Track 29

Bella: Have you seen *The Lion King* yet?
Eliza: Do you mean the musical?
Bella: Yeah! We've got a spare ticket for the Friday show. Fancy coming?
Eliza: Um…
Bella: Please! We've been good friends for three years but we haven't been to a show together since last summer.
Eliza: Yes I know but I've already seen it. I saw it with my cousins last month but I'd love to do something else with you. How about Saturday? I haven't seen the new Robin Hood film yet. Everyone's talking about it and it's on at the cinema near us. Have you seen it?
Bella: 'Fraid so. I saw it last night with my flatmate. Let's have a look at the guide to see what else is on. What about *Carmen*? It says here that it's an incredible show with dancing and live music. Sounds good.
Eliza: *Carmen*? Fantastic idea. I've just learnt how to play one of the songs on the violin and my sister is learning to sing one of them too.
Bella: Oh no! It's not an opera, is it? I don't fancy that!
Eliza: Why don't you come round to my house on Saturday and we can watch a film.
Bella: Great! And why don't I get a pizza on my way to your house?

2 When the students have completed the sentences, elicit the spelling of *seen* as this may be a new form for the students and ask them which verb it comes from (*see*). Elicit that we call this the past participle.

Answers
1 seen **2** seen **3** seen **4** learnt

3 Stronger classes could look at the example sentences and try to decide the rules in small groups.

Answers
The present perfect is formed with *has/have* + past participle. We can use it to connect the past with the present. It usually describes something with a connection in the present, something that continues in the present, or an experience that happened at an unspecified time in the past.

4 Tell the students to look at the sentences in Exercise 2. Ask: *Do you think the speaker in sentence 3 will go to the Robin Hood film at sometime in the future?* (yes). *Did the speaker learn how to play one of the songs a long time ago or a short time ago?* (a short time ago) *Why does the speaker in sentence 2 use already?* (to emphasise that this has happened and they don't want to go again).
When the students have completed the rules, give other examples of how to use the words in sentences.

Answers
1 just **2** already **3** yet

5 Allow the students to work in pairs but make sure that they both write the sentences from the email in full in their notebooks. Monitor and help where necessary.

Answers
2 My brother hasn't (has not) found a new job yet.
3 But he's (has) started a course in computing.
4 My flatmate has just won a prize in a photography competition.
5 Have you seen the new *Star Wars* film yet?
6 I've already seen it three times.
7 Have you taken your driving test yet?

Fast finishers
Students write three sentences about themselves using *already, just, yet.* When all the students have finished Exercise 5, elicit these extra sentences as well.

Students could do the Grammar reference: Present perfect, Exercise 1, page 128, at this point or for homework.

6 Look at the instructions and example sentences and elicit that *for* and *since* show us how long this activity or state has been true for. When students have finished, elicit some time expressions you could use with both words.

Answers
1 since **2** for

7 Tell the students to underline the time expressions in each sentence before they start. Elicit these (*four months, you arrived, March, three weeks, then*). When they have finished, ask them how they could say the same thing using the other word.

Answers
1 for **2** since **3** since **4** For **5** since

Students could do the Grammar reference: Present perfect, Exercise 2, page 128, at this point or for homework.

8 Elicit that the question: *How long have you* + past participle is used to talk about things that started in the past and are still true. *Have you* + past participle + *recently* asks about things which happened a short time ago and are still true. Monitor and help where necessary and encourage stronger students to answer the questions using both *for* and *since*.

▶ **Grammar reference page 128: Present perfect**
▶ **Grammar reference page 128: *since* and *for***
▶ **Workbook page 26**

Present perfect or past simple? SB page 55

Lead-in
Put students into groups. Set a time limit of two minutes for them to discuss musicians that they like and their favourite tracks by those musicians.

Background information
Martin Garrix became interested in being a DJ when he saw DJ Tiësto, performing at the 2004 Olympic Games in Athens. In 2018, Martin headlined the closing ceremony of the Winter Olympics in South Korea.

1 Ask the class if they have heard of Martin Garrix. When students have read the text, ask what they learned about him. Help students with any words they might need and check the meaning of *a single* (a track released and sold on its own).

Answers
He's a DJ and his single *Animals* is famous.

2 When students have found the answers, elicit the three forms of each verb – base form, past simple and past participle: *be – was/were – has/have been; become – became – has/have become; tour – toured – has/have toured*. The verb '*be born*' is a passive construction. It may be better to focus just on the verb *to be* here.

Answers
Present perfect: 's been, 's toured; past simple: was (born), was, became
We normally use the expression in bold with the past simple.

3 When students have completed the table, point out that some expressions can be used with both tenses, e.g. *for – I have been at secondary school for three years* (and I am still there). *I was at primary school for four years* (but I am not there now).

Answers
the present perfect – already, since 2010, this week, today, yet
the past simple – at 8 o'clock in the morning, last year, two months ago, yesterday

4 Look at the example with the students and elicit why the present perfect is correct (today is an unfinished time period). Allow students to work in pairs and explain their choice of verbs for each question (1, 5, 7 – present perfect with an unfinished time expression 2 – present perfect with yet 3, 4, 6 – past simple with a finished time expression).

Answers
2 yet; Have (you) read **3** three months ago; saw
4 last year; won **5** for ages; haven't swum
6 last night; did (you) go **7** since; have (you) taken

Fast finishers
Students write sentences about themselves using some of the time expressions in Exercise 4. When all the students have finished Exercise 5, ask the students who wrote extra sentences to read them out without a time expression. The other students have to guess what the correct time expression is.

5 Look at the example questions in Exercise 6 with the students. Elicit more possible questions and point out that we use the past simple with questions such as *When/Where did you buy it?* because we are talking about one, completed action in the past. We use the present simple for questions such as *Do you like it?* because we are asking about present facts.

6 As there are six topics, tell the students to ask about three each. Set a time limit of four minutes. Elicit some of the interesting information that they found out from their partner.

Students could do Grammar reference: The present perfect or the past simple? Exercises 3 and 4, page 129, at this point or for homework.

▶ **Grammar reference page 129: The present perfect or the past simple?**
▶ **Workbook page 26**

Vocabulary SB page 56
been/gone, meet, get to know, know and *find out*

Lead-in
Dictate the following words to the students: *cook, exercise, break, fail, lose, journey, trip*. In small groups the students discuss any problems students might have learning these words. Set a time limit of two minutes and elicit ideas.

1 Set a time limit of three minutes. Elicit the answers and allow another two minutes for students to explain the differences between the different words.

Answers
1 Paul is at his friend's house.
2 Sophia is at home (she's returned from the cinema).
3 *Been* means go and come back. *Gone* means hasn't come back yet.
4 Lucas and Nick became friends years ago at university.
5 They see each other, often on Saturday afternoons.
6 Lucas sometimes sleeps at Nick's house.
7 No, he didn't.
8 The neighbours.

2 Point out that *Have you ever* is a common way of asking questions in the present perfect. Ask what time period it refers to (*at any time in your life*). When the students have finished, elicit the answers and the reasons why the other choice is wrong.

Answers
1 been **2** gone **3** known, meet **4** stay **5** getting to know **6** find out

3 Set a time limit of five minutes and encourage students to give details or reasons for their answers.

▶ **Workbook page 24**

Listening Part 1 SB page 56

1 When the students have found the items in the pictures, elicit the meanings of the adjectives.

Answers
2 2 A, B or C **3** 1 A or C **4** 1 C **5** 3 A **6** 1 B

2 Look at the first question with the students. Elicit the words they think are important and why.

Suggested answers
1 What would the woman like to try on? A a plain sweater with a round neck, B a plain sweater with a V-neck, C a striped sweater with a round neck
2 Where has Matt left his keys? A in his coat pocket, B in the front pocket of his rucksack, C in his jeans' pocket
3 What did Karen buy last weekend? A a dress, B a top, C a skirt
4 Which one is Sarah's cousin? A a girl with short hair and no earrings, B a girl with long hair and no earrings, C a girl with long hair with huge earrings.
5 Where did the man get the trainers that's he's wearing now? A in a sports shop, B on a website, C on a market stall.
6 What's the latest time visitors can buy a ticket today? A half past five, B a quarter to six, C a quarter to seven
7 What sort of TV programmes does the girl like watching? A a football match, B a comedy, C a wildlife documentary

Listening Part 1 (multiple-choice with pictures)
Discuss the advice with the students. Give an example of the second point, e.g. in the first listening, Jane might say that she doesn't like one of the jumpers.

3 Tell the students to do this exam-style task alone as if they were in an exam. When they have listened for a second time, allow them to compare answers in pairs and discuss the reasons for their choices.

Answers
1 A **2** B **3** C **4** B **5** B **6** A **7** C

Track 30

Narrator: Part 1. For each question, choose the correct answer.

1

Narrator: What would the woman like to try on?
Woman: Excuse me. Could I try on one of the jumpers in the window please?
Shop assistant: Sure. Do you mean one of the striped ones? They'd look good on you.
Woman: I was actually thinking of a plain one. Have you got it in a small?
Shop assistant: I think so. I'll check. Did you want it with a V-neck?
Woman: I'd rather have a round one.
Shop assistant: OK. I'll just get it for you to try on.

2

Narrator: Where has Matt left his keys?
Matt: Ava, I think I've lost my keys, have you seen them? I put them in my jeans' pocket a minute ago but they're not there now.
Ava: Not again! You were wearing your coat just now. Have you checked all the pockets? You usually leave your keys there.
Matt: I've looked in all the pockets. Was I carrying my backpack when I came in?
Ava: I think so. I bet they're in there.
Matt: You're right again, Ava!

3

Narrator: What did Karen buy last weekend?
Man: Did you have a good weekend, Karen?
Karen: Yes, I did, thanks. On Saturday I went to the new shopping centre with my aunt. She wanted to get a dress for the summer.
Man: Did she buy one?
Karen: They were all the wrong size. Then she tried on loads of tops.
Man: What about the red one you're wearing?
Karen: Isn't it lovely! She didn't like the colour so I got it instead.
Man: So, she didn't buy anything but you did!
Karen: That's right! It'll look good with that skirt I got for my birthday.

4

Narrator: Which one is Sarah's cousin?
Man: Sarah, did you manage to get your cousin something for her birthday?
Sarah: Don't ask! We got her some earrings in the end but then we found out that she never wears jewellery.

Man:	Oh no! I thought that girl over there with long hair and huge earrings was your cousin.
Sarah:	That's my sister, but they look alike, don't they? They even used to have the same length hair.
Man:	Has she had it cut?
Sarah:	Yeah but she says she's going to grow it long again.
5	
Narrator:	Where did the man get the trainers that he's wearing now?
Woman:	Nice trainers! Have you just been to that new sports shop?
Man:	Yeah! It's a great store with some amazing bargains. I bought some trainers there last week, but they weren't the right size so I had to take them back. Then one of my friends suggested looking in the market, so I did and found these. They fit perfectly.
Woman:	My flatmate keeps telling me to look on the web. She buys everything there.
Man:	She's right! You know the boots I wore to the party? I got them online.
Woman:	They're really cool! Were they expensive?
6	
Narrator:	What's the latest time visitors can buy a ticket today?
Man:	You have reached Lansdown Art Museum. We're sorry that there's no one to take your call right now. If you are interested in seeing the Photographer of the Year exhibition, the ticket office is open from nine a.m. to half past five. You need to leave the museum at quarter to seven but remember that last admission to the gallery is at quarter to six. Thank you for calling.
7	
Narrator:	What sort of TV programmes does the woman like watching?
Connor:	You look tired. Did you go to bed late last night after the football?
Laura:	I think my flatmate was watching the match in his bedroom. I don't even care who won it, to be honest! I watched this comedy instead, about two men who get lost in a department store.
Connor:	I saw that! I haven't laughed so much for years. Wasn't the ending good?
Laura:	Well, I'd kind of lost interest by then. I'd much rather watch a wildlife documentary.
Connor:	Oh? I didn't think you liked those sorts of programmes.

Extension idea

Make photocopies of the audioscript on page 125. After Exercise 3, give each pair a copy so that they can identify exactly why the two wrong choices are incorrect.

/P/ Contrastive stress

4 Before the students start, ask which kind of words they think will be stressed (words which contain important information). Elicit ideas and then play the recording. Students practise saying the dialogue in pairs, taking turns to play both parts.

5 When the students have listened and answered the question, drill the three sentences.

Answers

Oh? I didn't think you liked those sorts of programmes.= The man didn't know this about the woman.
Oh? I didn't think you liked those sorts of programmes. = I knew that other people liked serious stuff but I didn't know that the woman liked serious stuff.
Oh? I didn't think you liked those sorts of programmes. = I knew that the woman liked a certain sort of TV programme but I didn't know she liked that sort.

Track 31

1 Oh? I didn't think you liked those sorts of programmes.
2 Oh? I didn't think you liked those sorts of programmes.
3 Oh? I didn't think you liked those sorts of programmes.

6 Put the students into groups and tell the students to choose one occasion each so that they are each asking about different things. The students take turns to ask each other about their topic.

▶ **Workbook pages 26–27**

Speaking Part 3 SB page 58

Lead-in

Put the students into small groups. Ask them to think about a special celebration that they have been to in their town or while on holiday.

1 Ask the students to underline the key words and then decide which will make a difference to their answer.

Answers

The different events the university could organise and which would be most popular with students.

2 Set a time limit of two minutes and tell the students to think of reasons for their answers. Elicit ideas from the class and have a vote on the best idea.

3 When the students have finished, elicit why the other choices are not good ideas

Answers
1 ✓ 2 ✗ Students should discuss their ideas with their partner in this part.
3 ✓ 4 ✓ 5 ✗ Ideally the students should talk about as many of the pictures as they can BUT they won't lose marks if they don't talk about all of them. If they only talk about one picture then they may not complete the task successfully.
6 ✗ They should aim to reach an agreement towards the end of the two minutes
7 ✓ Ideally they should carry on speaking until the examiners asks them to stop – this is what happens to Noa and Greta.

4 Elicit the answers and the fact that they did all the things that the students said they should do in Exercise 3 and didn't do the things the students said they shouldn't do, so they did the task well. Ask the students what Noa and Greta's final choice was (*the exhibition*).

Answers
1 ✓ 2 ✗ 3 ✓ 4 ✓ 5 ✗ 6 ✗ 7 ✓
Noa and Greta do the task well.

Track 32

Examiner: Now, in this part of the test you're going to talk about something together for about two minutes. I'm going to describe a situation to you. A university would like to celebrate its 25th anniversary with a special event. Here are some events the university could organise. Talk together about the different events the university could organise, and say which would be most popular. All right? Now, talk together.

Noa: Let's start with the photography exhibition. I think it would be a great idea. The university could collect pictures and photos from now and the past. It would be really interesting.

Greta: I agree. Students could see how things have changed.

Noa: Yeah! For example, my mum showed me a picture of her university library with loads of old books all over the desks. My mum used to spend hours in the library looking for information. Now we can go online and do most of our research there. Another difference is that there used to be more men than women.

Greta: That's right! Let's talk about another one. What about a concert? Everyone loves music and everyone could take part. What do you think?

Noa: I'm not sure about that one. Some people like rock music and other people hate it. And have you thought about the noise?

Greta: Perhaps you're right. Shall we talk about the student fashion show?

Noa: OK. I think the student fashion show is a great idea. Past and present fashion students could show the clothes they've designed.

Greta: Um… I'm not very interested in fashion, I'm afraid. We haven't talked about the bike ride yet. Do you think it's a good idea?

Noa: Perhaps, but if it rains, they won't be able to go very far. Don't you think?

Greta: Yes, I agree. That leaves the talent show and the disco. Well, you know lots of people love dancing but do you think everyone would enjoy it?

Noa: I don't think so. I can't stand discos. How about the talent show then?

Greta: I'm not sure I understand. How would it work?.

Noa: Yes, you know, groups of friends perform something different. One group could sing and do a dance, for example.

Greta: Oh I see! But remember some people don't like dancing.

Noa: You're right. Well, what do you think? Shall we choose the photography exhibition?

Greta: Yes, I think that's the best idea. Do you…

Examiner: Thank you.

Extension idea
Play the recording again and ask the students to note down the reasons why Noa and Greta rejected the other choices.

5 Elicit the expressions and ask the students about other expressions they could have used in place of *Shall we …*, e.g. *Let's talk …, How about talking ….*

Answers
Shall we talk about the fashion show? We haven't talked about the bike ride yet. Do you think it's a good idea?

Speaking Part 3
Go through the advice with the students. Elicit that, if there are six pictures or ideas to discuss in two minutes, this means that they have about 20 seconds for each one.

6 Read the instructions to the class so that students all start at the same time. When they have finished, put them in groups of three to practise the task with an examiner. The student playing the examiner uses the check list in Exercise 3 and gives them feedback on their performance at the end of two minutes. Repeat the activity three times so they all have a chance to play the role of the examiner.

▶ **Speaking bank pages 159-160: Part 3**

Writing Part 2 SB page 59

Lead-in
Split the class into an even number of small groups. Half of the groups think about celebrations in Venice and the other groups about those in China. They then write down as many related words as they can. They then try to guess the China and Venice words from the other groups.

Background information
The Venice Carnival lasts for just over two weeks. The carnival attracts about three million visitors each year. People wear masks and costumes and there are concerts in the city.

Chinese New Year lasts for 16 days and everyone has a week off work. It is a time to visit family but there are firework displays, street processions and a lantern festival on the last day.

1 Elicit *costume* and *mask*, then put students into pairs to discuss the photos.

Answers
The festivals are Chinese New Year and the Venice Carnival; Students' own answers.

2 Put students into small groups to discuss the questions. Set a time limit and then ask the students for ideas for Exercises 1 and 2 together.

3 Ask students to say why the words they chose are important, e.g. your *country* – you can't write about something in a different country.

Suggested answer
a celebration in your country, What people wear, What people do, Why special, article, answering questions, about 100 words.

4 Set a time limit of one minute. Elicit ideas and the differences between an article and a story and the sort of language used in each.

Answer
The second answer is better. She has written an article and not a story. The first answer is a story and not an article.

5 When the students have read the article, ask them what facts they found out about the carnival, what opinions and what people do.

Answer
Yes

6 Tell the students to read the text again and tick the questions which have the answer *Yes*. Elicit the answers and then ask why the first paragraph is interesting (It makes the celebration sound exciting and gives a personal opinion).

Answer
The answer is 'yes' to all the questions.

Writing Part 2 (an article)
Discuss the exam advice with the students and elicit why it is important. (*If you write the wrong kind of text, you will lose points. Tell students that, as well as an interesting first paragraph it is important to answer the questions in the instructions and use a variety of grammatical structures and vocabulary.*)

Exam advice

7 Tell the students that the total time they have for each writing task in the exam is 22.5 minutes but, because of planning time, you are going to allow them fifteen minutes for the actual writing.

Fast finishers
Tell students to note down the nouns, verbs and adjectives they used in their text.

8 When students have checked their own text, allow them to swap articles in pairs to see what they think about their partner's writing.

▶ **Speaking bank pages 159–160: Part 3**
▶ **Writing bank page 148: Writing Part 2 an article**
▶ **Workbook page 27**
▶ **Complete Preliminary new edition Test Generator Unit 6**

Vocabulary

Television programmes

advert
cartoon
chat show
comedy series
cooking show
quiz show
reality show
sports
the news
wildlife documentary

going out

accompanied by
acting
admission
admission fee
audience
book early
display
explore
interval
live music
perform – performance
refreshments
review
screen
stage
subtitles
ticket

been/gone, meet, get to know, know and *find out*

been
find out
get to know
gone
know (about)
meet

Vocabulary activity 1

Put the students into pairs. The students choose a word from the word list and use a dictionary to write a definition of the word. They read the definition and the first pair to guess the word wins a point.

Vocabulary activity 2

Put the students into small groups. They write the ten types of TV programme from the word list on ten separate pieces of paper which they place in the middle of the group. All the words should be visible. Students close their eyes and one student removes one word. Students open their eyes and try to say the missing word first. The first one who does so wins a point. The word is then placed back on the desk and the process is repeated.

Vocabulary and grammar review Unit 5

1 **2** of **3** with **4** on **5** of **6** about **7** about **8** about **9** of **10** of

2 When I was tidying my room last Sunday, I found some surprising things. Among all the ~~bored~~ **boring** exercise books from my school days, there was something ~~amazed~~ **amazing** - my diary, from when I was eight years old. It was really ~~interested~~ **interesting** to read my thoughts from back then, though at times I felt a bit ~~embarrassing~~ **embarrassed**, too. For example, I was still very ~~frightening~~ **frightened** of the dark in those days. It was also funny to read how ~~exciting~~ **excited** I was about being nine soon – I thought I would be really grown up then.

3 **Across: 1** mean **5** anger **6** afraid **8** jealous **9** bored
Down: 2 negative **3** sad **4** nervous **6** awful **7** love

4 **2** can't **3** should **4** Could **5** don't have to **6** might **7** have to

Vocabulary and grammar review Unit 6

1 **2** Audiences **3** live **4** reviews **5** performances **6** admission **7** interval

2 **2** B **3** A **4** B **5** C

3 **2** since = for **3** he's gone = he went **4** gone = been **5** Already I've been = I've already been **6** I looked = I've looked **7** I've never been = I've ever been **8** has given = gave **9** didn't decide = haven't decided **10** has opened = opened

4 **2** for **3** have **4** since **5** got **6** already

7 Getting around

Unit objectives

Topic: weather

Listening Part 4: multiple-choice, long dialogue: Listening to find specific information and detailed meaning, not the main message.

Reading Part 1: short texts, multiple choice: reading notices and other short texts to identify text purpose

Speaking Part 2: individual picture description: adding new points and correcting yourself; describing things you don't know the name of

Writing Part 1: an email: useful email expressions

Grammar: *extremely, fairly, quite, rather, really* and *very*; *too* and *enough*; the future; prepositions of movement

Vocabulary: weather; compound words

Pronunciation: word stress in compound nouns

Starting off SB page 62

Weather

Before students open their books, put them into small groups. Ask them where in the world they would like to spend the winter and the summer and why. Set a time limit of two minutes and then elicit ideas and reasons. Look at the photos with the students. Remind them of the phrases *look(s)/look(s)* like and encourage them to imagine the people's feelings.

1 When the students have finished question 1, elicit the answers and ask the students to try to explain the difference in meaning of words with similar meanings, e.g. *rain/showers; storm/thunderstorm/lightning/ (thunder); frost/ice.*
Set a time limit of three minutes for students to discuss questions 2 and 3. Monitor and help where necessary. Elicit ideas from different groups and then ask about the advantages and disadvantages of living somewhere which is always hot in the summer and one where the weather is more unpredictable.
Look at the first sentence in question 4 with the class. Ask what is happening now in the sentence (there is no sun; it is behind a cloud). Elicit what the person wants – for it to be sunny. Students discuss the other sentences in the same groups as before. Set a time limit of two minutes and elicit ideas.

Answers
1 **1** hot, sunny, sunshine; **2** cold, foggy; **3** freezing, frost, ice, icy, snowy; **4** lightning, rainy, showers, storm, thunderstorm, windy;
2 & 3 Students' own answers
4 chilly = cold; It's pouring = It's raining hard; It's boiling = It's very hot; nippy = cold; cleared up = the sky became clear; soaring temperatures = rising temperatures

Listening Part 4 SB page 62

Background information
The snowfall described in the recording took place on March 5, 2015, when 2.56 metres (101 inches) of snow fell in 24 hours in the town of Capracotta in the Province of Isernia, in the Italian region of Molise. It was widely recognised as a new world record.

1 Set a time limit of two minutes for the students to do this in pairs. Tell them to underline key words in the questions to answer question 4 but not to worry about the different options yet. Elicit answers from different students.

Answers
1 Olivia **2** an interviewer **3** travelling in Italy during the world's heaviest – ever snowfall **4** What Olivia and her friend were doing when the heavy snow began, how she felt when it started to snow heavily, why the car stopped moving, how they tried to keep warm in the car, why they stayed in the car all night, how they travelled to a village the next day.

Listening Part 4 (multiple-choice)
Students have about 45 seconds to read through the questions before the recording starts, which will help them to understand what the recording is about and what information they have to listen out for. Remind them that the words in the text might be different from the words with the same meaning in the choices. When reading the instructions and questions, it is a good idea to underline key words to remind them of what they need to listen out for.

Exam advice

Extension idea

To help prepare the students, make a copy of the photocopiable audioscript and ask them to look at the start: *Then, while we were trying to decide how to get back to the main road, some really heavy snow started coming down.*

Ask them to read it and decide which answer is correct (1A: *we were trying to decide* matches *we were talking about what to do next*). Ask students why the other two answers are incorrect (1B: she says we stopped for a quick meal before carrying on, not that they were already having a snack; 1C: she says they were trying to decide how to get back to the main road, not that they were driving along the main road).

2 Tell the students to do the listening under exam conditions, i.e. without talking or comparing answers.

3 When the students have listened for a second time, allow them to compare their answers and, if they have different answers, try to justify their answers by referring to information in the text that they remember.

Answers
1 A **2** B **3** B **4** A **5** B **6** C

Track 33

Narrator: For each question, choose the correct answer. You will hear an interview with a woman called Olivia talking about her experience of travelling through a snow-storm – with her friend Grace.

Interviewer: Today I'm talking to Olivia Richardson, who was with a friend on a skiing holiday in central Italy when over two metres of snow fell in 24 hours. Where were you, Olivia, when that happened?

Olivia: Grace and I were near Capracotta, in the mountains. There'd already been some light snow and we stopped for a quick meal before carrying on to a crossroads, but there we took a wrong turning and got completely lost. Then, while we were trying to decide how to get back to the main road, some really heavy snow started coming down.

Interviewer: Was that frightening?

Olivia: At first I was quite certain it wouldn't last long. It was March in Italy so I wasn't worried worried. Of course, it was rather annoying we'd gone the wrong way, but I couldn't blame Grace because it'd been my idea. And we were still moving, but not very fast.

Interviewer: When did you have to stop?

Olivia: Well, it was getting quite difficult to see and we nearly crashed into a parked car. There was more and more snow on the road, so when we tried to go up a steep hill the wheels started going round really fast but it was so deep the car just wouldn't move forwards. It looked as if we'd be stuck there, but we didn't have much petrol left so we switched off the engine. Grace tried to phone for help but couldn't get through.

Interviewer: How did you stay warm? With the car heater?

Olivia: That meant having the engine on so we only used it a bit. Instead we got all our jumpers, trousers and socks from our suitcases and wore them all night. We were still frozen, though, and wished we had some coffee or tea with us.

Interviewer: So you spent the whole night inside the car?

Olivia: Yes, I'd at last managed to contact the emergency services. They knew our location from my phone and they advised us to 'stay in our vehicle until help could be sent the next day'. That's what we did, but by then the snow was starting to cover the car completely so we cleared a space next to the doors in case we needed to get out.

Interviewer: How did you get moving again?

Olivia: The rescue vehicles didn't get there until the afternoon. They'd called to ask if we needed an ambulance and luckily we didn't, so they just cleared the snow and led us along the road to the nearest village. There we stopped for an enormous hot meal of roast fish and pasta with cheese, the most delicious I've ever tasted!

4 Set a time limit of two minutes. Elicit examples of students' experiences, good or bad, with bad weather, from the class.

▶ **Workbook page 30**

Grammar SB page 63

extremely, fairly, quite, rather, really and *very*

Lead-in

Give students an example of normal and strong adjectives, e.g. *good-amazing.* Put the students into small groups and set a time limit of one minute to think of more pairs of adjectives. Elicit these and then elicit words we can use to make them stronger, e.g. *very* for normal adjectives, *absolutely* for strong adjectives and *really* for either.

1 Students stay in their groups to answer the questions. Elicit the answers and remind the students that we can't use *very* with strong adjectives but we can use *really* with all adjectives. We don't generally use *fairly* or *rather* with strong adjectives because the point of using them is to make the adjective stronger. Point out that, when we use *quite* to make adjectives stronger, it is stressed more than when used to make adjectives less strong. *I was **quite** certain.*

Answers
1 really **2** rather **3** quite

2 Look at the example with the students and elicit the adverbs used (*extremely, very, really, quite*). Encourage students to use a similar range of adverbs in their own discussion. Elicit ideas from different students.

Students could do Grammar reference: Adverbs of degree: *extremely, fairly, quite, rather, really* and *very*, Exercise 1, page 130 for homework.

▶ **Page 130 Grammar reference: Adverbs of degree: *extremely, fairly, quite, rather, really* and *very***
▶ **Workbook page 30**

too and *enough*

Lead-in
Write the word *hot* on the board. Put the students into pairs and set a time limit for them to think of any disadvantages with hot weather. Elicit ideas and note them down on the board, e.g. *can't sleep, difficult to work*. Keep these on the board to look at after Exercise 1.

1 Read the instructions with the students and direct their attention to grammar box. Tell the students to work in pairs. When they have finished, elicit the answers and look at the rules in more detail. Write the forms below on the board and, for each one, elicit some example sentences:
too + adjective (+ *to* + base form of the verb); *too* + *much* + uncountable noun
too + *many* + countable noun; *not enough* + countable or uncountable noun
not + *adjective* + *enough* (+ *to* + base form of the verb); *enough* + noun / adjective + *enough*
Ask how the last is different from the others (it is the only one which doesn't describe a problem). This is less common than the negative use to denote a problem. Elicit which exam task types could test these, e.g. multiple choice or open cloze and, especially, in transformations: *I'm too poor / not rich enough to go to Las Vegas.*
If you used the lead-in activity, ask the students to make sentences using their ideas on the board, e.g. *It is too hot to sleep.*

Answers
1 more than you need or want
2 before, *to* + infinitive
3 uncountable, countable
4 as much as
5 before, after, *to* + infinitive

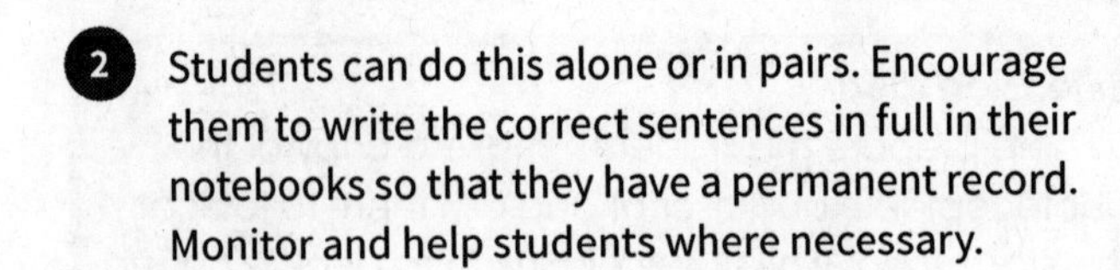

2 Students can do this alone or in pairs. Encourage them to write the correct sentences in full in their notebooks so that they have a permanent record. Monitor and help students where necessary.

Fast finishers
Ask students to make sentences that are true for themselves using *too / enough*, e.g. *I haven't got enough money to buy a new phone*. When all the students have finished, elicit some of the extra sentences that students wrote.

Answers
1 correct
2 In the streets, there are too ~~much~~ **many** cars.
3 My sister is ~~very~~ **too** young to travel alone.
4 correct
5 We did not have ~~plenty of~~ **enough time** to see the University of Cambridge.
6 I think you are ~~enough old~~ **old enough** to spend this summer with your friends.

Students could do Grammar reference: Adverbs of degree: *too* and *enough*, Exercise 2, page 130 at this point or for homework.

3 Give the groups one minute to think of their six places. Encourage them to choose a variety of places near their home town, in other parts of their country and in different countries. When they have chosen, look at the example with the class. Set a time limit of two or three minutes to discuss the other questions. Elicit the best place to go from each group and reasons why.

Extension idea
Write on the board: *too* + adjective, *too much, too many, not enough* + noun, *not* + adjective + *enough*, adjective + *enough*, *enough* + noun. Elicit ideas about the students' town and write these under the appropriate headings, e.g. *It's too small, There's too much crime*. Students work in groups of four to think of more ideas for each column. Set a time limit of five minutes and then elicit ideas.

▶ **Grammar reference page 130: Adverbs of degree: *too* and *enough***
▶ **Workbook page 30**

Reading Part 1 SB page 64

Lead-in
Discuss signs that the students can see in their town, especially those with pictures on them. Put the students into small groups. On a piece of blank paper they draw a made-up sign with no writing on it at the top of the page. They should have an idea of what the sign represents. The groups then pass their signs to a new group. The students discuss the sign and, at the bottom of the piece of paper, they write what they think it means. They then fold the paper so that their idea is hidden and pass the papers to a new group for them to write their own idea about what the sign means. Demonstrate this with a piece of paper so they can see exactly what to do. Repeat as many times as required and then pass the papers back to the group who originally drew the sign. They unfold the paper to see what other people thought their sign meant. Elicit what each group drew, what it represented and how accurate the other groups' guesses were.

1 Discuss the signs with the class and ask them if there are any similar signs in their town or if they have seen similar signs elsewhere.

Answers
A next to a lake in winter **B** on a ferry **C** on a bus
D on a phone or tablet screen **E** in a street

2 Look at the example with the students. Ask what information about prices the sign gives, e.g. children's prices on trams. Also elicit that *free* means without paying. Students now do the same for the other four signs alone or in pairs.

Answers
1 C NOTICE, £3, only
2 E No (+*ing*) – for prohibition
3 A DANGER
4 B Leave, Go, Return – use of imperatives
5 D Sign up, extra credit

Reading Part 1 (multiple-choice, texts, signs, messages and notices)
Discuss the advice with the students and ask why they think it is useful. Try to elicit that all the information helps the students to understand the signs better. However, they will still have to look at the choices and read the information carefully to decide the correct answer.

Exam advice

3 Set a time limit of five minutes for the task. This task has less information to read and the students should be able to complete it more quickly than some of the other reading tasks. Don't elicit the answers yet.

Answers
1 C **2** A **3** B **4** A **5** B

Extension idea
Look at Reading Part 1, Exercise 1, A with the students and give them these options about what it means:

A You shouldn't swim here because the water is deep. **B** There is a possibility that the ice will break if you walk on it. **C** The lake often freezes in winter. Elicit the correct answer (B). Put the students into small groups and ask them to write similar sentence for one of the other four signs. When they have finished, elicit their ideas and ask the other students to choose the correct answers.

▶ **Workbook page 28**

Grammar SB page 66
The future

Lead-in
Write the words: *plan, arrangement, timetable, prediction* on the board. Elicit or tell the students what these mean and give examples of them all for you:

e.g. *plan* – mark homework this evening, *arrangement* – teachers meeting on Thursday evening, *timetable* – 8am Mondays Business English class at a local company, prediction – everyone in the class will pass their English exam this year.

Students now write their own examples. Set a time limit of one minute. When they have finished, allow them to share ideas in pairs.

1 Play the recording while the students have their books closed. Ask them to listen to find where the people are going and what the problem is. (*They are going to the train station and the problem is the weather*). They then open their books and discuss in pairs what the missing verb forms could be. Play the recording again for them to complete the exercise.

Answers
2 's going to rain **3** 'm meeting **4** leaves **5** 'll take

Track 34

Mia: Look at the rain, Owen.

Owen: Yes, I know. I'm hoping it'll stop soon, but I don't think there's much chance of that.

Mia: No, the weather forecast said it's a big storm, so it's going to rain for hours. What time do you have to be at the station?

Owen: I'm meeting Jason and Mark there at 8.30, in the café near the main entrance. The train leaves at 8.45.

Mia: It's quite a long walk to the station, isn't it? And it's 8.15 already. Look, I'll take you in the car.

Owen: Thanks!

2 Elicit the answers and the structures used (a present simple; b, c *will* + base form of the verb; d present continuous; e verb *to be* + *going to* + base form of the verb). Point out that we usually use the short form of *will* and the verb *to be*.

Answers
b 5 'll take **c** 1 'll stop **d** 3 'm meeting **e** 2 's going to rain

Extension idea
If you used the lead-in activity, put the students into pairs. They use their ideas from the lead-in to make full sentences with the correct future form, e.g. *I'm going to mark homework this evening. We're having a teachers meeting on Thursday. My Business English class starts at 8a.m. on Mondays. (I think) everyone in this class will pass their English exam this year.* Elicit ideas from the students to check they are using the structures correctly.

3 Tell the students to write the full questions in their notebooks . Elicit these to check they are correct. Look at the example with the class and point out that, although we often use the same structure in the response as in the question, we don't have to, e.g. if you have already thought about sending the photos, you could reply *I'm going to send them to you tomorrow.* Monitor the students and help them where necessary. Question 5 is an example of an indirect question. Here, the word order is the same as in a normal sentence, not a question (*it will be*, not *will it be*).

Suggested answers
2 Where are you going to go this evening? I'm going to go to the cinema.
3 When will you take your next English test? I'll take my next test in two weeks' time.
4 Is the Earth going to get hotter? Yes, it's going to get a lot hotter.
5 Do you think it will be cloudy tomorrow? No, I think it'll be sunny.

Fast finishers
Ask students to think of similar questions about the future that they could ask other students in the class, e.g. *What do you think you will study at university?* They can then work in pairs with other fast finishers to ask and answer their questions for extended practice.

Students could do Grammar reference: Future forms: *will, be going to,* present continuous and present simple, Exercise 1, page 131 for homework.

4 Look at the example with the class and ask if this is an example of *going to*. (No. There is no second verb. It's a present continuous form with the verb *go*.) If you think the class need more help with future forms, elicit which structure they will use for each response and why before they start working in pairs. (1 present continuous if you have an arrangement, *going to* if you have a plan 2 *'ll* for a decision made at the time of speaking, 3 Present simple for a timetabled future 4 *going to* for a prediction made based on evidence 5 *going to* for a plan)

Answers
2 I'll help you/fix it (if you like).
3 It starts / begins on July 1st (etc.).
4 I think there's going to be a storm soon.
5 I'm going to study French./I don't know which I'm going to study.

▶ **Grammar reference page 131: Future forms: *will, be going to,* present continuous and present simple**
▶ **Workbook page 31**

Vocabulary SB page 66
Compound words

Lead-in
Write the word *classroom* on the board. Elicit that this is a combination of two words: *class* and *room*. Tell students this is called a compound word. Put the students into small groups and set a time limit of two minutes to think of other compound words. Elicit ideas from each group.

1 Allow the students to work in the same groups as for the lead-in so that stronger students can help the weaker ones. Elicit the answers and, if no one said the word during the lead-in activity, ask which weather word is a compound of two nouns (*thunderstorm* – a storm in which there is thunder).

Answers
2 suitcase **3** crossroads **4** backpack **5** signpost
6 overnight **7** campsite **8** sightseeing

2 Tell the students to work alone Don't elicit the answers until the students have listened and checked their answers. When eliciting the answers, also elicit the meaning of the compound words, e.g. *2 a book with information about Australia.*

Answers
2 guidebook **3** sightseeing **4** campsite **5** backpack
6 suitcase **7** crossroads **8** signpost

Fast finishers
Ask the students to think of more compound words which could be made using a word from A or B and another word, e.g. *bookcase* (both words are in B), *crossword* (*cross* is in A). Students can share any ideas they have with the other students at the end of the activity.

Track 35
Lewis: Next week I'm going to Australia! I'm arriving in the north, so first I'm going to stay overnight in Darwin. My guidebook says it's an interesting city, so I think I'll do a bit of sightseeing there. Then I'm getting the train to Alice Springs, right in the middle of the country, where I'll spend the night at a campsite. The next day I'm hoping to get a lift down the main road. I'm taking all my things in a backpack so that I don't have to carry a heavy suitcase around. About 200 kilometres south of Alice, I'll reach a crossroads where there's a signpost that says 'Uluru 247 km'. Uluru is also known as Ayers Rock – one of the most amazing sights in the world.

/P/ Word stress in compound words

3 Make sure students are clear that the audio starts from question two by pointing to the section of the text in the book. Pause the recording after he says: *My guidebook says it's an interesting city* and model and drill the word *guidebook*, showing the students that the first syllable is stressed. When they have listened to the whole text, elicit the answers and drill each individual word with the class. Ask why they think that *overnight* doesn't have the same stress pattern (it's a compound word but not a compound noun).

Answers
First part of all words 2–8. Point out that *overnight* is not a compound noun.

4 For weaker classes, before the students discuss their ideas, allow them to work in pairs to think of where they would go and individual sentences they could use containing compound words. They then change pairs so they discuss their journey with a different student.

Extension idea
Tell the students that they have been asked to write a guidebook about their town. Put them in pairs to decide what sections the book should be split into (e.g. *historic buildings, places to eat* and what illustrations they would use on the cover to show the biggest attractions of the town. When students have finished, elicit ideas from different groups.

▶ **Workbook page 29**

Grammar SB page 67
Prepositions of movement

Lead-in
Have a class survey on how the students usually get to work or college. Tell them to put their hands up for the form of transport they use the most and write the results on the board. Ask about: *car, bike, bus, train, walking, other* and tell the students you will come back to this after Exercise 2.

1 Allow the students to read through the text and discuss their ideas in pairs. If they aren't sure of the missing words, they should have a guess then listen to see if they were right.

Answers
2 on **3** on **4** off **5** in **6** out

Track 36

Toby: Hi Leon, Toby here. I'm really pleased you're coming to our new house next week. The quickest way here is by train to the city centre, which takes an hour and is usually on time. Then you can get on the number 64 bus to Edgely, getting off by the stadium. From there it's a fifteen-minute walk. Or, if you don't feel like walking, you could jump in a taxi and ask the driver to take you to the end of Valley Road. When you get out of the taxi, you'll see our place right in front of you. See you soon!

2 Allow the students to discuss the rules in pairs. All the answers can be found in the text in Exercise 1. Elicit the answers and elicit or tell the students that the rule for point 1 also includes *taxis* and if we walk we don't go *by foot* but *on foot*.

Answers
1 in, out of **2** on, off **3** by, by **4** on

Extension idea
Put the students into small groups and ask them to talk about how they get to school using full sentences. Encourage them to add more details, e.g. *I usually go by car. My mum takes me. I get out in Market Street.*

3 Encourage the students to write full sentences in their notebooks. When the students have finished, ask them if they recognise any of the mistakes as ones that they have made in the past.

Answers
1 in → by **2** correct **3** correct **4** at → on **5** with → by

Students could do Grammar reference: Prepositions of movement, Exercise 1, page 132 for homework.

4 Elicit the instructions for a journey from the students' language school to a place in their town from the whole class. Ask for details to ensure that they use as many prepositions of movement as possible. Now put the students into small groups and set a time limit of three minutes for them to do the same thing for a different journey. Elicit their ideas and check their use of prepositions.

▶ **Workbook page 31**

▶ **Grammar reference page 132: Prepositions of movement**

Speaking Part 2 SB page 68

Lead-in
With books closed, tell the students to close their eyes and imagine a scene. Say: There's a railway station, some passengers and a train. Give students ten seconds to imagine the scene then describe it in pairs. Elicit some of the ideas the students had.

1 Before the students start, elicit any useful topic vocabulary that the students can see in the photo and write this on the board e.g. *waiting, woman.* Put them in groups and set a time limit of one minute to describe what they can see in sentence form. Elicit ideas from different groups.

2 When the students have listened, allow them to discuss in pairs or small groups any details they remember from the recording, e.g. *on their way to work, sunny day*

Track 37

Lorenzo: It's a picture of a railway station, quite a small one I think. There are some trees on the left and I can see some green fields, too, so it might be in the countryside. There's a train coming into the station and it's probably going to stop there. There are some people waiting to get on it, a woman and a man and maybe others. They're very close to the railway lines, on the place where people stand, and maybe they're on their way to work in the morning. The woman has a dark coat on and she's wearing, I mean carrying, a large bag on her shoulder. She's doing something on her mobile phone, perhaps sending a message to someone. The man's wearing a suit and he also has a bag on his shoulder. The front of the train has big windows but they're a bit dark and I can't see the person who is driving it. It looks like quite a sunny day, but I don't think it's hot because the woman is dressed for winter weather.

3 Tell the students to read through the sentences before they listen again to prepare themselves for what they need to listen for and see if they can guess or remember any of the missing words.

Answers
2 There's, coming **3** There are, waiting **4** place where
5 I mean **6** also **7** person who

4 Look at a) with the whole class and elicit the words *also, too*. Monitor and help where necessary. When the students have finished, elicit that *also* comes between two ideas whereas *too* usually comes at the end of the sentence, e.g. *There are also a lot of people. There are a lot of people, too.*

Answers
a too (1); also (6) **b** I mean (5)
c There's, coming (2); There are, waiting (3)
d place where (4); person who (7)

Extension idea
The students work in small groups and think of five people or objects that you could see at a railway station, e.g. *ticket office*. They then think how they could describe their words if they weren't sure of the word in English, e.g. *It's the place where you buy tickets*. Elicit descriptions from different groups and ask the other students to guess what the words are.

Speaking Part 2 (describing a photo)
Discuss the advice with the students. Point out that it is important to get as much practice in speaking tasks as possible which is why you sometimes ask them to do this even in sections of the book which aren't primarily focused on speaking.

Exam advice

5 Tell the students not to start speaking until you tell them and that you will also let them know when one minute has passed. When both students have described their photos, ask if anyone's partner had to correct themselves or describe something they didn't know the word for. If so, elicit details.

▶ **Speaking bank pages 154–158: Speaking Part 2**

Writing Part 1 SB page 68

Lead-in
Write the words music festival on the board. Put the students into small groups and set a time limit of two minutes for them to think of vocabulary for things or activities associated with music festivals, e.g. *stage, crowd, bands*. Elicit the words and remind students of how to describe them if other people don't understand: *It's a place where …; It's a thing which …* .

1 Allow the students to work in pairs and try to elicit that although the expressions have the same function, i.e. they are to start or finish an email, we use different ones when writing to different people. More than one answer is often possible but some choices would definitely sound wrong, e.g. writing *Looking forward to seeing you soon* to a friend you were going to see the next day or *Lots of love* to someone you don't know well.

Answers
Hi (B), Looking forward to hearing from /seeing you (E), Well, that's all for now (E), All the best (E), This is just a quick message to say (B), It was great to hear from you (B), Give my love to everyone (E), Take care (E), See you soon (E), Don't forget to write soon (E), Sorry I've taken so long to write back. (B) Bye for now (E), Dear (B)

2 When students have completed the exercise, elicit the functions of the different future forms Thomas uses, e.g. *I'm going to an international* – an arrangement; *we'll probably get* – a prediction. Point out that *There will be* is often used for future facts.

Answers
1 Your English-speaking friend Thomas; arranging a trip to a music festiavl next Saturday
2 Hi, Sorry I've taken so long to write back, All the best
3 I'm going, will be, We'll be, we'll … need, will you meet; very
4 a, c, e; you should also agree to go and say whether you prefer to take your own food or pay for something to eat at the festival.

3 Elicit the answers and ask the students why they think he has used one paragraph for each note, e.g. it makes the email very easy to read and understand. This also helps students to make sure they have covered all of the notes.

Answers
1 Yes **2** No problem!: 1st paragraph, Yes, say why: 2nd paragraph, Tell Thomas: 3rd paragraph, Suggest: 4th paragraph **3** a Hi … , See you soon b really, very c It'll be, will be, that'll be, will take me, I'll text d enough time, be enough

Writing Part 1 (an email)
Discuss the advice with the students and elicit which endings Marco could have finished his email with, e.g. *All the best, Take care* or *Bye for now* would all sound fine.

Exam advice

4. Encourage the students to cover Marco's email so that they use their own ideas as much as possible. Tell them to plan their ideas for five minutes and not start writing until you tell them. You can allow students to plan together if you think it will help them. Then allow a maximum of fifteen minutes for the students to write the email. This should be done alone and without help.

Fast finishers
Students check their email is the correct length and addresses all of the notes and to make sure they have used a variety of tenses and adverbs of degree.

5. When the students have finished the task, ask them if they think this is a good way to correct written work and why/why not. If you don't use this method of marking written homework, you could ask if the students would like you to do it.

Extension idea
Tell the students to imagine they are doing something interesting at the weekend and they can invite their partner. They should write an email similar to Thomas's but using their own ideas. The email should contain at least three questions. The students then swap these with their partner who writes a reply, answering all the questions, for homework.

▶ **Speaking bank pages 154–158: Speaking Part 2**
▶ **Writing bank pages 145–147: an email**
▶ **Workbook page 31**
▶ **Complete Preliminary new edition Test Generator Unit 7**

Vocabulary list

Weather

cold
foggy
freezing
frost
hot
ice
icy
lightning
rainy
showers
snowy
storm
sunny
sunshine
temperature
thunderstorm
windy

Compound words

backpack
campsite
crossroads
guidebook
overnight
sightseeing
signpost
suitcase

Vocabulary activity 1

Put the students into groups. Tell them to write all the compound nouns from the word list but each word should go on two pieces of paper, e.g. *back* on one piece and *pack* on another. All the pieces of paper should be about the same size. They then lay the cards on the desk face down. The students then take it in turns to turn over two bits of paper to see if they form a compound. If they do, they keep the cards. If not, they turn them back over and try to remember where each word is for the next go. Stop the activity after a few minutes. The person who makes the most compounds is the winner.

Vocabulary activity 2

Students work in pairs and think of five towns or cities in their country. Alone they each draw a very simple outline map of their country and each add five of the cities to their map. They then write the weather in each place, e.g. *Madrid: sunny*; *Barcelona: raining*. They then tell each other, in sentences, what the weather is like in their five cities. Their partner should draw the map and add their partner's cities to their map and draw a weather symbol for each to match what their partner told them. When they have both finished, they can compare maps.

8 Influencers

Unit objectives

Topic: social media influencers

Listening Part 3: information completion

Reading Part 6: open cloze: understanding grammar in a short text

Speaking Part 1: general questions; talking about your daily routine and what you like

Writing Part 2: an article: using correct spelling and punctuation

Grammar: zero, first and second conditionals; *when, if* and *unless* + present, future

Vocabulary: phrasal verbs; describing people; adjective prefixes and suffices; adjective order

Pronunciation: conditional sentences: contracted words

Starting off SB page 70

Lead-in
Put students into small groups. Ask them to think about all the people in their family, including cousins, aunts and uncles, and to tell their group who the most talented person is and what their talents are.

1. Students now discuss any information they know about each person. Don't elicit any information at this stage and don't give the students the answers.

2. If students recognised the people in the photos, this will be very easy so ask them to find one interesting piece of information about each person.

Answers
1 B **2** D **3** A **4** C

3. Elicit a few advantages and disadvantages from the class before they work in groups.

Reading Part 6 SB page 71

Lead-in
Ask if anyone shares anything they have done online, e.g. films, photos, drawings or writing. Discuss why they do it.

Background information
Tanya Barr studied to become a make-up artist and then got a job at a beauty counter in a department store. Her company is called Tanya Barr Cosmetics. She has also written three books about beauty, vlogging and baking.

Marc Forne started using Instagram in 2014. In addition to his Instagram work he is now a model. He tries to be true to his own style and personality and believes that is why he is successful.

1. Elicit the meaning of *influence*: to change the way someone thinks.

Suggested answer
'Someone who affects or changes the way that people behave' from the Cambridge Online Dictionary

2. Ask the class if anyone has ever heard of Emma Watson and, if so, elicit any information they know. Set a time limit of one minute for the students to read the text and discuss the question in pairs before you elicit the answers.

Suggested answer
She tells her fans what she thinks and supports issues through her social networks.

Reading Part 6 (open cloze)
Discuss the advice with the class. Elicit the kinds of words which are tested (pronouns, relative pronouns, auxiliary verbs, e.g. *do, be*) and that there can only be one correct answer.

Exam advice

3 Look at the example with the students and ask what kind of word this is (a preposition and the gap is testing adjective + prepositions). Set a time limit of six minutes for students and check their answers.

Answers
1 was **2** when **3** than **4** as **5** to **6** on

4 Look at the first sentence with the class. When the students have completed the rest of the exercise, ask them if they recognise any of these mistakes from their own work and what other spelling mistakes they make.

Answers
1 to | too **2** where | were **3** an | and **4** quite | quiet
5 whit | with **6** becouse | because

5 Set a time limit of five minutes for the discussion and then elicit the most interesting thing students found out from their group.

Extension idea
Ask students to choose one website, channel or influencer to present to the class. Get the groups to present their ideas.

▶ **Workbook page 33**

Vocabulary SB page 72
Phrasal verbs

1 Allow students to compare their ideas in pairs. Look at the differences between the two pairs of similar words: *grow up / bring up*. *Growing up* involves moving from childhood to adulthood naturally. *Bringing someone up* includes teaching them how to behave and telling them what's right and wrong; *set up / take up*: *you set up something* such as a company or website; *you take up* an activity, e.g. a sport.

Suggested answers
1 became older **2** started/created
3 take care of a child until it is an adult **4** start doing

2 Look at the example with the whole class. When the students have matched all the phrasal verbs, go through the meaning of each with the class and other situations in which the new verbs can be used.

Answers
2 runs out of **3** set up **4** take up **5** get on with **6** make up
7 found out **8** brought up

3 Look at the example sentence and elicit that we use the preposition *in* with countries or cities (*in Naples, in Rome [in Italy]*). Set a time limit for students to write the sentences alone and tell quicker students to continue making sentences using as many of the phrasal verbs as they can.

4 Elicit the phrases: *two of us, none of us, all of us, some of us* so that the students can report their findings to the class when they have finished comparing their sentences.

▶ **Workbook page 32**

Grammar SB page 72
Zero, first and second conditionals

1 Elicit phrases we can use for giving advice, e.g. *Why don't you; You should; How about … ing*. When students have listened, elicit what a reality TV show is (one which involves real people in unscripted situations such as in a house, on an island etc). Elicit ideas for advice from the class.

2 Ask students to guess what advice Ed will give. Elicit the answers and ask the students what they think of the advice.

Suggested answers
1 He should talk to the university and Channel Seven.
2 Students' own answers.

Track 38

Ella:	Kristian! Kristian?
Kristian:	Oh hi, Ella.
Ella:	Are you ok? What's the matter?
Kristian:	You know I've always wanted to work in television. Well, Channel Seven have just got in touch. They'd like me to take part in their new reality show.
Ella:	Wow! What's it about?
Kristian:	It's a bit of a secret actually, but the idea is that twelve of us are going run a youth hostel for twelve weeks.
Ella:	But that's amazing! Haven't you always wanted to be on TV?
Kristian:	Er, yes, but filming starts next week. If I take up the offer, I'll have to give up my degree. And if I don't finish my degree, what will everyone say?
Ella:	I'm sorry? I don't understand.
Kristian:	I have to give in a project by Thursday and then my exams start next week.
Ella:	Oh, I see. Have you spoken to your tutor yet?

Kristian: No. Why? She's never in her office anyway.
Ella: If you spoke to your tutor, I'm sure she'd understand.
Kristian: But you know the rules, if you don't hand in your project on time, you can't do your exams. If you don't do your exams, you don't pass the year. And you have to leave if you don't pass the year!
Ella: Yes, but this is an incredible opportunity. You can't afford to miss a chance like this. If I were you, I'd talk to the university and also to the people at Channel Seven. There must be a way around this.
Kristian: I hope so! And thanks for your support, Ella.

3 Elicit the verb forms used but don't talk about them yet as there will be a more complete look at how we form conditionals in Exercise 5. Explain that these are all conditional sentences. These are split into two halves: an *if* clause which gives the situation and a result clause which tells you what the result of that situation is or will be.

Answers
2 spoke, 'd understand **3** have, don't pass

Track 39
1 If I take up the offer, I'll have to give up my degree.
2 If you spoke to your tutor, I'm sure she'd understand.
3 And you have to leave if you don't pass the year!

4 It may be easier to do the matching with the class in order to look at each kind of conditional in more detail. Look at the zero conditional: *You* in this kind of sentence is used to talk about people in general, e.g. *You (anyone) have to leave university,if you don't pass the year.* It can also be used for scientific truths, e.g. *If you heat ice, it melts. if* can often be replaced by *when*. First conditional sentences refer to a specific likely situation, e.g. *If you* (now talking about a specific person*) heat that ice there, it will melt.*
The second conditional can refer to something unlikely or completely imaginary. The situation could be about now or the future.

Answers
1 c **2** a **3** b

5 Elicit that the past form used in the second conditional doesn't mean that the sentence is talking about the past. Elicit that, in sentences 1 and 2, the sentences start with the *if* clause and sentence 3 starts with the result clause. Point out that we can always reverse the order of the sentence but elicit that sentence 3 doesn't require a comma. Elicit the reversed forms of each sentence from Exercise. Elicit that, apart from the comma, there is no other change in structure.

Answers
Type 0 – present, present; **Type 1** – present, future;
Type 2 – past, *would* + infinitive; We use a comma when the conditional sentence begins with the *If* clause (the situation). We don't use commas when the sentence begins with the result.

/P/ Conditional sentences: contracted words

6 Look at the example and elicit that there are five words (don't = 2). Elicit the number of words and any contractions used in each.

Answers
2 8 **3** 5

Track 40
1 And if I don't finish my degree, what will everyone say?
2 If you don't do your exams, you don't pass the year.
3 If I were you, I'd talk to the university.

7 Allow students to discuss the two gapped sentences to see if they can remember the words used then play the recording and elicit the sentences.

Answers
2 don't do your exams, you don't **3** were you, I'd talk

8 If you think the students need more help, elicit the type of conditional in the example and why this conditional is used (first – possible future situation). Tell students to look at the other sentences in pairs and think of which conditional each uses and why. Elicit the answers and allow students to practise saying the sentences, using unstressed contracted forms.

Answers
2 is **3** get **4** won't go out **5** 'll buy **6** don't sleep

9 Tell the students to keep the first half of each of the sentences in Exercise 8 unchanged and write different endings. Monitor and help students with the form and with ideas. When students have compared ideas elicit ideas from each pair.

10 Look at the sentence stems with the class and elicit what conditional each one is (1, 3, 4 – second conditional; 2 – first conditional; 5 – could be either first or second). Students then work alone to write their ideas and then compare them in small groups. Elicit the best idea for each sentence from each group.

Students could do Grammar reference: Conditional sentences, Exercises 1 and 2, page 133, at this point or for homework.

11 Elicit a question for question 1: *What would you do if you lost your mobile phone?* Elicit that questions in the second conditional always start: *(Question word) + would + pronoun/noun + verb + if + past form* and in the first conditional: *(Question word+ + will + pronoun/noun + verb + if + present simple form.*

▶ **Grammar reference page 133: Conditional sentences**

▶ **Workbook page 34**

when, if and *unless*

1 Elicit the answer and ask students why sentence 2 uses *when* but the other two don't (they will definitely get to the conference but Josh might not need anything and they might not get to the conference really late).

Answer
2 Hayley

2 Students complete the rules. Elicit that, to decide whether a sentence needs *if* or *unless*, they should try both and see which makes sense: *if* or *except, if.* Write an example on the board: *I'll go swimming if/except if the sea is really cold.* Ask the students which makes sense and elicit that *unless* would be the correct word.

Answers
1 when **2** if / unless **3** unless / if **4** unless

3 Elicit the answers and reasons for their choices.

Answers
1 when **2** if **3** unless **4** if **5** unless **6** when

Students could do Grammar reference: Conjunctions: *when, if, unless* + present, future, Exercise 3, page 133, for homework.

▶ **Workbook page 34**

Listening Part 3 SB page 74

1 Look at the questions with the class and tell them your own answers to the questions. Set a time limit of two minutes for students to discuss the information and elicit interesting answers from different students.

2 Elicit as much information about the type of words needed as possible e.g. 2 a noun, a topic/theme 3 an adjective – a positive, personality adjective / a reflexive pronoun 6 a time – a plural form. Ask the students to guess what the missing words and numbers could be.

Suggested answers
1 a number **2** a noun **3** an adjective or pronoun **4** a noun **5** a noun **6** a time (e.g. days, weeks, months etc.)

Listening Part 3 (information completion)
Discuss the exam advice with the students. Also elicit that they won't be asked to write much; one or two words, such as compound nouns, only. Also remind the students that if a real name is used, it will be spelt for them on the recording.

Exam advice

3 Tell the students to treat this as if it was an exam. Don't elicit any answers after the first listening. When they have listened once, tell them to listen carefully on the second listening to check or complete their answers and check their spelling. Play the recording again and elicit answers.

Track 41

Narrator: Part 3. For each question, write the correct answer in the gap. Write one or two words or a date or a number or a time. You will hear a man called Ben Richards talking about how to get famous on YouTube.

Presenter: Hi! Ben Richards here. About a billion people around the world use YouTube. While some people just watch videos, others upload around 300 hours of them a minute. That means that by the time I finish this introduction there'll be 500 hours of new videos on YouTube. Have you ever dreamt of becoming a famous YouTuber? Here's my advice to help you get started.

Do your research! Find out what kind of videos people are into right now by searching for 'Popular on YouTube' and then choose your style. Everyone loves watching animals doing funny things – in fact, the first ever video on YouTube was a visit to a zoo – but the ones with the most likes are often music videos.

Next think about how you can make something bigger, better and different, something that you and the people you know would like to watch. Your audience will also want to get to know you, so avoid being a clown or a film star, just act like yourself.

Practise making very short high-quality videos first. Tell your friends about your videos and ask them for their opinion. However, aim to upload at least 10 good ones before letting them know about your channel. You'll need to create a video for this which attracts attention.

Make sure you upload new videos with new information at least once a week. Choose a day and let the people who follow you know. To increase the number of people watching your videos, each one should have an unforgettable title and a clear description, but once again, try to be a bit different.

Many people give up after two or three months because nobody's watching but attracting a large audience takes time, often two or three years. It's hard work, but definitely worth it!

Answers
1 300 **2** music **3** yourself **4** channel **5** description **6** years

4 Look at the instructions and elicit ideas of what the video could show and how it could be presented, e.g. a student-led video or a more professional-looking video with an introductory film showing the university with music playing in the background. Set a time limit of two minutes to think of a basic outline and then another three minutes to think about their ideas in more detail.

5 Each group presents their ideas to the class. Encourage each member of each group to do some of the talking and allow other students to ask questions if there is anything they aren't sure about.

Extension idea
Allow the class to vote on the best idea for the video presentation. Discuss why it was the best idea.

▶ **Workbook page 35**

Vocabulary SB page 74
Describing people

1 Put the students into small groups and give them two minutes to look at the four people and discuss the differences between them. Elicit the answer and the key words which helped them decide. Elicit the meaning of *scar.*

Answer
B

Track 42
Carter: Hey Will! Is that you?
Will: Carter! How's things?
Carter: Great! You know I've been creating a new YouTube channel? Well, I'm looking for someone to present it. Would you do it?
Will: Me? Sorry. I'm too shy. I'd be terrible. What would your perfect presenter look like?
Carter: You know, someone with an interesting face. He should be medium height, look around twenty-five years old with straight hair. He should probably be good-looking, too.
Will: Um … there's John. He's got a great voice.
Carter: Yeah but I think I'm looking for someone without a beard or moustache.
Will: So no beard or moustache, right?
Carter: Right!
Will: What about Robert? He's got that cool scar on his chin.
Carter: He's got blue eyes, hasn't he?
Will: That's right and everyone says he's honest and reliable. Do you want his phone number?

2 Ask students to draw the mind map in their notebooks. Elicit the meanings of all the words.

Suggested answers
Skin: dark, fair, pale **Hair:** bald, beard, blond(e), curly, dark, fair, grey, long, moustache, red, straight, wavy
Build: broad shoulders, medium height, short, slim
Other: attractive, beautiful, good-looking, plain, scar

3 If you think the students need more help, elicit the meanings of either the adjectives in the box or the adjectives in the list. Allow them to work in pairs and ask the students to say which adjective in each pair is the most positive and why.

Answers
2 lazy **3** stupid **4** quiet **5** generous **6** polite **7** anxious **8** shy

4 Elicit the meaning of *honest* and *reliable* and then allow the students to work in pairs to complete the task. Elicit the answers and tell students they should try to learn negatives when they learn new adjectives. Try to elicit the two adjectives from Exercise 3 that can take a negative prefix (*impolite, unconfident*).

Answers
impatient, unpleasant, dishonest, unreliable

5 Tell students that prefixes can make words negative and suffixes change them from one kind of word to another, e.g. a verb to an adjective. Elicit examples from the adjectives they have already looked at in the lesson, e.g. *attract–attractive*. Students then look at the exercise in pairs. Elicit the words and the fact that the suffix *-ful* only has one *-l* . Note that *helpful* and *helpless* aren't opposites and have different meanings (the opposite of *helpful* is *unhelpful*).

Answers
2 cheerful **3** beautiful **4** helpful **5** helpless

6 Ask the students to read the six sentences (a–f) before they look at the rules to see if they can identify what is wrong and why.

Answers
a In my tennis club, there are two ~~coaches very nice~~ **very nice coaches.**
b My best friend has ~~hair and eyes brown~~ **brown hair and brown eyes.**
c At the beginning of the film, a ~~young handsome~~ **handsome young** man is sitting in a café.
d She is wearing a ~~white beautiful~~ **beautiful white** dress.
e I've made a new friend with ~~black short~~ **short black** hair.
f He lives in a house with a ~~green big~~ **big green** garden.

7 Look at the example with the class and then elicit a famous celebrity and ask students to describe his or her looks and character. When the students have discussed some ideas in pairs, put the pairs together to compare ideas with a different pair.

▶ **Workbook pages 32–33**

Speaking Part 1 SB page 76

1 Tell the students to read through all the questions. Tell them that they don't have to worry about writing full answers.

Answers
1 Switzerland **2** Tokyo in Japan **3** I work in my mum's shop, but I'd like to go to university. **4** I'm an engineer in a large company. **5** I love it! **6** too often **7** playing sports

Track 43

1

Examiner: What's your name?
Chiara: My name's Chiara.
Examiner: Where do you live?
Chiara: I live in Italy.
Examiner: Do you work or are you a student?
Chiara: I'm a student.
Examiner: What do you study?
Chiara: I'm studying to be a teacher. I'd like to be a primary school teacher.
Examiner: Thank you. Do you enjoy studying English?
Chiara: I love it!
Examiner: Why?
Chiara: Because the classes are fun and we've got a really good teacher. And also, as I said, I want to be a teacher and I know that I'll need English for my work.

2

Examiner: And what's your name?
Celine: My name's Celine.
Examiner: Thank you. Where do you come from?
Celine: I come from Switzerland.
Examiner: Do you work or are you a student?
Celine: At the moment, I'm working.
Examiner: What do you do?
Celine: I'm working in my mum's shop but I'd like to go to university next year.
Examiner: How often do you use a mobile phone?
Celine: Sorry, can you say that again, please?
Examiner: Do you often use a mobile phone?
Celine: Oh yes! My friends say I use it too often. I use it for everything. It's my alarm clock, I check it for messages and I also use my phone for the internet and to watch videos.

3

Examiner: What's your name?
Akihiko: Akihiko.
Examiner: Where do you live, Akihiko?
Akihiko: I live in Tokyo in Japan.
Examiner: Do you work or are you a student?
Akihiko: Er … I work.
Examiner: What do you do?
Akihiko: I'm an engineer in a large company.
Examiner: What do you enjoy doing in your free time?
Akihiko: Um … I really enjoy playing sports. I play table tennis and I also like baseball. I also like travelling to new places.

2 Before the students listen again, ask them to read the questions and discuss what they remember in pairs.

Answers
1 Yes they do because they answer the examiner's questions and they give more than one-word answers.
2 Sorry, can you say that again?
3 No, he repeats it in a slightly different way: 'Do you often use a mobile phone?'

Speaking Part 1 (general questions)
Discuss the advice with the students and ask why the last sentence is important. Elicit that, the question probably won't be exactly the same as what they practised. It's better to practise answering unknown questions and becoming more confident in all situations.

Exam advice

3 Look at the dialogue with the class. Put them in pairs and ask them to practise the dialogue but with Enrico giving full sentences as answers. Ask a confident pair to role-play the Speaking test, then elicit ideas.

Suggested answers
Examiner: What's your name? **Enrico:** I'm Enrico (*or* My name's Enrico). **Examiner:** Where do you live, Enrico?
Enrico: I live in Porto which is in Portugal.
Examiner: Do you work or are you a student?
Enrico: I work. **Examiner:** What do you do?
Enrico: I'm a journalist for an important newspaper in my country.

4 Tell the students playing the examiner to see if the students are answering the questions correctly and giving extra information. They should also listen out for common mistakes as well as good use of linking words like *because*, *but*, etc.

▶ **Speaking bank pages 152–153: Speaking Part 1**

Writing Part 2 SB page 77

1. Set a time limit of two minutes for students to discuss the similarities and differences and elicit ideas.

2. Look at the first sentence with the whole class. Write the sentence as it is in the book on the board, then elicit the punctuation needed and add it so that everyone can see. For the other sentences, when students have finished, elicit the punctuation items needed for each one (e.g *2 – 2 capitals, 2 question marks; 3 – 3 capitals, 1 apostrophe, 1 full stop; 4 – 1 capital, 2 commas and a full stop; 5 – 3 capitals, 2 full stops, 1 apostrophe; 6 – 1 capital, 1 apostrophe, 1 full stop*).

Answers
1 **D**ear **S**am**,** **I** had a great time with my friends last weekend too.
2 **W**hat about you**?** **W**ho is your best friend**?**
3 **O**n Saturday **I** took my cousin's (or cousins**'** *if more than one cousin owns the dog*) dog to the beach.
4 **A**fter that**,** we ate salad**,** chicken and ice cream.
5 **H**e loves **E**nglish**.** **H**e thinks that **it's** easy.
6 **I'm** looking forward to seeing you soon.

3. Elicit that the important words are those which tell them what they need to write. Elicit the words they chose and reasons for them.

Suggested answers
Who? – member family, friend, someone famous; What / look like? What / like? Why / admire? Article answering questions; about 100 words

4. Tell the students to work alone and decide whether or not the student answered the question correctly and also whether they made any grammar, spelling or punctuation errors. Set a strict time limit as this should be an initial general impression of the text. Don't elicit any answers yet.

5. This time the students look at the text in more detail. Elicit the answers and examples of adjectives used.

4 & 5 Suggested answers
Although Zahra answers the questions well, she doesn't get full marks because she makes several mistakes with punctuation and spelling.
1 Yes **2** Yes **3** Yes **4** No **5** Yes

6. Look at the instructions with the class and ask them how many errors they have to look for in total (ten). Elicit what the errors are and what they should be.

Answers
Spelling: 1 with curly dark hair and brown eyes
2 gets on well with him **3** because he's
4 Hasan is hardworking and generous too
5 he set up his own online company which sells
Punctuation: 1 If I had to choose **2** He's medium height
3 he's easygoing, honest and reliable
4 to help an international children's charity.

Writing Part 2 (an article)
Discuss the advice with the students and ask why the first point is useful (the examples and reasons show that you understand what the adjectives mean and aren't just listing all the words you can remember). The second point is important for all exam tasks where students need to write anything, e.g. open cloze tasks, Listening Part 3 and Writing.

Exam advice

7. Elicit how long they should spend planning their answer and vocabulary (about five minutes). Tell the students not to start writing the actual text until you tell them to. First they should decide who to write about and some adjectives and reasons for them. After five minutes, tell the students to start writing.

Model answer
If I had to choose one person who I admire, it would be my grandmother. She was born in 1930 in the south of England. She's quite short with grey hair but when she was younger, she had short, brown hair. She's also got one green and one brown eye. She's very independent and active. She plays bridge, paints and loves going to the theatre.

As well as enjoying herself, she also helps others. She visits other elderly people who can't get out on their own and volunteers at the local hospital. She's amazing. I think she's got more energy than most people half her age.

8. This could be done in pairs. Once the students have checked their own writing and made any corrections necessary, they swap with a partner and use the checklist to rate their partner's work.

▶ **Writing bank pages 148–149: Writing Part 2: an article**
▶ **Complete Preliminary new edition Test Generator Unit 8**
▶ **Complete Preliminary new edition Test Generator Term Test Units 5–8**
▶ **Workbook page 35**

Vocabulary

Phrasal verbs

bring up
find out
get on with
grow up
make up
run out (of)
set up
take up

Describing people

attractive
bald
beard
beautiful
blond(e)
broad shoulders
curly
dark
fair
good-looking
grey
long
medium height
moustache
pale
plain
red
scar
short
slim
straight
wavy

Adjectives and opposites

calm–anxious
confident–shy
easygoing–strict
generous–mean
hard-working–lazy
polite–rude
quiet–noisy
stupid–smart

Negative adjectives

friendly–unfriendly
honest–dishonest
patient–impatient
pleasant–unpleasant
reliable–unreliable

Adjectives from nouns

cheer–cheerful
beauty–beautiful
help–helpful
help–helpless
success–successful

Vocabulary activity 1

Tell the class they are going to have a race to find a word in the vocabulary list. As soon as they know the word, they should say it. Say: *Name a hair colour* (red); *Name the opposite of polite* (rude), etc. Put students into small groups. Each student takes turns to give a similar order starting: *Name ….* The other students get one guess each.

Vocabulary activity 2

Tell the students to work together in pairs to make a short story using one vocabulary item from each list. Read them an example and ask them to identify the five words you use: *My uncle is a successful business man. He set up his company five years ago and is now very rich. He is very confident but he is quite impatient with the people who work for him.*
Set a time limit for the students to do the same. When they have finished, invite the students to read out their stories. The other students listen for the words from the vocabulary lists. Make sure the story makes sense and they have used the words correctly.

Vocabulary and grammar review Unit 7

1 **2** big enough **3** too dark **4** thick enough **5** too sleepy **6** old enough **7** too cold **8** too expensive

2 **2** 'm meeting **3** 'll go **4** leaves **5** 'll **6** are going

3 **2** f **3** a **4** b **5** c **6** e

4 **Across:** **1** freezing **4** cold **6** crossroads **7** backpack **8** extremely **9** lightning
Down: **2** guidebook **3** sightseeing **5** foggy

Vocabulary and grammar review Unit 8

1 **2** B **3** A **4** C **5** D **6** B **7** A **8** C **9** D **10** C

2 **1** I only go shopping if I have to ~~becouse~~ **because** most of the shops are expensive.
2 I've just received your email. You ask me ~~wich~~ **which** film stars I like.
3 Since ~~than~~ **then** we have been very good friends.
4 You asked me if ~~i~~ **I** had fun last weekend.
5 On ~~friday~~, **Friday**, my family and I got on a boat to the island.
6 I think you ~~now~~ **know** him. He is called Patrick.

3 **2** I feel tired / I'll be tired tomorrow **3** I'd take it to the police station **4** you don't come too **5** I'll start learning French **6** I lost my mobile phone **7** I'll go to the beach **8** I would live in Australia.

4 **2** with **3** a **4** up **5** for **6** to

9 Stay fit and healthy

Unit objectives

Topic: health and sports

Listening Part 2: identifying the situation and what you need to listen for

Reading Part 3: multiple choice: identifying opinion and attitude

Speaking Part 4: discussing sport, fitness and health; showing agreement and polite disagreement

Writing Part 2: a story: using a range of past tenses to explain what happened

Grammar: relative clauses (defining and non-defining); past perfect

Vocabulary: illnesses and accidents; sports; *do, go* and *play*

Pronunciation: word stress: agreeing and disagreeing

Starting off

Lead-in
Elicit the name of the lesson in which students do sports (PE/*Physical Education*). Elicit some of the activities the students used to do during PE, e.g. *football, basketball, running*. Put the students into small groups. Set a time limit for them to discuss what they liked and disliked about PE lessons when they were at school and how PE lessons are similar or different from the exercise they do now. Elicit ideas from each group and discuss their ideas as a class.

Background information
Padel is a mixture of tennis and squash. The rackets are solid, not stringed as in squash or tennis. The court has walls and you can hit the ball against the walls like in squash but you also hit the ball over a net, as in tennis. The game was invented in Mexico and is now becoming more and more popular in South America and Europe.

1 Tell students that 'these kinds of activity' means it doesn't have to be exactly what is shown. Put students into pairs and set a time limit of two minutes for them to discuss the questions.

2 Tell students to complete the quiz alone and then compare their answers in pairs. Find out who is the most active person in each pair and elicit things they do.

3 Before they look at what it means, ask the students to think together what it might say about them. When they have looked, ask if they agree with the results. Elicit ways that students could change their lifestyles.

Listening Part 2 SB page 81

1 When the students have found the answers to the questions, elicit why this information is useful.

Answers
1 a conversation about running 20 kilometres, a woman and her friend, the reason she decided to run in the race
2 a conversation about a film after two people watched it, two friends, what they agree about
3 a conversation about a bicycle, two friends, the reason he wants to sell it
4 a conversation about a concert one of the speakers went to, two friends, his opinion of it
5 a conversation about an illness, a man and his friend, how he feels now
6 a conversation about a sports centre, two friends, what they agree about

Listening Part 2 (multiple-choice, short dialogues)
Discuss the advice with the students. Tell the students that each recording starts with a narrator reading out the situation so they will be able to see which question they are listening to. For the second point, elicit that each conversation has one question, which is why they can forget each conversation when they have the answer to the question.

Exam advice

2 Tell the students to work alone and do the listening as if they were in an exam. After the first listening, they should remain silent and not share their answers. When the students have listened for a second time, either elicit the answers or use the Extension idea below.

Answers
1 B **2** A **3** B **4** A **5** C **6** B

Track 43

Narrator: Part 2. For each question, choose the correct answer.

1

Narrator: You will hear a woman telling her friend about running in a 20-kilometre race. Why did she decide to run in the race?

Man: Why did you run in that 20-kilometre race over the weekend? To get fit?

Woman: Well, as you know, I do a lot of athletics training most weeks so a single race wouldn't really make any difference. But my friend Julia, who keeps fit by running in other races like this, told me the winner gets £500. I thought if I could somehow manage to come first, I'd be able to give that to charity, so I went online, found the website and registered for it straight away.

Man: Did you win?

Woman: I came second. But I still made £200 for charity.

2

Narrator: You will hear two friends talking about a film they have just watched.

Woman: So what did you think of the film?

Man: It was pretty good, I thought. It was quite long but it was certainly more interesting than the last one we watched here.

Woman: Well, I found it rather slow and a bit hard to follow in places. And I noticed a lot of people in the seats around us left before it ended.

Man: Yes they did, and it was a shame because they missed the best bit in the last few minutes. I really didn't expect it to finish like that.

Woman: That was quite a shock, wasn't it?

3

Narrator: You will hear a student telling his friend about his bicycle.

Female student: I think I've just seen an ad on the notice board for your bike. Are you really selling it?

Male student: Yes, it's in great condition and I should get a good price for it. Then I can get a brand-new phone.

Female student: I'm really surprised. I often see you riding it when I'm going to university, even on cold winter mornings.

Male student: Yes, I know I'll miss it but I can't afford to replace it with a new one as well as buy a phone. The screen on the one I've got is just too small and it's damaged, too.

4

Narrator: You will hear a young man telling his friend about a concert he went to.

Woman: I heard you went to the concert in the park on Saturday night. How was it?

Man: Well, I know normally you'd pay a lot of money to see a top band like that so it was good in that way, but it was still a bit of a disappointment. They didn't play any of their big hits, just a load of new songs from their latest album and they all seemed to go on for hours. Like a lot of other people there, I went home quite a while before the end because it wasn't interesting. The only good thing really was that the concert was free.

5

Narrator: You will hear a man telling his friend about his illness.

Woman: I saw you were off work at the end of last week and someone said you were ill. What was the matter?

Man: Yes, I had a nasty cough, a sore throat and a stomach ache, but fortunately that's gone now.

Woman: So do you feel better today?

Man: I've still got a bit of a headache and I don't have any energy at all, maybe because I wasn't eating properly until today. But at least I've got rid of the fever I had.

Woman: Good. Remember to keep warm and have plenty of drinks, especially hot ones.

6

Narrator: You will hear two friends talking about their local sports centre.

Male student: There are definitely lots of things to do at that new sports centre next to the park.

Female student: If you like team sports or racket sports, yes, but they need things like athletics and gymnastics, too.

Male student: Their swimming pool's a really good size, though, and there's a reduced admission fee for students.

Female student: That's true. Actually, I should go more often because it's only about ten minutes by bus from my place.

Male student: And even less from mine. Actually, I could walk there instead and save a bit of money.

Female student: If we have enough time, let's go next weekend!

Extension idea

Put the students into groups of three. Tell the students that you are going to play the recording again and will stop it after each dialogue. One student is A, one B and one C (if the number of students isn't divisible by 3, either have a group of four where two students work together or a group of two where one student has to be B and C). The students have to listen for information why their letter is correct or incorrect. After each dialogue elicit the correct answer and the reasons why.

▶ **Workbook page 36**

Vocabulary SB page 81
Illnesses and accidents

Lead-in
Put the students into small groups. Ask them to think about a time they had to stay at home because they were ill. They should tell each other when it was, what was wrong (they should explain how they felt or symptoms if they don't know the name of the illness) and how long they had to stay at home. Elicit one idea from each group.

1 Put the students into pairs to see if they know what the words mean and how they think the words are pronounced. When they have listened, drill the sentence and elicit the meaning of each word.

Answers
1 Phonetic script for underlined words: cough: /kɒf/; sore: /sɔː/; throat: /θrəʊt/; stomach: /stʌmək/; ache: /eɪk/
2 Meanings: *cough*: make air come out of your throat with a short sound; *sore throat*: pain inside the throat; *stomach ache*: pain in your stomach

Track 45
I had a nasty cough, a sore throat and a stomach ache.

2 Look at the headings in the table and elicit what the three words mean. Students then work in pairs. Set a time limit of two minutes and tell the students to leave any words they don't know. Elicit answers and model and drill each word.

Answers
Illnesses: earache, fever, flu, high temperature
Accidents: bruise, cut, fracture, sprain, wound
Treatments: aspirin, bandage, medicine, operation, pill, plaster, plaster cast, test, X-ray

3 Put the students into pairs and ask them to discuss which word they think changes and how. Elicit ideas or give them the correct answer if they can't guess.

Answers
2 cut **3** bruise **4** cough **5** sprain

4 When the students have looked at the example sentences and completed the rules, look at the vocabulary that has been introduced and how it is used in sentences, pointing out any irregularities and possible problems.

Answers
1 parts of the body **2** illnesses **3** treatments

Extension idea
Each person works alone and writes an illness or injury on a piece of paper. They don't show this to anyone else. Put the students into small groups. The students take turns to mime their problem for the other students to guess. When they have guessed correctly, they give the student advice.

5 Look at the example conversation with the students and elicit the tenses that are used and why (present perfect to talk about general experience that has happened at some point in their lives; past simple to ask about and give details about a specific time in the past).
If some members of the class have never suffered from any of these problems, they should think about a problem they have had. Set a time limit of three minutes, then ask each group to tell the class about one of the problems they talked about and encourage other students to ask questions about what happened.

▶ **Workbook page 37**

Grammar SB page 82
Relative clauses

Lead-in
Write on the board: *do exercise, training, warm up*. Put the students into small groups and ask them to discuss what the similarities and differences are between the three words. Set a time limit of two minutes and elicit ideas from the students.

1 Before the students look at the words in italics, ask them to read the text quickly and, in small groups, discuss a good idea for a title, e.g. *Stay safe while exercising*. Set a time limit of one minute for the reading and one minute for the discussion. Elicit ideas and reasons for them. Students then work together or alone to look at the relative pronouns.

Answers
1 that **2** who **3** which **4** when **5** that **6** whose **7** where **8** that

2 Before the students look at the rules, write an example on the board: *That's the shop*. Ask the students if this, on its own, makes much sense (no). Now complete the sentence: *That's the shop where I bought my new T-shirt*. Ask if it now makes sense (yes). Tell the students that

the phrase *where I bought my new T-shirt* is a defining relative clause and the word *where* is a defining relative pronoun. Elicit what the relative pronoun refers to (*the shop*).
When the students have looked at the text and rules, elicit that we can use *that* for both people and things.

Answers
2 who **3** that/which **4** which/that **5** when **6** where **7** whose

3 Look at the example with the students and ask what the relative pronoun refers to (*The TV series*). Ask if this is a person, thing, place, time or possession (*thing*) and why two answers are possible (rules 3 and 4 from Exercise 2).

Fast finishers
Ask fast finishers to identify what each relative pronoun refers to. When you elicit the answers, also elicit this information to check that the correct choices have been made.

Answers
2 who **3** where **4** which/that **5** whose **6** when

4 Look at the example with the students and elicit other possible endings, e.g. *everyone loves*. Tell the pairs to write one ending for each sentence first.

Suggested answers
2 I watch TV / I listen to music **3** I hate / I really like **4** I stay in bed late / I go swimming **5** always helps you / listens to you **6** name is the same as mine / best friend works in the same place as me

5 Before the students look at the rules, write an example on the board: *My brother lives in the USA.* Ask if this, on its own, makes much sense (yes). Now complete the sentence: *My brother, who is two years older than me, lives in the USA.* Tell the students that the phrase, *who is two years older than me,* is a non-defining relative clause and the word *who* is a non-defining relative pronoun. Elicit what the relative pronoun refers to (*who – my brother*).
The students now answer the questions alone or in pairs.

Answers
1 which **2** which is very healthy **3** yes **4** no

6 Look at the example sentence with the students. Ask them which word in the second sentence refers to the person's arm (*it*). *What kind of word is it?* (a pronoun). Ask them if they can see 'it' in the answer (*no*). Point out that *which* (a relative pronoun) refers to the arm and we only need one pronoun. If you feel the students need more help, elicit which word they can omit in the other sentences (*her, there, his, then, it*).

Answers
2 you met, works at the hospital. **3** we hired a boat, is in the next valley. **4** sister is a teacher, is my best friend. **5** I was 19. **6** is popular in my country.

Fast finishers
Write an alternative version of 2 on the board: *My cousin, who works in the hospital, is a doctor.* Ask students to look at sentence 4 and ask them to try to write a second answer starting: *Ricky, who …*

Students could do Grammar reference: Defining and non-defining relative clauses with *which, that, who, whose, when, where*, Exercises 1–3, pages 134–135 at this point or for homework.

7 Ask the class to look at the first sentence and elicit what the mistake is (the relative pronoun) and why (we use *who* to refer to people but this is referring to sport).

Answers
1 I want to know ~~who~~ **which** sport is your favourite.
2 I can play my favourite sport, ~~that~~ **which** is tennis.
3 They filmed students ~~which~~ **who/that** were playing football.
4 This is the book ~~who~~ **which/that** my best friend Joey gave me.
5 One sport ~~who~~ **which/that** I think is good is swimming.
6 I want to learn more about tennis, ~~that~~ **which** is my hobby.

Extension idea
Write a simple sentence on the board, e.g. *Tapas is Spanish.* Elicit how this could be made longer, e.g. *Tapas, which is a small dish of food, is Spanish.* Students work in small groups and write three similar sentences about a thing, a person and a time, place or possession. They then swap these with a different group who try to make them longer using non-defining relative clauses. Monitor and help where necessary. When they have finished, they hand them back to the original group to check and decide which one they like the best.

▶ **Grammar reference page 134–135: Defining and non-defining relative clauses with *which, that, who, whose, when, where***
▶ **Workbook page 39**

Vocabulary SB page 83
Sports

Lead-in
Put the students into pairs. Give each pair 30 seconds to write as many sports as they can in English. When they have finished, put the pairs together in groups of four. The pairs take it in turns to mime one of their sports for the other pairs to guess.

1 When the students have matched the photos, ask the class if they can explain the difference between Taekwondo and more popular martial arts such as judo (e.g. it is Korean, the focus is on head high kicks).

Answers
1 A **2** C **3** B

2 When the students have matched the verbs to the activities, ask them if they know what the rule is for which word to use. If you think the students have some ideas, you can ask them to complete the table in pairs. If not, you could look at the rules in Exercise 4 first and then ask the students to complete the table.

Answers
do: Taekwondo; **go:** surfing; **play:** volleyball

3 Tell the students to only write the words they are sure of. Monitor and help where necessary. Elicit the answers but don't tell the students the rules at this stage.

Answers
do: athletics, gymnastics
go: climbing, cycling, jogging, mountain biking, rollerblading, running, skateboarding, skiing, swimming
play: baseball, basketball, football, golf, ice hockey, tennis, volleyball

4 Ask the students to work in pairs to try to decide the rules. They may say that activities ending in *-ing* are used with *go*. Although it is almost correct, *boxing* and *wrestling*, for example, are used with *do* (or as verbs *to box*, *to wrestle*).

Answers
1 play **2** go **3** do

5 Look at the first sentence with the students. Ask them how they could guess the verb to use is *go* (it's an outdoor activity which we do alone and there isn't a ball). Allow students to look at the other sentences in pairs and elicit reasons for their answers.

Answers
2 make – do **3** make – go **4** done – played **5** made – did
6 played – went

6 Look at the words and elicit that the two words following *in* are buildings. The words following *on* are the playing area inside the building so, for example, football is played *on* a pitch *in* a stadium. Other sports could also be matched to more than one place.

Suggested answers
on a court: tennis, squash, basketball, volleyball, etc.
in a gym: gymnastics, aerobics, martial arts, etc.
on a pitch: football, rugby, hockey, baseball, etc.
in a stadium: football, rugby, baseball, etc.
on a track: athletics, running, cycling, etc.

7 Elicit which words have similar meanings and how they are different, e.g. we use a bat and a racket to hit a ball but a racket usually has strings. Allow students to work in small groups and discuss their ideas. Elicit ideas and the meanings of each word.

Suggested answers
Clothes: boots (football, rugby, skiing, etc.); gloves (boxing, football goalkeeper, ice hockey, skiing, etc.); helmet (horse riding, motorcycling, baseball, etc.); trainers (running, jogging, tennis, etc.)
Equipment: bat (baseball, cricket, table tennis, etc.); racket (tennis, squash, badminton, etc.); net (tennis, table tennis, volleyball, etc.)

8 Students can work in pairs. Elicit the answers to the exercise.

Answers
2 score **3** draw/lose/win

9 Before the students get into groups, ask them to work alone and write down the sport they like most and the sport they like least. When they get into groups, they can discuss these sports and see which ones they agree with. Elicit ideas and reasons for their answers.

Extension idea
Students work in small groups and think of a sport. They list the equipment and clothes required and where it is played. Each group takes turns to read out their words and the other students guess what the sport is.

▶ **Workbook page 37**

Reading Part 3 SB page 84

Lead-in
Put the students into pairs. Tell them to imagine they are doing a Speaking task and have to describe one photo from the top of page 84 and say where they think it is and how the people are feeling. Set a time limit of 30 seconds for each photo and elicit ideas.

1 Tell the students to try to talk about each question for 30 seconds, so one and a half minutes in total. When they have finished, elicit interesting information that the students heard.

2 Look at the first question with the class. Ask them to quickly read the exam questions and find which ones ask about the text as a whole (1 and 5). Ask the students to work in pairs to do the other three questions in Exercise 2. For question 4, they should try to decide on an answer without looking at the options or underlining the text which answers the question. Don't elicit the answers to question 4 yet.

Reading Part 3 (multiple-choice)
Discuss the advice with the students and ask how they can get the general meaning of the text (by reading the whole text quickly first). Elicit that if questions focus on opinion and attitude, there will often be clues in the text, e.g. *I believe, I feel.*

Exam advice

3 Tell the students to do this as under exam conditions. As they have already found where the answers are, set a shorter time limit than usual. Allow five minutes and tell the fast finishers to find information in the text which shows that the other choices are incorrect. When everyone has finished, the fast finishers can explain which answer is correct, e.g. *1 B office jobs are mentioned but there is no warning; 1 C is mentioned in paragraph 3; 1 D back pain is mentioned but no advice is given.*

Answers
1 A **2** D **3** C **4** C **5** B

4 Tell students to do this as if it was a Speaking exam Part 3 task. Tell them they have three minutes to discuss all six points and how important they are, and to agree on the best three pieces of advice to give to a friend. When they have finished, elicit their ideas and reasons for them.

Extension idea
Put the students into small groups. Elicit some questions they could ask each other about exercise and work using different structures, e.g. *Do you sit at a desk for a long time? How often do you walk to work?* Set a time limit for the students to discuss and write down five questions. They should all write the questions. When they have finished, put students into pairs, making sure that the two students weren't in the same group as each other. They ask and answer each other's questions.

▶ **Workbook page 38**

Grammar SB page 86
Past perfect

Lead-in
Ask students how they felt when they arrived at work or university in the morning, e.g. *cheerful, hungry, tired.* Put the students into small groups to discuss their feelings at the start of the day and their feelings now. Ask how many students have different feelings now from when they left home and why.

1 Discuss the sentences with the students and elicit why the past perfect is important (without it, we might not know what order the events happened in). Elicit that, as well as in their own writing, this might be tested in multiple-choice gap-fills or open cloze tasks.

Answers
1 *had* + past participle, *had not* + past participle
2 the first action

2 Look at the example sentence with the class and elicit which event happened first. Allow the students to work in pairs and elicit the answers. There is nothing wrong with the first sentences in the exercise, but if the students can use the past perfect correctly it shows they know a greater range of grammar structures.

Students could do Grammar reference: Past perfect, Exercise 1, page 135, at this point or for homework.

Answers
2 I had/'d walked all the way home
3 arrived at the stadium, the match had started
4 had/'d left my trainers at home, I couldn't run in the race

3 Elicit that the first two sentences are written in the order that the events happened.

> **Suggested answers**
> **2** … I went to hospital. **3** … had left their trainers there.
> **4** … the film had (already) started.

▶ **Grammar reference page 135: Past perfect**
▶ **Workbook page 39**

Writing Part 2 SB page 86

> **Lead-in**
> Put students into small groups and tell them that they are going to talk about a time when they were frightened. Allow them thirty seconds to think alone and then thirty seconds each to tell their group about the experience. The other students can ask questions if it is necessary.

1 Students look at the instructions and answer the questions in pairs. Elicit the answers and ask how the key words will affect their story (*it has to have the topic of the first line; it will use past tenses to talk about something that happened to the writer in the past; it may also use present and past perfect where necessary).*

> **Answers**
> **1** the first line **2** first person
> **3** story, begin, frightening, experience, my

2 Tell the students to read the story quickly. Set a time limit of one minute and elicit what the frightening experience was (snowboarding). Students then do the task in Exercise 2. Elicit the answers and what the text says for each, e.g. 1 main events – *Lucy disappeared, the writer went faster, she turned, she came to some cliffs, she thought her friend had fallen over the edge.*

> **Answers**
> **b** 1 **c** 3 **d** 3 **e** 3 **f** 1

3 When they have found the examples, ask questions to check their understanding: *Why is the verb 'go' used with snowboarding?* (*It's an outdoor activity, done alone and without a ball.*); *Why is the relative pronoun 'who' used in the first sentence?* (*It refers to a person: Lucy.*); *Why does the writer use 'had started' in sentence 1?* (*The snow started before they got to the top of the mountain.*)

> **Answers**
> **1** went (go) snowboarding
> **2** who is a champion snowboarder
> **3** it had started; she had disappeared; had she gone; I'd gone; she'd heard; she'd found

4 Tell the students to work in pairs and, when they have answered the questions, to discuss a few ideas that they could write about in the story. Elicit the answers and then discuss the students' ideas. This will give the class more ideas to think about for their own stories.

> **Answers**
> **1** the first line **2** first person **3** I, nervous, game, began

> **Writing Part 2 (a story)**
> Look at the exam advice with the class before the students write their stories. Discuss why this idea is important: using a range of tenses can help the students to get a better mark for their writing if they can use them correctly.
>
> Exam advice

5 Tell the students that they will have five minutes to think of their own story and note down some useful vocabulary and grammar points to include and fifteen minutes to write the story. When everyone has finished, put the students into small groups. The students take turns to read out their stories, making them sound as interesting as possible. The rest of the group should try to think of positive ways to make them better, e.g. by setting the scene using the past continuous.

> **Model answer**
> I felt nervous when the game began. Fifty thousand people were watching me in the stadium, as well as a television audience of millions. I had always dreamed of playing football for my favourite team, and at last I had my chance. For the first hour, everything went fine. We were playing well and I had started to feel less nervous. Then, suddenly, it all went horribly wrong: I made a terrible mistake and the other team scored. I felt awful.
> Then I thought back to what the coach had said to me, about never giving up, and I knew that I had to win the match for my team. So, in the last few minutes, I scored the two most important goals of my life.

Extension idea

Students stay in their groups and choose one of their stories. They imagine that a Hollywood studio has decided to turn their story into a film. They discuss who could play the roles in the film and how the story might have to change to be made into a film. Set a time limit of 3 or 4 minutes and invite each group to present their ideas to the class.

▶ **Writing bank pages 150–151: A story**
▶ **Workbook page 39**

Speaking Part 4 SB page 87

Lead-in

With books closed, ask students if they have any opinions which they believe strongly, e.g. *I believe that there shouldn't be any zoos.* Allow them one minute to think alone and then put them into groups to share their ideas and explain them.

1 Allow the students to stay in the same groups as in the lead-in or put them in pairs to discuss the sentences and try to guess the missing words before they listen. Play the recording before eliciting the correct words.

Answers
2 sure **3** totally **4** so **5** way **6** all **7** true **8** too

Track 46

1. You **may** be **right**, but …
2. I'm not really **sure** about that.
3. Yes, I **totally** agree with you.
4. I don't **think** so because …
5. That's not the way **I** see it.
6. I don't agree at **all**.
7. That's **true**.
8. **I** think so **too**.

2 When the students have finished, elicit or point out that, especially in British English, when people disagree they do so as politely as possible, e.g. *You may be right, but …* . Sometimes, they start by apologising: *I'm sorry, but I think you're wrong …* .

Answers
a agree: 3, 7, 8 **b** disagree strongly: 5, 6
c disagree politely: 1, 2, 4

/P/ Word stress: agreeing and disagreeing

3 Ask students to guess the stressed words before they listen again. Play the recording and allow the students to check their ideas in pairs.

Answers
(Same as track 46)

4 Pause the recording after each sentence for the students to repeat. Use different techniques to try and make the activity more fun, e.g. have the whole class repeat a sentence, then ask one side of the class to repeat it, followed by the other side. You can also have a quiet or loud drill, still stressing the correct words.

Speaking Part 4 (general discussion)

Look at the advice with the class and elicit why it is useful, e.g. it is easier to think of ideas if you have personal experience of something. If you change the subject, the examiner may think you don't know what to say about the topic or you have learned something else by heart. For the second point it is important because you can add comments, agree and disagree with reasons. For the last point, elicit that the examiner isn't judging you on your opinions, just your use of English.

Exam advice

5 You could encourage the students to make some obviously wrong sentences so that their partner has a chance to disagree strongly, e.g. *I think cricket is the most popular sport in our country. I don't agree at all. No one plays cricket here.* Elicit opinions from different pairs.

Extension idea

If you did the lead-in activity, put the students back into their original groups. They again tell each other their opinions but this time the other students have to respond appropriately. Tell the students that, whether they agree or disagree, they should give reasons why. Elicit one opinion and other students' responses from each group.

▶ **Speaking bank page 161: Speaking Part 4**
▶ **Complete Preliminary new edition Test Generator Unit 9**

Vocabulary

Illnesses and accidents

aspirin
bandage
bruise (n, v)
cough (n, v)
cut (n, v)
earache
fever
flu
fracture
high temperature
injury
medicine
operation
pill
plaster
plaster cast
sprain (n, v)
test
wound
X-ray

Verb phrases

break a bone
have the flu / a sore throat / a stomach ache
put a plaster / bandage on
sprain an ankle
take an aspirin / medicine

Sports

athletics
baseball
basketball
climbing
cycling
football
golf
gymnastics
ice hockey
jogging
mountain biking
rollerblading
running
skateboarding
skiing
surfing
swimming
Taekwondo
tennis
volleyball

Places

in a gym / stadium
on a court / pitch / track

Sports equipment and clothes

bat
boots
gloves
helmet
net
racket
trainers

Sports verbs

beat
draw
lose
score
win

Vocabulary activity 1

Tell the class to choose an activity or sport from the vocabulary list for you to guess. If possible, leave the room for ten seconds for them to confer. When you come back, ask questions about the activity. When you have guessed, students do the same thing in small groups, taking turns to choose an activity for the others to guess. Monitor and check students are using grammatically correct question forms.

Vocabulary activity 2

This is best done in groups of three. Write the words: *Different? The same?* on the board. Choose two words from the list, e.g. *football, tennis*. Ask the class: *How are they the same?*, e.g. they are both sports, they both use a ball. Ask: *How are they different?*, e.g. one we play on a court, the other on a pitch, one is a team sport, the other is an individual sport (or for two players on each side). Students do the same in small groups. They must have an idea of how the words they choose could be the same or different.

10 Looks amazing!

Unit objectives

Topic: food, shops and services

Listening Part 1: multiple-choice real-world notices and other short texts: listening carefully for information

Reading Part 2: matching people to places to eat; reading to find specific information and detailed comprehension

Speaking Part 2: individual picture description: explaining what things are made of or used for

Writing Part 2: an article: writing an article

Grammar: commands and instructions; *have something done*

Vocabulary: *course, dish, food, meal* and *plate*; shops and services

Pronunciation: connected speech: linking sounds

Background information

Carbohydrates provide the body with energy. They can be healthy (e.g. whole grains) or unhealthy (e.g. white bread). Proteins build and repair things in our bodies, e.g. muscles, bones. Dairy products are foods which are made from milk. Fats give and store energy. The healthiest fats are found in nuts, olive oil, seafood and other items. The fats found in meat and dairy products are unhealthy. The most unhealthy fats are found in fast food and many baked products such as cakes and biscuits.

Starting off SB page 88

Lead-in

Put the students into small groups and tell them to draw a Venn diagram with three connected circles on a blank piece of paper. The three circles will be: *healthy food, tasty food* and *food one of us can cook/prepare*. Elicit a food item and where it should go on the diagram, e.g. *salad* is healthy, tasty and easy to prepare so goes where all three circles intersect. Set a time limit for students to put a variety of food items in their diagram.

1 Elicit that most food products could appear under more than one heading, e.g. cheese is a dairy product but also contains protein and fat. Elicit ideas for extra foods for each heading from the groups.

Answers
A Carbohydrates **B** Fruit and vegetables
C Milk and dairy products **D** Protein
E Fats, e.g. chocolate, crisps and cake

2 Allow the students to stay in the same groups as before to discuss the questions. Elicit that *eat out* means to eat in a restaurant or café. If you get a takeaway and eat at home or cook at home, we say you are *eating in*. Elicit ideas from each group when they have finished their discussion.

Extension idea

Ask students if they have ever eaten something abroad (or on holiday in their own country) that they found either very good or very bad. Students then work in small groups to think of one food from their country that they would definitely advise visitors to try and something they would advise visitors to be careful of. Set a time limit of two minutes and elicit ideas.

Reading Part 2 SB page 88

Lead-in

Students imagine they are a visitor to their town and want something to eat. They write down what sort of food they want.

1 Tell the students not to read the information in Exercise 2 but just look at the pictures and the headings in the guide. Elicit their ideas.

Suggested answer
Choose the most suitable street food stall for each group of people.

2 Elicit what the important information might include, e.g. likes, dislikes, things they can't eat, lack of money, lack of time. Set a time limit of one minute. Elicit the information in description 1 and why it is important.

Suggested answers
1 try something new on Tuesday, Both of them would really like fish, a hot drink with their meal
2 some of the stalls have won prizes, vegetarian main meal, short of money
3 light lunch on Saturday, are not willing to pay very much, sit down to eat
4 meal on Sunday, doesn't want to walk too far, proper meal, wants a dessert
5 trying a spicy vegetable dish, won't have much time, need to take away their dessert

3 Look at the first question with the class and elicit ideas about different kinds of hot drinks. Students look at the other questions in pairs. Elicit ideas from the class.

Suggested answers
1 tea, coffee or hot chocolate
2 they don't want to eat meat or fish
3 not expensive, reasonable, cheap
4 near the entrance or front door
5 Jack: a complete meal, a heavy meal, main dish; Sara: a sandwich, salad or snack

Reading Part 2 (matching people to things they want)
Discuss the advice with the students and elicit that, even if they match two of three requirements for one person, it isn't enough. They have to match all three points identified in Exercise 2.

4 Set a time limit of five minutes for students to do the reading task. Elicit the answers and ask students to justify them using the key words they underlined in Exercise 2.

Fast finishers
Tell the students to list useful vocabulary items that can refer to food: adjectives, nouns or verbs. When everyone has finished, elicit these useful words and encourage all students to make a note of them in their notebooks, e.g. *delicious, spicy, light, top-quality, reasonably priced, grilled, homemade, vegan; served with, barbecue, filled with; soft drink, main meal, chef, hot pepper (sauce), flatbread.*

Answers
1 B **2** G **3** F **4** E **5** H

5 Set a time limit of three minutes and ask the students to discuss each place and try to come to an agreement about where to eat. Elicit final decisions made by different pairs.

Extension idea
If the students did the lead-in activity, put them into small groups. They take it in turns to tell their group what they wrote and the other students try to decide on the best place in their town for them to go to. Elicit ideas from each group.

▶ **Workbook pages 40–41**

Vocabulary SB page 90
course, dish, food, meal and *plate*

Lead-in
Write the following on the board in four columns:

1	2	3	4
lunch	meat	starter	fish and chips with peas

Dictate more words and ask students to say which number they match: banana (2), dessert (3), supper (1), cheese (2), breakfast (1), fried chicken with salad (4).

Leave the writing on the board until the students have finished Exercise 1.

1 Allow the students to discuss their ideas in pairs. Elicit the answers and ask questions to check their meaning. If you did the lead-in, ask what the headings for the four columns are (1 = meals 2 = food 3 = courses 4 = dishes).

Answers
1 d **2** a **3** e **4** c **5** b

2 Ask the question to the whole class. When they have found the answer, elicit how this affects the words (they have plural forms and can be counted). Point out that the word *food* is usually uncountable but if we are referring to things like national dishes we can use a countable form, e.g. *They sell different foods from all over the world.*

Suggested answer
They are all countable but *food* can be both countable and uncountable. We know by the *C* and *U*.

3 Look at the example with the students and elicit why *food* is the correct answer (the examples given after the gap are not dishes, courses or meals, they are general words for types of food). Ask the students to do the exercise alone and then compare answers in pairs.

Answers
2 meals **3** plate **4** courses **5** dish

Extension idea
Ask the students to imagine they received the email from Elsa. Tell them to write back with a similar email about food in their own country.

▶ **Workbook page 41**

Grammar SB page 90
Commands and instructions

Lead-in
Students work in small groups. Ask them to think of five things that a boss, parent or partner tells them to do and five things that they tell them not to do. When they have completed the list, they discuss which of the things they don't like doing the most and why.

1 Check: *ingredients* (all the food items you need to make a dish). When the students have answered the questions together, ask them which they would choose if they were the only things on the menu. Don't elicit ingredients yet as this is done in Exercise 2.

2 Tell the students to tick any of their ideas from Exercise 1 that are mentioned and to write down any ingredients they didn't discuss earlier. Elicit these and then the ingredients they thought of before which weren't mentioned in the recording. Tell the students that a *dosa* is a pancake made from rice.

Suggested answers
1 Mexico: tortilla, rice, beans, lettuce, tomato, meat, avocado
2 Japan: rice, seaweed, fish, carrots, avocado, cucumber
3 India: pancake, potatoes, curry, spice

Track 47
1 On today's programme, we're going to learn how to make chicken burritos from Mexico. First of all, mix the chicken together with salt, pepper and chilli and then fry it. Don't cook it on a high heat or the burrito will be rather dry. Next, boil some rice until it is just soft. Then prepare the other ingredients.
2 Everyone loves Japanese sushi and this is actually something you can make at home quite easily. Wash one and a half cups of sushi rice and then boil it for twelve minutes. Next, decide on your ingredients. Use cucumber, carrot and tuna for your first sushi rolls and then try other things.
3 Masala dosa is a vegetarian breakfast dish from South India. To make it at home, buy the dosa from an Indian supermarket and fill it with spicy boiled potato. Don't forget to serve your dosa with lassi, an Indian yoghurt drink.

3 Tell the students to look at the sentences before they listen again and to try to guess the missing words. Check the meaning of: *mix.* Elicit that these verbs often come at the start of a sentence but can also follow sequencing words such as *then*, *next*.

Answers
2 Don't cook **3** Wash **4** Use, try **5** Buy **6** Don't forget

4 Elicit the form of the verbs and that we don't say: *You* before the verb. If you used the lead-in activity, elicit that instructions for things like cooking use the same form as instructions given by parents or teachers.

Answers
We use *wash*, *use*, *try*, etc. (infinitive without *to*) to tell people what to do.
We use *don't cook*, *don't forget*, etc. (*don't* + infinitive without *to*) to tell people what not to do.

Students could do Grammar reference: Commands and instructions, Exercise 1, page 136, at this point or for homework.

5 Students may need some extra support with this. Allow the students to work in pairs or small groups. They may also need extra verbs: *add* (salt), *chop* (the onions, carrots), *peel* (the carrots), *fry*, etc. Write these on the board before they start. Monitor and help where necessary.

6 Before the students read out their instructions, tell them to write a list of ingredients for the dish. They read these out first and then the instructions. When all the students have read out their recipes, have a short class discussion about cooking and what dishes students can prepare/cook.

Extension idea

Put students into small groups and ask them to look back at the different food stalls in the guide in the Reading section on page 89 and think of a similar idea that they think would be successful.

▶ **Grammar reference page 136: Commands and instructions**
▶ **Workbook page 42**

Listening Part 1 SB page 91

Lead-in

Split the class into an even number of small groups. Tell half of the groups to imagine they are going on a picnic and the other half to imagine they are going to a party. Each person in the group chooses one thing to take to their event. Now put the students into pairs so there is one student from a picnic group and a party group together. They tell each other their group's ideas and reasons for them. Elicit some of the food chosen.

1 Ask the students not to look at question 1 yet but just at the three pictures. Elicit what the similarities and differences between them are (they all show bread and water, one has chocolate, one crisps and one cups). Students now do Exercise 1 alone.

Answers
2 bottle of water **3** bar of chocolate **4** cups **5** crisps

2 Play the first sentence of the recording only and ask the students what they have to listen for (what she will buy). When the students have listened, elicit what she says she is going to buy (bread and water). Ask if this helps them (no, all three photos show these two items).

Track 48

1

Narrator: What will the woman buy for the picnic?
Natalie: Have we got everything we need for the picnic, Sam?
Sam: Hang on! I'll check. Do you know what? We haven't got any bread.
Natalie: You're joking! I'll get some from the bakery on our way there. No, I've got a better idea. I'll cycle down to the supermarket now to get some and I'll buy another bottle of water. I'll also get some crisps while I'm there.

3 Play the recording and elicit the answer from the students. Elicit that this is why it is important to listen to the whole recording and not make up their mind too early.

Answer
B

Track 49

Sam: Great! But please don't get any more crisps or chocolate. We've got plenty. We need some cups though. Could you buy some?
Natalie: Sure.

4 Elicit that in the exam the students have about 45 seconds to look through the pictures and key words. Encourage them to think of just one or two key words for each one. Allow them one minute and then ask them to compare ideas in pairs.

Suggested answers
2 What did the <u>woman take</u> to the party?
Did she take A two pizzas, B some homemade biscuits or C a cake?
3 What food will the <u>man try</u>?
Does the man try A a plate of steak and chips, B a plate of mixed fried fish or C a bowl of soup?
4 <u>Where</u> did the <u>woman go yesterday</u>?
Did she go to A a concert, B the theatre or C the cinema?
5 What do they need to <u>bring</u> for <u>training</u> tomorrow?
Do they need to bring A a pair of gloves, B a helmet or C a tracksuit?
6 What activity did the man do for the <u>first time</u> on <u>holiday</u>?
Did the man try A waterskiing, B diving or C windsurfing?
7 <u>Where</u> has the <u>woman</u> <u>been</u>?
Has she been to A a jewellery shop, B a gallery or C a bookshop?

Listening Part 1 (multiple-choice, pictures)

Discuss the advice with the students. Ask if there is any part of the recording the students don't have to listen carefully to (no). Ask how many questions there are for each recording (1). They can then look quickly at the next question and choices to prepare themselves for what they are going to hear.

Exam advice

5 Tell the students to work alone. Ask them to tick the correct choice if they are sure of it and write a question mark if they are unsure. When students have listened for a second time, elicit the answers and reasons for them.

Answers
1 C **2** A **3** B **4** A **5** A **6** A **7** B

Track 50

Narrator: Part 1. For each question, choose the correct answer.

2

Narrator: What did the woman take to the party?

Man: Hi Katy! How was the party? Did everyone like the biscuits you made?

Woman: I didn't make them in the end. I baked a cake instead. But then, I phoned Mark to see what time his party was and he mentioned that he had already made a huge chocolate one. I didn't know what to do so I bought a couple of pizzas on the way and we ate those at the party.

Man: What a shame! Perhaps we can have it for dessert today.

3

Narrator: What food will the man try?

Presenter: And I've just got a few minutes left to tell you about a new programme where we send our presenters around the world to try local dishes. Today, Paul's in Milan, Italy where his favourite food, *fritto misto de pesce*, is on the menu. This is a plate of mixed fried fish, and will make a change from his usual favourite of steak and chips. Then next week his sister's going to Granada, Spain to try *gazpacho*, a cold soup made with tomatoes, peppers and cucumber.

4

Narrator: Where did the woman go yesterday?

Man: Hi. Are you doing anything later? We're going to the early-afternoon performance of that new spy film. The reviews are incredible. Do you want to come?

Woman: Oh! I saw it yesterday with my cousin. He wanted to see a play but I didn't fancy it. I heard it was very long with no interval.

Man: Would you recommend the film, then?

Woman: Oh yes! It's brilliant, but I don't think I want to see it again. Are you going to the concert tomorrow? It's going to be amazing.

5

Narrator: What do they need to bring for training tomorrow?

Trainer: Shh! Great work today guys! Now listen carefully, because as you know, tomorrow we're going to train at the sports centre on their indoor climbing wall. Remember to wear comfortable clothes. A tracksuit is much better than shorts. The sports centre will provide you with a helmet and a pair of climbing shoes. Your hands may get a bit sore, I'm afraid, but it isn't really a good idea to wear gloves because you might slip on the wall.

6

Narrator: What activity did the man do for the first time on holiday?

Woman: You're looking well. How was your trip to Egypt?

Man: Great, we've just got back. We had an amazing time. We went diving on the first day and we took some beautiful underwater photos.

Woman: But you've done that before, haven't you?

Man: Yeah, that's right! Then my friend persuaded me to try waterskiing. I'd never done that before and by the end I was quite good at it. It was fun but my favourite watersport is still windsurfing. Do you remember when we both tried that for the first time at university?

7

Narrator: Where has the woman been?

Woman: Sorry I'm late. I've been trying to find a present for Mum. I was on my way to the bookshop, but then I remembered it was closed today.

Man: What did you get her in the end?

Woman: Well, I went to the art gallery to see if they had a nice picture in a frame for her, but I didn't really like any of them and they were quite expensive. I think I'm going to get her some earrings or a necklace from that new jewellery shop on the corner.

/P/ Connected speech: linking sounds

6 When students have listened to the recording, drill the whole sentence and the individual connected words. Point out that there is almost no difference in the sound between, for example, *a nap* (a short sleep) and *an app* (that you use on a smartphone). Drill more simple connected words, e.g. *an apple*, *put on*, *find out*.

Suggested answer
The consonant sound at the end of a word connects with the vowel sound at the beginning of the next word.

Track 51
I'm going tomorrow to get her some_earrings_or_a necklace from that new jewellery shop_on the corner.

7 Put the students into pairs to practise saying the sentences to each other and then mark the sentences. Play the recording and drill the sentences and then elicit where the lines are.

Suggested answers
1 I baked_a cake_instead.
2 This_is_a plate_of mixed fried fish.

Track 52
1 I baked_a cake_instead.
2 This_is_a plate_of mixed fried fish.

8 Put the students into small groups and tell them to discuss each question for two minutes.

Extension idea
Dictate the following to the students: *find out, making, life in, it's no, wait in*. Say: *find out* several times and write *fine doubt* on the board. Students work in small groups and do the same for the other words and try to write two different words with the same sound (*may king, lie fin, it snow, way tin*).

▶ **Workbook pages 42–43**

Vocabulary SB page 92
Shops and services

Lead-in
Put students into small groups and ask them to discuss the kind of shops you can find in their town and some adjectives to describe them (e.g. *bright, crowded, boring*). Elicit ideas and discuss the students' favourite place to shop.

1 Put the students into pairs. When they have described the photos, ask the class which place looks most attractive and why.

2 Elicit what you can buy at a bakery (bread), butcher's (meat) and chemist (medicine, sometimes make-up) and what you take to a dry cleaner's (clothes that you can't wash in a washing machine). Put students into pairs or small groups to share their ideas.

Suggested answers
1 dentist, garage and hairdresser's
2 bakery, bookshop, butcher's, chemist, garage, hairdresser's, supermarket
3 library
4 travel agent's
5 dentist, garage, dry cleaner's
6 probably in all the places except the library

3 Tell the students to note down any key words which can help them to identify the correct places. Elicit these as well as the answers, e.g. 1 hair, hair cut 2 accident, scooter, repaired 3 spilt, dress, cleaned.

Answers
1 hairdresser's **2** garage **3** dry cleaner's

Track 53

1

Madison: What have you done to your hair, Layla?
Layla: Oh don't. I normally have my hair cut at Gabrielle's but I wanted something different, so I went to that new place on the High Street.
Madison: Oh no! Was it very expensive?

2

Andrew: Are you coming to the party tonight, Lewis?
Lewis: I can't. I need to save up some money.
Andrew: Why's that?
Lewis: I had a little accident on my scooter. All my fault, I'm afraid.
Andrew: What about your scooter? You only got it last week.
Lewis: That's why I can't afford to go out. I'm having the scooter repaired and I'm going to have to look for another job to pay for it.

3

Vicki: Oh no, Charlie! That's cola you've spilt down my dress.
Charlie: Sorry, Vicki. It was an accident.
Vicki: My sister's going to go mad. I borrowed this dress from her and I had it cleaned last week for this party. The cleaning wasn't cheap, either.

4 Before the students listen again, ask them to discuss what the problem was in each case. Play the recording and then elicit the three problems (a bad haircut, a damaged scooter, a dress with cola spilt on it). Set a time limit for the students to discuss the question in pairs or small groups and elicit ideas from the class

Extension idea
Students work in pairs and write a similar dialogue about going to one of the other places. Write prompts on the board for students who need them, e.g. *dentist / broke a tooth, butcher's / invited people to lunch – no food, travel agent's / want to go abroad, the library / need book for homework.* The dialogue should have them explaining the problem and the other person giving some advice.

▶ **Workbook page 41**

Grammar SB page 92
Have something done

Lead-in
Read out the names of some places from the vocabulary section and tell students to write something that people there do to help you, e.g. hairdresser's – cut your hair. Say: *hairdresser's, garage, dentist, dry cleaner's, travel agent's, butcher's*. Students compare their ideas in groups.

1 Put the students into pairs to discuss the rules. Elicit the answers and ask them what form of the main verb they use (the past participle; the same form as they use in the present perfect). Elicit the past participle of some irregular verbs, e.g. *do – done, go – gone, take – taken.*

Answers
1 somebody does for us **2** informal

Extension idea
The students work in pairs or small groups and look at their ideas from the lead-in. They then make sentences about what people have done in each place (e.g. *they have their hair dyed, they have their car fixed*). Monitor and help where necessary.

2 Put the students into pairs and ask them to describe one picture, each saying what they can see. Ask the class how they would describe the two women (Polly is messy/dirty; Ginny is tidy/clean). Students now read the sentences and match them to the right person.

Answers
1 Polly **2** Ginny **3** Polly **4** Ginny **5** Ginny **6** Polly **7** Polly **8** Ginny

3 Elicit that sentences 1–5 in Exercise 2 are in the present simple and 6–8 are in the past simple. Ask what part of the sentence changes (the verb *to have*) and what part doesn't change (the main verb). Students now look at the sentences in the table. Point out that you can use the structure with any tenses, e.g. *I have just had my hair cut.*

Answers
2 having my flat cleaned. **3** had my hair cut.

4 Look at the instructions with the class and ask why both *have* / *get* might not be possible (if the situation is formal). Elicit the answers and the structure used in both (infinitive with *to*, *will* future).

Answers
1 *have* (*get* is not possible here because the situation is formal) **2** *have* and *get*

5 If you think the students need more help, elicit the tense they need to use for each sentence before they start. Monitor and help the students where necessary.

Fast finishers
Students write questions about what people do or have done, e.g. *Do you repair your own bike or do you have it repaired?* When everyone has finished the exercise, fast finishers can ask their questions to the other students.

Answers
2 I can't finish this report because I'm having my laptop mended at the moment.
3 My bike is broken again and I had it repaired a week ago.
4 Jack isn't at work. He's having his teeth checked today by the dentist.
5 Keith and Pete are going to a New Year's Eve party. They had their suits cleaned last week.

Students could do Grammar reference: *Have something done*, Exercises 1 and 2, page 136, at this point or for homework.

6 Look at the example with the students and elicit how they would answer a question starting *When did you last … (I last had my haircut one month ago)*. Set a time limit and elicit questions and answers from groups.

▶ **Grammar reference page 136: *Have something done***
▶ **Workbook page 42**

Speaking Part 2 SB page 94

1 Put the students into groups of three and ask each person to describe one of the photos. When they have finished, ask what happened when there was something they didn't know the words for.
Play the recording and ask the students to note down key words which help them to identify the correct photo.

Answers
Photo 1. She describes all five things.

Track 54

Examiner: Now I'd like each of you to talk on your own about something. I'm going to give each of you a photograph and I'd like you to talk about it. Luna, here is your photograph. It shows people shopping on a rainy day. Lidia, you just listen. Luna, please tell us what you can see in your photograph.

Luna: Uh-huh. In this picture, I can see a lot of people outside. It's a rainy day and the people are shopping. The street is quite crowded. I can see many shops, for example: a mobile phone shop and a shoe shop. In the middle of the picture, there are two women. One of them is carrying something. I can't remember the word for this object. It's used for the rain … we open it when it rains. She's wearing a long black coat, and black shoes. The other woman is wearing a coat and a red scarf, grey jeans and boots. On her back, she's got … a … it's something like a bag. In front of them, there's another woman. She's wearing a blue coat. She's got a … a … two bags. One is on her back. It's made of leather. The other bag is black and it's enormous. It looks heavy. In the background, I think I can see some flags, I'm not sure …

Examiner: Thank you.

2 Tell the students to read the sentences before they listen again. Elicit the answers. The first phrase is an example of the passive but at this stage it can be introduced as a phrase (similar to *it is made of*).

Answers
1 It's used for **2** it's something like

Track 55
1 One of them is carrying something. I can't remember the word for this object. It's used for the rain ... we open it when it rains.
2 On her back, she's got a ... a ... it's something like a bag.

3 Look at the exam advice box, then tell students that this exercise practises both skills: describing a photograph clearly and using phrases to describe objects you don't know the word for. Look at the table with the class and elicit ideas for each phrase using vocabulary from the unit, e.g. *It's a kind of shop where you can buy meat (butcher's).* Set a time limit of two or three minutes for the task and then elicit one description from each pair for the other students to guess.

Speaking Part 2 (individual picture description)
Look at the exam advice before the students do the task. Elicit how long students have to do this task in the exam (about one minute) and that they speak alone. Elicit some of the objects described in the recording and how the students described them.

Exam advice

4 Encourage students to use at least two of the phrases from Exercise 3 in their description. When they have both finished, the students give each other feedback about how many things they mentioned and what they didn't mention.

Extension idea
Tell the students to look back to the Vocabulary section on page 92 and the photos of shopping streets. They take turns to play the part of the examiner and ask each other to describe one of the photos. The students swap roles and give each other feedback on their performance.

▶ **Speaking bank pages 154–158: Speaking Part 2**

Writing Part 2 SB page 95

Lead-in
Put the students into pairs and ask them to describe one of the photos each for one minute. They note down useful phrases that their partner used. Elicit phrases their partner used in their descriptions.

1 Allow the students to do the task in pairs. Elicit ideas for the key words and how these will affect the writing, e.g. *you and your friends* – don't talk about shoppers in general; *prefer* – indoor / town centres – mention why you prefer one to the other.

Suggested answers
Where do you and your friends go shopping nowadays?
Do you prefer going to indoor shopping centres or to town centres?
Or perhaps you'd rather do all your shopping online?
Answer these questions and we will publish the best articles in our next magazine.
Write your article in about 100 words.

2 Set a time limit of two minutes for students to discuss their ideas. Don't elicit any ideas yet. Encourage all the students to make notes of the ideas in order to use them later.

3 Set a time limit of three minutes. First the students find and underline the key words, then they discuss the questions and make notes of the ideas their group comes up with. When they have finished, ask each group which task they would write about and why.

Writing Part 2 (an article)
If you didn't look at this before the students started writing, discuss the advice now and elicit which exercise allowed students to check that they have followed the advice (Exercise 5).

Exam advice

4 It may be better to look at the exam advice before the students start writing. Tell the students to work alone and set a time limit of fifteen minutes for the writing.

5 Give the students a minute to check their own work and then ask them to check their partner's article too and to think about things they like better about theirs and things that they like better about their partner's. They don't have to share this information with their partner but can think about it when they next have to write something.

Model answer
A good meal doesn't have to be expensive or complicated to prepare. The simplest ingredients can be delicious. For example, a piece of fish with a few herbs cooked on a barbecue can taste amazing.

In my opinion, what makes a good meal is eating delicious food with good friends, whether that's at home or in a restaurant.

I think it is important to try food from different countries but I can't afford to go to restaurants a lot. That's why I use recipes on the internet to make different dishes from all over the world in my own kitchen.

Extension idea
In pairs, students think of a shop or restaurant that they like and try to create a short (30-second) radio advert for it. They can present these to the class.

- **Writing bank pages 148–149: An article**
- **Complete Preliminary new edition Test Generator Unit 10**
- **Workbook page 43**

Vocabulary list

Food

carbohydrates
course
dairy products
delicious
dish
fats
filled with
flatbread
food
fruit
grilled
heavy (meal)
homemade
juicy
light (lunch)
meal
plate
protein
(a) range of
reasonably priced
served with
soft drink
spicy
vegan
vegetables

Shops and services

bakery
bookshop
butcher's
chemist
dentist
dry cleaner's
garage
hairdresser's
library
supermarket
travel agent's

Vocabulary activity 1

Tell the students you are going to write a word on the board and they have to think of any related words on the same topic, e.g. SCHOOL: – *students* – *teachers* – *staff room* – *coffee* – (the next word must return to the topic of school, not move away to food and drink).
Put students into small groups with a different topic, e.g. FOOD. Students see how long they can think of new words without changing topic.

Vocabulary activity 2

Tell the students that they have five clues to find a word. The quicker they guess, the more points they can win, but they only have one chance and, if they are wrong, they can't guess again. Give an example:
5 points: It's a fruit.
4 points: It comes from warm countries.
3 points: We don't eat the skin.
2 points: It's yellow.
1 point: Monkeys like eating it.
(banana)
Put the students into groups. They think of a word and clues and present it to the class for other groups to guess.

Vocabulary and grammar review Unit 9

1 **2** d which **3** f when **4** a who **5** b where **6** e whose

2 **2** In summer, when the weather is good, we play tennis.
3 Stevie, whose team won, was the best player of all.
4 In the city centre, where we live, there is a lot of pollution.
5 My brother, who had an accident, is feeling better now.
6 Volleyball, which is a team sport, is played on a court.

3 **2** had practised **3** felt **4** had/'d brought **5** had/'d put **6** was **7** had/'d rained **8** didn't seem **9** was **10** had left **11** started **12** realised **13** had/'d played **14** was **15** slipped **16** fell **17** knew **18** had/'d injured **19** went **20** had not/hadn't broken **21** wore

4 **2** sore **3** beat **4** bat **5** athletics **6** pill **7** bruise

Vocabulary and grammar review Unit 10

1 **2** complain **3** book **4** borrow **5** repair/mend

2 **2** D **3** B **4** D **5** A **6** D

3 **2** have it cut **3** had it taken **4** have them cleaned **5** had it repaired

4 **2** ago **3** had **4** have **5** had **6** were

11 The natural world

Unit objectives

Topic: nature and the environment

Listening Part 4: multiple-choice long interview: listening for detailed meaning

Writing Part 1: an email

Reading Part 5: multiple-choice cloze: understanding vocabulary

Speaking Part 4: general discussion; talking about likes/dislikes, preferences, habits and opinions. Giving reasons and examples to support arguments.

Writing Part 1: an email: checking your work for mistakes

Grammar: the passive: present simple and past simple; comparative and superlative adjectives

Vocabulary: the natural world; noun suffixes

Pronunciation: word stress in passive forms

Starting off SB page 98
The environment

Lead-in
Before the students open their books, put them into small groups. Ask the students to imagine they are walking in their town. Ask them what good things they can see, e.g. flowers, old buildings, and what bad things they can see, e.g. graffiti, rubbish. Set a time limit of two minutes and elicit ideas from each group.

1 Set a time limit of three minutes for students to discuss questions. Elicit ideas and ask which of the things in 1-5 they do.

1
1 2 Packaging creates waste that harms the environment.
3 Destroying rainforest by cutting down trees. Many animals and plants then have nowhere to live and disappear forever.
4 Air pollution, often the result of too many cars. People's health badly damaged.
5 Cruelty to animals. Poor-quality food.
2
2 – A Buy fruit without packaging in your local market (and take it home in non-plastic bags).
3 – E Use less paper and reduce the need for wood, for instance by getting paperless bills sent online.
4 – B Drive an electric car and reduce air pollution where you live.
5 – C Buy free-range chicken and eggs, from animals that can move freely and lead healthy lives.
3 (Suggested answers)
2 Avoid buying items packed in plastic, paper, etc. Recycle packaging.
3 Save data on a memory stick, not paper. Use cloth handkerchiefs you can wash, not paper tissues.
4 Use public transport. Work from home to avoid travelling into the city.
5 Buy cheese, eggs, meat, etc. from local farmers or markets.

2 Elicit one or two problems from the class and then set a time limit of two minutes for students to discuss the questions together. Elicit ideas from different pairs.

Listening Part 4 SB page 99

Lead-in
Ask the students to look at the photos and elicit what the animal is (*lynx*), what animal family it is a member of (*cats*) and any other wild cats they can name (e.g. *lion, tiger, panther, jaguar, puma, leopard, cheetah*).

Background information
The Iberian lynx is a medium-sized animal of the cat family, with pointed ears and a short tail. Its fur is grey or brown, with black markings. It eats smaller animals such as rabbits. It almost completely disappeared early this century, but conservation work has now helped increase its numbers.

1 Look at the questions with the students. Set a time limit of two minutes for the students to discuss the questions.

Listening Part 4 (multiple-choice, long interview)
Elicit what the Listening Part 4 consists of (*a long interview with multiple-choice questions to answer*). Discuss the advice with the students and ask them why it is important (looking at the key words prepares them for what they are about to hear, often the speakers use alternative words to those in the questions so students have to be aware of words giving the same or opposite information).

Exam advice

2 Look at the key words in question 1 and what students would have to listen out for to find out which choices are wrong, e.g. *A Maybe only one of them had been there before. Maybe they had both heard about the stream but not visited it. B Maybe a different animal had been seen there. Maybe a lynx was seen there but a long time ago. C Maybe there were a lot of rabbits in the area. Maybe there weren't any rabbits or maybe there were very few of a different animal.*
Give the students 45 seconds to look at the other questions and underline key words in the questions and options to prepare themselves for what they are about to hear. Play the recording twice and then allow the students to compare their ideas and reasons for them.

Answers
1 B **2** A **3** A **4** C **5** A **6** B

Track 56

Narrator: Part 4. For each question, choose the correct answer. You will hear a young woman called Ellie talking about a trip to southern Spain to see the Iberian lynx.

Interviewer: With me today is Ellie Johnson, who went to Spain with her university friend Marta to see the beautiful Iberian lynx, one of the world's rarest wildcats. So, Ellie, which location did you choose, and why?

Ellie: A place with a stream next to the forest, with plenty of rabbits. The huge fall in the number of rabbits is the main reason why the lynx is so rare, because an adult lynx needs to eat three rabbits a day. Marta knew the area but I didn't until I saw on TV photos of a lynx taken there a few days before.

Interviewer: How easy was it to get there?

Ellie: Well, it was summer and temperatures were really high during the daytime, so it made sense to set off really early – at five a.m. in fact, when it was still cool. The moon was bright, and we were pleased about that because it's easy to go in the wrong direction in the dark. The track was really challenging in places – it went up and down a lot. We didn't actually find it too exhausting, but it did mean we got to the stream later than we'd expected. Once we were there, we looked for somewhere to hide.

Interviewer: Where did you hide?

Ellie: There was an empty hut nearby but it was locked, so it looked like the best place was behind some large rocks. There was no shade there, though, so instead we lay down just inside the forest and waited. In fact, we waited there for ages. I was going to suggest leaving, when suddenly we heard something running through the bushes.

Interviewer: What was it?

Ellie: Well of course we hoped it'd be a lynx and we both grabbed our cameras, but it was just a frightened-looking little rabbit. Just then, though, another creature appeared, running after it. It was grey and brown, about the size of a small cat: it was a young lynx!

Interviewer: I can imagine your excitement! What did it do?

Ellie: Well, by then the rabbit was far away and the lynx's chance of catching it had gone so it stopped and looked around, though it didn't notice us. We were so busy taking photos of that cute little animal that we didn't see a much larger one approaching. It was an adult female, and clearly the little one was hers. That was why it had stopped.

Interviewer: How long did you stay there?

Ellie: The sun had almost set but we stayed another hour, taking photos of them until we couldn't see anything. Marta wanted to stay overnight to see them again at sunrise, but we didn't have a tent, so we set off, reaching the hostel just before midnight.

3 Elicit one or two ideas from the class, then set a time limit of one minute for students to discuss their ideas. Put students into small groups, making sure no-one is in the same group as their partner, to share the ideas they thought of. Elicit ideas from each group.

▶ **Workbook page 44**

Vocabulary SB page 99

Noun suffixes

Lead-in
With books closed, elicit the meaning of *prefix* and *suffix* (a prefix is something attached to the start of a word, e.g. to make it negative, a suffix is something added to the end of the word, e.g. to change its form). Students work in small groups. Set a time limit of one minute for them to write as many adjectives as they can ending in *-ful*, e.g. *beautiful*. Elicit their ideas and the words the suffix is attached to, e.g. *beauty–beautiful*.

1 Students can do this in pairs or the same groups as they did the lead-in activity in. Discuss the answers and elicit that we don't drop the *-e* before the suffix *-ment*.

Answers
1 locate, excite, direct
2 (suffixes are underlined) locat<u>ion</u>, direct<u>ion</u>, excite<u>ment</u>
3 location drops the final 'e' from the verb form locate because the suffix begins with a vowel

2 Tell the students that, if they aren't sure, they should write the words in pencil so they can change them later. Elicit the answers and the spelling of nouns formed from verbs ending in *-e*.

Answers

-ment	-ation	-ion
announcement	admiration	attraction
development	confirmation	celebration
disappointment	examination	collection
enjoyment	exploration	completion
entertainment	information	connection
improvement	invitation	creation
movement	relaxation	discussion
replacement	reservation	education
		invention
		pollution
		prevention
		protection
		translation

Background information

The robot was invented by a team of scientists, who found that when they were trying to get close to the penguins, the penguins moved away into other penguins' areas, which caused fighting. At first, some penguins tried to attack the robot penguin but their stress levels reduced more quickly than when humans approached. The scientists tried five different looks for the penguin and finally gave it black arms, a black and white face and a black beak. Finally, the penguins accepted it.

3 Re-elicit the noun forms of the verbs in the box and the meanings of the words if necessary. Tell the students to read through the text quickly before they start doing the gap-fill. Set a time limit of one minute and elicit what the text is about. Students then do the gap-fill alone or in pairs. Don't elicit the answers yet.

4 Play the recording and elicit the answers. If students say the words with the wrong stress, don't say anything at this point. When you have elicited the words, then tell the class that you are now going to look at how they are pronounced. Write the words from the text on the board.

Answers
2 exploration **3** information **4** movement
5 disappointment **6** improvement

Track 57

Presenter: Scientists in Antarctica have used a new invention to help them study penguins close up: a tiny robot on wheels that looks lik a baby penguin. The robot, similar to those used in the exploration of the moon and Mars, provided lots of exciting new information about the birds. Scientists, working some distance away, controlled every movement the robot made and it was immediately accepted by penguin families as one of them. The adults even sang to it, though to their great disappointment the 'baby' didn't reply. The scientists are now working on a new model with one important improvement – it will be able to play penguin songs.

/P/ Word stress in longer nouns

5 Tell students to write the six nouns from Exercise 3 in their notebooks. Write three stress patterns on the board: *Oo, oOo, ooOo*. Look at the first one, *Oo*. Model the stress pattern it represents by humming. Elicit that it gives the stress pattern of a two-syllable word with the stress on the first syllable. Do the same with the other two patterns and elicit the words which match each pattern: *Oo – movement, oOo – invention, improvement, ooOo – exploration, information, disappointment*. Students now work in pairs to find the word in Exercise 2 which doesn't follow the same pattern. Elicit ideas until someone guesses correctly. Show the stress pattern: *oOoo* (*development*).

Answers
2 exploration **3** information **4** movement
5 disappointment **6** improvement
Patterns: the stressed syllable is normally before the suffix, or the *a* in the case of *-ation* (although there are exceptions, e.g. *advertisement*, *argument*).
Exception in Exercise 2 table: development

6 Students practise in pairs. Then drill the words with the class and encourage students to make a note of the stress patterns of any new vocabulary.

Answers
(word stress underlined): admiration, attraction, celebration, collection, completion, confirmation, connection, creation, development, disappointment, discussion, education, enjoyment, entertainment, examination, excitement, exploration, improvement, information, invention, invitation, movement, pollution, prevention, protection, relaxation, replacement, reservation, translation

▶ **Workbook page 46**

Grammar SB page 100
The passive

Lead-in

Ask the students to write two sentences with *have something done*; one using the present simple and the other using the past simple. Students then work in small groups to compare their sentences.

1 Allow the students to work in the same groups as in the lead-in activity. When the students have discussed the questions, look at the sentences with them in more detail. Elicit that when we change the tense of a passive sentence, we change the tense of the verb *to be*, not the main verb. Elicit why we sometimes use *by* and sometimes not (sometimes it is important; sometimes it isn't or it's so obvious that we don't need to say it).

Answers
1 A and C are active; B and D are passive.
2 C and D describe an event in the past.
3 B and D
4 A: subject – this new technology; object – air pollution. B: subject – air pollution; agent – this new technology (using *by*)
5 C: subject – guides; object – tourists. D: subject – tourists; no object
6 information not in sentence D: *who* allowed the tourists to take photos (the guides)

2 You could do this exercise with the whole class, eliciting the answers one at a time, or allow the students to discuss the sentences in pairs. When looking at questions 4 and 5, point out that we can use the passive to avoid blaming someone or taking responsibility, e.g. *The food wasn't cooked properly* = *I didn't cook the food properly.*

Answers
2 passive **3** active **4** active **5** passive **6** by

3 Look at the two examples with the students and elicit why the tenses are used (1 present simple – a fact; 2 past simple – the discovery happened in the past). Elicit how we form questions in the passive (question word + verb *to be* + noun + past participle). You could also add that, for *Who* questions, we write *by* at the end, e.g. *Who was the island discovered by?* Allow the students to work in pairs and monitor and help where necessary.

Answers
3 was closed **4** was spoilt **5** is blamed
6 weren't / were not noticed

4 Look at the instructions with the students and elicit that the underlined words will come at the start of their sentences. You could ask the students to do this alone or allow them to work together in pairs. Elicit why 'by' is needed in 1 and 7 (the agent is important).

Students could do grammar reference: The passive: present simple and past simple, Exercises 1 and 2, page 137 at this point or for homework.

Answers
2 Two giraffes were seen near the trees.
3 The moon was hidden by one small cloud.
4 Cars aren't/are not allowed in the National Park.
5 Rice is grown in the east of the country.
6 A poem was written about this waterfall.
7 The forest was partly destroyed by fire.

Fast finishers
Ask fast finishers to make passive sentences about what happens to them at school, e.g. *We are given homework. We are told to be quiet.*

5 Look at the example with students. Ask how they know it is a passive form (verb *to be* + past participle) and what the infinitive form is (*turn*). Set a time limit of three minutes for students to find the other verbs. Monitor and help where necessary.

Fast finishers
Ask students to make some of the passive forms active, e.g. *people turned huge areas of forest and open countryside into farm land.* Elicit these when everyone has finished the exercise.

Answers
In the past, bears and wolves were considered a danger to both people and farm animals, so their numbers were reduced, often to zero. Nowadays, however, a lot more is understood about how they form an essential part of nature, and some years ago, international agreements were made to bring back these magnificent creatures. A lot of money was spent, large areas where they could move freely across borders were created, and they are now protected by law. In Europe, bears and wolves are once again found in many countries, from Spain to Scandinavia, where they are allowed to live in places with few people. They are sometimes seen in mountain areas or forests, but usually they prefer to keep away from humans. So if we keep well away from them, we are not in any danger.
Infinitives: consider, reduce, understand, make, spend, create, protect, find, allow, see

/P/ Word stress in passive forms

6 Elicit the answer and why they think the main verb is stressed (it gives us the important information).

Answers
The main verb is stressed. The weak form of the auxiliary verb is used: /wə/

Track 58
… bears and wolves were considered a danger to both people and farm animals.

7 Allow the students to discuss the question in pairs. Play the recording all the way through and then one sentence at a time to drill each sentence. Allow students to practise the sentences again in pairs.

Track 59

1 A lot of electricity is wasted by those machines.
2 Two giraffes were seen near the trees.
3 The moon was hidden by one small cloud.
4 Cars aren't allowed in the national park.
5 Rice is grown in the east of the country.
6 A poem was written about this waterfall.
7 The forest was partly destroyed by fire.

Extension idea

Write the following prompts on the board and elicit possible sentences for *Employees eat lunch*, e.g. *Employees eat lunch at 1 pm. Employees don't eat lunch in the office.*

Employees ...
eat lunch
make personal phone calls
check their social media pages
write reports
attend meetings

Put students into small groups to make more sentences using the prompts. Set a time limit of two minutes. When finished, elicit passive forms for the example sentences, e.g. *Lunch is eaten at 1 pm. Lunch isn't eaten in the office.* Students swap sentences with a second group and try to make the sentences passive.

▶ **Grammar reference page 137: The passive: present simple and past simple**
▶ **Workbook pages 44–45**

Reading Part 5 SB page 102

Lead-in

Pre-teach *expedition* (a journey made for a specific reason, e.g. to learn, discover, help or fight). With books closed, tell them to imagine that they see an advert for volunteers to join an expedition which will teach them something about nature and the environment. Put the students into small groups and set a time limit of two or three minutes to think of where they would like to go, what they would like to do and how their expedition would help. Elicit ideas from each group.

Background information

Because of the isolated location, the Galapagos Islands offer an opportunity to see how species evolve without any external inluences. Charles Darwin spent five weeks on the islands in 1835. He noticed that species had evolved differently depending on the environment, for example the shape of tortoise shells was slightly different on each island. His observations led him to write his theory *The Origin of Species.*

1 Tell students to discuss what they think the text will be about. They then complete the text. Elicit the answers and ask the students if they know anything else about the Galapagos Islands.

Answers
2 west **3** South **4** Pacific **5** Ecuador **6** unique **7** hard **8** weight **9** tail **10** wings

2 Tell the students not to worry about the gaps yet. Set a time limit of about 30 seconds to give them practice of scanning a text to find only the information necessary to answer the questions. Elicit the answers.

Answers
1 a news report in a local paper
2 San Cristóbal Island, one of the Galápagos Islands
3 They will work on environmental projects, without payment.
4 the environment and the wildlife there
5 see the countryside, study the wildlife, sail and dive

3 Tell the students to cover the options. Allow them to work in pairs to try to think of the missing words. Elicit ideas but don't tell students if they are correct or not.

4 Tell the students to work alone. Set a time limit of five minutes. When they have finished, ask how many of the missing words they guessed correctly before they saw the choices. Elicit the answers and encourage the students to make a note of any phrases they weren't sure of, e.g. *in order to, take part in, prevent ... from, surrounded by.*

Answers
1 D (team) **2** A (include) **3** B (prevent) **4** D (part) **5** C (explore) **6** A (surrounded)

Fast finishers

Tell fast finishers to look at the text about bears and wolves on page 101 and think of a sentence which they could test with a multiple-choice question. They should also think about the four options that they could give. Elicit ideas when everyone has finished the reading task.

5 Tell students to discuss how important each idea is in their country and try to come to an agreement about the most useful ideas. Allow about five minutes to give each student a chance to give their opinions. Elicit ideas and reasons for choosing the best one from different groups.

▶ **Workbook page 46**

Grammar SB page 103
Comparative and superlative adverbs

Lead-in

Elicit the difference between an adjective and an adverb (an adjective describes a noun, an adverb describes a verb).

Ask them to write down one thing they can do well, one thing they do badly, one thing they do quickly and one thing they do slowly.

When they have finished, allow them to compare ideas in small groups. Students will look at these again after Exercise 4 (in the extension activity).

1 Allow students to work in pairs to do the exercise. When they have answered the questions, go through the differences between comparative and superlative adjectives and comparative and superlative adverbs (only longer adjectives form comparatives and superlatives with *more/most*; all adverbs, except for *well*, *badly* and those which have the same form as an adjective, form comparatives and superlatives with *more/most*; with superlative adverbs we can use the word *the*, or leave it out, so sentence D could also be … *sing most beautifully* …).

Answers
1 Students should underline – comparative adverbs: more quickly, more quietly, worse;
superlative adverb: most beautifully
2 by adding *more* in front of the adverb
3 worse **4** than **5** by adding most in front of the adverb

2 Tell the students to follow the rules from Exercise 1. If it is a form with *more/most* + adverb, (e.g. *most carefully*), then they know it is a regular adverb formed with *-ly*. If it is a form without *more/most* (e.g. *faster*), they know that the adverb and adjective have the same form (or are the adverb forms of *good* and *bad*). Elicit the adverbs which have the same form as adjectives: *fast, hard, early* (and *late* although it isn't in the table).

Answers

adverb	comparative	superlative
quietly	more quietly	(the) most quietly
carefully	more carefully	(the) most carefully
slowly	more slowly	(the) most slowly
easily	more easily	(the) most easily
fast	faster	(the) fastest
badly	worse	(the) worst
hard	harder	(the) hardest
well	better	(the) best
early	earlier	(the) earliest

Students could do Grammar reference: Comparative and superlative adverbs, Exercises 1 and 2, page 137, at this point or for homework.

3 Look at the example question with the class and elicit what else could be compared using *the fastest* as a superlative adverb, e.g. *Which person in the group drives the fastest?* Monitor and correct where necessary, then elicit questions and answers from different pairs.

Answers
2 harder **3** more brightly **4** (the) most frequently
5 (the) most heavily **6** worse

4 Look at the example with the students and note that the first person says *fastest* and the second *the fastest*. Point out that A could have used *the fastest* but, because of the phrase *in the world* B couldn't leave out the word *the*. Set a time limit of two minutes and tell students to give a reason when answering Yes/No questions, e.g. 2 *Yes, we should because …* Elicit ideas from different pairs.

Extension activity

If you did the lead-in activity, elicit a sentence that one of the students used, e.g. *I can speak English well.* Ask the student to now make a comparative sentence using the same information, e.g. *I can speak English better than my parents.* Students go back to the groups they were in for the lead-in activity and change their sentences to comparative ones.

▶ **Grammar reference page 137: Comparative and superlative adverbs**
▶ **Workbook page 45**

Speaking Part 4 SB page 104

Lead-in
Before the students open their books, put them into small groups and ask them to think about all the times they use water at home, e.g. *when they wash their hands before a meal, when they flush the toilet.* Set a time limit of one minute and elicit ideas from the groups. Check the words: *tap, flush.*

Background information
A survey shows that 26.7% of water is used to flush toilets, 21.7% for washing clothes and 17% for baths and showers.

An average bath uses 164 litres of water compared to 11 litres per minute for a shower. So, a 15-minute shower uses as much water as a bath.

1 Tell the students to describe what they can see in each picture. Elicit how they can describe unknown words, e.g. *It's something like …; It's used for …; It's made of … .* Set a time limit of two minutes for this part and then another minute to answer the questions about wasting water. Elicit ideas and any useful vocabulary students used or needed, e.g. *hose(pipe), bucket, sink, leave the tap running, turn on/off the tap, dishwasher, half-full/ half-empty, wash by hand.*

Suggested answers
A: She hasn't turned the tap off . She should turn it off when she isn't using the water
B: Using a lot of water to wash the car. They could wash it by hand using a bucket and sponge.
C: He's using a dishwasher for just a few plates when he could wash them by hand or wait until there is a full load.

2 Elicit the answers and ask the students which of these they do or don't do at home. Ask them who they think the worst person in their household is for wasting water.

Answers
Have a quick shower instead of a bath.
When you're brushing your teeth, turn off the tap when you're not actually using any water (and when washing your hair).
Check taps are completely turned off (especially in places like colleges).

Track 60
Ethan: Well, there's lots you can do to save water. At home, for instance, you can have a quick shower instead of a bath. I read in an article that having a bath uses 80 or 100 litres of water.
Lily: Right. And when you're brushing your teeth, let's say, you should turn off the tap when you're not actually using any water. And do the same when you're doing other things, such as washing your hair.
Ethan: Good idea. And it's important to check the taps are completely turned off, especially in places like our college. The article said that a tap which loses just one drop a second, for example, wastes 20 litres a day!

3 Look at the example with the students and tell them to read through the other sentences and try to remember the missing words. Play the recording and elicit the answers. Elicit or tell students that: *For example, for instance* and *let's say* all come after the example they are referring to. *Such as* and *like* both come before the example.

Answers
2 let's say **3** such as **4** like **5** for example

Extension idea
Write the expressions from Exercise 3 on the board: *like, for example, for instance, such as.* Dictate sentence stems and ask the students to complete them so they are true for them, using a different expression each time. When they have finished, students discuss their sentences in small groups. Elicit ideas from different groups.

4 If you used the lead-in activity, they should have some examples of water use which may give them ideas of how to save water. If not, elicit other examples of when they use water.

Speaking Part 4 (general discussion)
Discuss the exam advice with the students and why it is useful: giving reasons and examples allows them to extend their speaking, show they understand the topic and gives them a chance to use more vocabulary. Asking each other questions keeps the conversation going for longer and helps both students to demonstrate their ability in English.

Exam advice

5 Look at the first question with the class and demonstrate how it could develop, e.g. start by saying: *Let's start by looking at how we use electricity at home.* Ask a stronger student: *What do you use electricity for at home?* When they respond, suggest how we could save electricity, e.g. we should switch off computers when we aren't using them. When students are talking in pairs, tell them after each minute has passed so they have an idea of which question they should be answering. If they are still talking after four minutes, give them one more minute to finish off. Elicit ideas from different groups.

▶ **Speaking bank page 161: Speaking Part 4**

Writing Part 1 SB page 105

Lead-in
Tell the students to imagine that someone is coming to stay with them during the holidays and wants to spend some time in the town, any nearby cities that are worth visiting and in the countryside. Put the students into small groups and give them two minutes to discuss where they would take their friend and what they would do there. Elicit ideas from different groups.

1 Tell the students that they don't have to read the whole email yet, just find the information to answer the questions. Set a strict time limit of a minute.

Answers
1 She writes 'It was great to hear from you'.
2 visit her city
3 Agree with Chloe's suggestion that you should go to the countryside. Say whether you'd prefer to go by bus or bike. Say what wildlife you'd like to see there. Tell Chloe whether you want to go for a day or a weekend.

2 For weaker classes, it may be a good idea to look at the first question with the whole class and elicit the answer. Elicit that this was also done in a previous email where each point was answered with one, very short paragraph. Then put students into groups to answer the other two questions. Elicit the answers and what the grammatical error is an example of (it needs a passive structure).

Answers
1 *Good idea!*: 1st paragraph; *Tell Chloe*: 3rd paragraph; *Suggest*: 4th paragraph; *Say which and why*: 2nd paragraph.
2 polluteion – pollution (Sp). the weekend whole – the whole weekend (WO), drive – ride (V), find – are found (G).
3 walk – (get around) on foot, Saturday and Sunday – weekend, wildlife – animals, rather – prefer to

Writing Part 1 (an email)
Discuss the advice with the students. Ask why it is useful and elicit that the first piece of advice will help them to get more marks for a wide range of vocabulary while the other two pieces of advice will help them to avoid losing marks for errors or not answering the question fully.

Exam advice

3 Look at the instructions with the students and elicit what comparative adverb was used in the example (*We can get around much more quickly than on foot*) and another idea that they could use in this email, e.g. *You probably cycle more quickly than I do!* Set a time limit of five minutes for students to think of ideas in pairs before they start writing alone for fifteen minutes or do the writing for homework.

4 Alternatively, two students swap with another pair to discuss the two emails they have to check and decide together what mistakes there are, if any. They should also check that all the information has been included. They then get together with the other pair and give each other feedback.

Extension idea
Put the students into small groups. Each group looks at a different unit from the book. Tell them to write one sentence using the grammar of the unit which contains a deliberate mistake and one sentence using a vocabulary item from the unit which contains a deliberate spelling mistake. Each group takes turns to write their sentences on the board and the other students try to spot the mistakes.

Model answer
Hi Chloe,

Thanks for your email. I like the idea of going to the countryside. I love nature.

It's very kind of your grandparents to invite us over for a meal. Why don't we stay for dinner, then we'll have plenty of time to explore the countryside during the day? Thanks for offering to lend me your bike. I think that would be a great way to get some exercise and see some lovely scenery.
I'm keen on birdwatching so I'd love to see some species that I've never seen before.
See you soon,
Rita

▶ **Writing bank pages 145–147: An email**
▶ **Speaking bank page 161: Speaking Part 4**
▶ **Workbook page 47**
▶ **Complete Preliminary new edition Test Generator Unit 11**

Vocabulary

The natural world

battery farming
electric car
free range (eggs/hens)
ocean
packaging
plastic bottles
pollution
rainforest
recycling

Noun suffixes

admiration
announcement
attraction
celebration
collection
completion
confirmation
connection
creation
development
disappointment
discussion
education
enjoyment
entertainment
examination
excitement
exploration
improvement
information
invention
invitation
movement
pollution
prevention
protection
relaxation
replacement
reservation
translation

Vocabulary activity 1

Put students into small groups. Each group needs three pieces of paper on which they write *-ment, -ion, -ation* in letters large enough for you to see. Tell the class you are going to read out a verb and the students have to lift the correct suffix to change the verb to a noun. If they hold up the wrong one, they are out. After one or two rounds the last group to hold up a suffix can also be out to make them decide more quickly. The winning group is the last group left.
Say: *develop* (*-ment*), *inform* (*-ation*), *protect* (-ion), *discuss* (*-ion*), *replace* (*-ment*), etc.

Vocabulary activity 2

Play Pictionary. Draw an example of an environmental problem on the board, e.g. cut down trees. Whoever guesses what the problem is first decides on a different problem and comes to the board to draw it. You can insist that they only use words on the word list or allow other problems if the class is strong.

12 Express yourself!

Unit objectives

Topic: food, shops and services

Listening Part 3: information completion: listening for specific information

Reading Part 4: text insertion: putting the missing sentences into the correct part of the text

Speaking Part 1: general questions; talking about habits and routines

Writing Part 2: a story: using a range of tenses and reported speech

Grammar: reported speech and reported commands; reported questions; indirect questions

Vocabulary: collocations: using your phone: *ask, ask for, speak, talk, say* and *tell*; negative prefixes

Pronunciation: intonation in direct and indirect questions

Starting off SB page 106
Collocations: using your phone

1. Students order the things in the box depending on how often they do each one. Elicit the thing they do the most and least.

2. Set a time limit of one minute for each question. For each one, ask the students to think about their friends and people they know of different ages. Elicit ideas from each group and ask the students what they think the best and worst thing about smartphones is.

Reading Part 4 SB page 106

1. Tell students to work in pairs. Give them one minute to describe the photo and answer the questions together. Elicit ideas from different pairs.

Answers
1 Becky has to live without her smartphone for a week.
2 & 3 Students' own answers.

2. Ask students to find information in the text to justify their answer, e.g. *My mood changed (when I saw other people using their phones).* Elicit the positive things that she noticed too.

Answer
No, she didn't.

3. Elicit the pronouns in the two sentences (*her, them*) and what these pronouns replace (a female person, more than one person) and point out that, if their answer is correct they, will know who or what the pronoun refers to.

Answer
B, because the pronoun *them* is plural. In A, the pronoun *her* is singular.

Reading Part 4 (Matching sentences to paragraphs)
Elicit that, as well as verb forms and noun forms, they should check pronouns and other words which link parts of the text together, e.g. *because*. Point out that if they are unsure of one gap, they should complete other gaps first.

Exam advice

4. Set a time limit of five minutes and then another minute for the students to check their answers. Elicit the answers and the words in the sentences and text which helped them decide.

Answers
1 B **2** G **3** E **4** F **5** C

5. Elicit one idea for and against from the class before they start. Set a time limit of two minutes and then elicit ideas from different pairs.

6. Put students in groups so that they aren't with their partner from Exercise 5. Ask the students to discuss each reason that they wrote for Exercise 5 in turn. Set a time limit and then elicit ideas from different groups.

▶ **Workbook page 49**

Vocabulary SB page 108
ask, ask for, speak, talk, say and *tell*

1. Ask the students to read through the rules, then elicit more examples for each verb, e.g. *My friend asked me to help her cook dinner.* Elicit that we can say: *talk about something* or *talk to someone*, e.g. *I talked to my friends about the exam.*

Answers
1 ask **2** ask for **3** speak **4** talk **5** tell **6** Say **7** tell **8** say **9** tell

2. Ask the students to do the exercise alone, using the rules to help them. They compare answers in pairs before you elicit the answers.

Answers
1 speak **2** told **3** ask for **4** tell **5** talk **6** asked

3. Elicit that all the answers can be found in the rules box. Elicit the extra ideas.

Answers
1 talk **2** speak **3** say **4** tell **5** ask **6** ask for

4. Look at the first question with the class and elicit that the most appropriate missing word is *help*. Monitor and help where necessary.

Possible answers
1 help **2** 'hello' **3** joke / lie **4** languages **5** problems **6** lie / story / joke

5. If students worked in pairs in Exercise 4, put them in new pairs to ask and answer their questions.

6. Look at the example with the students. Students work alone, then compare ideas, before eliciting answers.

▶ **Workbook page 48**

Grammar SB page 109
Reported speech

Lead-in
Write the word *charity* on the board. Elicit the meaning (*an organisation which collects money to help people or animals in need*). Put the students into small groups and ask them to discuss charities that they know.

1. When the students have listened to the recording and found the answers, they work in groups to discuss which of the three events they like best and why.

Answers
Adam: an event like a street party; **John:** a football match; **Nina:** a technology-free day

Track 61

Helen: Shh! Be quiet! Close the door, Paul! Thanks. Sonia, can you take notes today?
Sonia: Oh, is it my turn to be secretary? OK.
Helen: Right. As you know, we have to decide what event we're going to organise for the charity weekend. Any ideas? Yes, Adam?
Adam: OK. Last year we organised a street party to collect money. We can organise a similar event again.
Helen: But the weather was awful and very few people came.
Adam: We don't have to hold it outside. We could decorate the gym in the sports centre and have the party there.
Helen: Mm ... That sounds expensive to me. Has anyone else got any other ideas? John?
John: Yeah, I've thought about organising a football match.
Helen: Another football match? Can't we do something different?
John: In my sister's town, groups of friends are going to play against each other.
Helen: But how are we going to raise money?
John: Everyone will have to pay to play.
Helen: Still not sure. Anyone else? Nina?
Nina: Yes. Look at everyone! We're all using our phones right now. How about something like a technology-free day?
Helen: A technology-free day? How does that work?
Nina: The idea is to have a day where we can't use any technology. We won't be able to use any screens, internet or phones.
Helen: And the money?
Nina: People will give us money not to use technology. We'll hold some old-fashioned, traditional events instead, like story-telling or a picnic if the weather is good.
Helen: Thanks. Right. Think about the suggestions. And don't forget the meeting tomorrow. We'll take a vote then.

2. Tell students that direct speech is what someone actually says, e.g. *My name's Tom.* Write this on the board. Ask: *How could I tell other people what Tom said?* Write: *He said that his name was Tom.* Write this next to the direct form. Tell students to look at the underlined words and say what has changed (pronouns and tense).

3. Play the recording and tell the students to check answers around the class.

Answers
1 had organised a street party
2 could organise a similar event again
3 didn't have to hold it outside
4 had thought about organising a football match
5 were going to play against each other
6 were all using their mobile phones
7 would hold

Track 62

Lisa: Hi Sonia. Sorry I didn't get to the meeting yesterday. What did you decide?

Sonia: Oh, hi Lisa. There's going to be another meeting today at one p.m. to take a vote. We have to think about the three suggestions.

Lisa: What three suggestions? Did anyone take notes?

Sonia: Yeah! I was the secretary. I've got them written here. Let me see. Oh yes, Adam said that they had organised a street party to collect money the year before and they could organise a similar event again.

Lisa: But the weather was really bad last year and very few people went.

Sonia: Yes, that's what Helen said, but Adam then said that they didn't have to hold it outside. They could use the gym in the sports centre.

Lisa: Good idea!

Sonia: Helen thought it sounded expensive. Then John said he had thought about organising a football match.

Lisa: Not another football match.

Sonia: Kind of …he said in his sister's town, groups of friends were going to play against each other.

Lisa: Mmm…You said there were three suggestions, didn't you?

Sonia: Yes, the third came from Nina. She said that they were all using their mobiles then. She suggested a day when they wouldn't be able to use technology at all. She said people would give them money not to use technology. They would hold some old-fashioned, traditional events instead.

Lisa: Like what?

Sonia: Like story-telling or a picnic if the weather's good.

Lisa: I like the sound of that one!

4 Students do this in pairs. When they have finished, elicit the answers and the fact that both the past simple and present perfect are reported using the past perfect. Point out that, if the original sentence uses the past perfect, *could* or *would*, it doesn't change in the reported form.

Answers
2 past continuous **3** past perfect **4** past perfect
5 *would* + infinitive **6** *was/were going to* + infinitive **7** *could*

5 Elicit the answers and elicit that in 6 *right now* changed to *then.* Elicit that if we report our own words, e.g. *I told my boss that …* we wouldn't change the pronoun. '*I don't want to work on Saturday*'. *I told my boss that I didn't want …*'

Answers
2 the year before **3** his **4** they **5** then

6 Look at the first example with the class. Elicit that the reporter added *because* to make it sound more natural. Ask what word we could add after the verb *said* in reported speech (*that*). Students do the rest of the exercise in pairs.

Answers
2 (that) someone had left their phone in the kitchen after the party.
3 (that) he was having a great time there.

7 Look at the example and elicit what Mark might say next, e.g. *He said that he wanted to play basketball but didn't want to upset me so he told a lie.* Tell students to choose one of the other situations for their stories. Allow students to work in pairs and monitor and help where necessary. Set a time limit of five minutes.

▶ **Workbook page 50**

Reported commands

8 Review the form we use for commands and instructions, i.e. (*Don't*) + base form of the verb, and some examples, e.g. *Sit down. Be quiet.* Look at the example with the students and elicit that to report these we use (*not*) + *to* + base form of the verb. Elicit the answers.

Answers
2 to close the door **3** to think about the suggestions
4 to forget the meeting

9 If necessary, elicit the answer to 1 to make sure the students choose the correct verb form (*to keep in touch*). Elicit the answers and ask the students to report things they have been told to do or not to do recently, e.g. *My friend told me to slow down when I was driving him to work.*

Answers
1 to stay/keep in touch. **2** not to be late
3 not to bring more pizza
4 not to forget to download Season 3

Students could do Grammar reference: Reported speech, Exercises 1 and 2, page 138, for homework.

▶ **Page 138 Grammar reference: Reported speech**
▶ **Workbook page 50**

Listing Part 3 SB page 110

1 Set a time limit of one minute for the students to read through the notes and allow them to discuss their ideas in pairs. Elicit what they know about the competition from the notes.

> **Suggested answers**
> You need to apply online, there are challenges with a subject. There is a judge called Fran Maddison. There are prizes. Food and drink will be provided. The next competition will be held in Prague.

2 Allow the students to work in pairs and elicit the answers and their reasons, e.g. June is a month, therefore we need to know which date in June.

> **Suggested answers**
> **1** date **2** noun (the subject of the challenges)
> **3** noun (name of book) **4** noun (prize)
> **5** noun (what you should bring) **6** noun (name of place)

3 Elicit the answer and reason for it and then elicit ideas for the other gaps.

> **Answer**
> A singular noun because of the *a* before the gap

Listening Part 3 (information completion)
Discuss the advice with the class. Elicit that students have to transfer their answers to a special answer sheet so they need to be able to read them. Elicit that if their answer is grammatically incorrect, it can't be the correct answer.

4 When you have played the recording once, tell them that they should listen carefully on the second listening to make sure their answers are correct.

5 After they have listened a second time, ask if they are confident about the spelling of 2 and 6. Tell them to think carefully about the punctuation of 6 as well. As it is a name, what do they have to remember? (capital letters). Elicit the answers and spellings.

> **Answers**
> **1** first, 1 or 1st **2** communication **3** are me
> **4** (unbelievable) trip **5** laptop **6** Grand Hotel

Track 63

Narrator: Part 3. For each question, write the correct answer in the gap. Write one or two words or a number or a date or a time. You will hear a woman called Catherine Bryant talking about a competition on the radio.

Catherine: Let me tell you about an app design competition which will take place in Lisbon, Portugal from the sixth to the seventh of June. All you need to do is fill in an online form by the first of June. If your application is accepted, you should hear from us before the fourth of June.

On the day, you can take part alone or join one of the teams. You'll need to choose one of the challenges from a list of four and create an app which solves a problem. Last year's challenges were connected to the environment. For example, one of the challenge winners created an app which finds the nearest recycling bin for the rubbish you want to throw away. All I can say about this year is that the challenges have something to do with communication. The rest is a secret!

The competition judge is blogger Fran Maddison, that's M-A-D-D-I-S-O-N. She presents the 'Apps Programme' on Channel Seven. Her latest book *Apps are me* will be on sale soon.

There are some amazing prizes. There's €1,000 and a tablet for the best app for each challenge. The four winners will then compete in the final for the first prize which is an unbelievable trip to California.

You won't be able to bring your own food into the event, but reasonably priced refreshments will be available. You mustn't forget your laptop, but you'll be able to hire headphones and chargers there.

And finally, if you can't make the Conference Centre in Lisbon in June, consider the Grand Hotel in Prague in October. There'll be more information about this event on our website at the end of August.

Now, any questions?

6 Elicit one or two examples of useful apps before the students work in groups. Set a time limit of three minutes for the discussion.

▶ **Workbook page 48**

Grammar SB page 111
Reported questions

1 Elicit who Catherine was (the organiser of the competition in the Listening section). Ask students to think of what they might ask her if they wanted to take part in the competition. Elicit some ideas before the students listen to the recording.

> **Answers**
> **2** Do we need to pay anything to take part?
> **3** How do we register for the competition?
> **4** What do we do if we have technical problems?
> **5** What are the prizes?

2 Ask the students if they remember the names of any of the speakers before playing the recording again. Elicit the answers.

Answers
2 Peter **3** Connor **4** Samir **5** Charlotte

Track 64

Presenter: Thank you Catherine. While you've been speaking, some of our listeners have phoned in with their questions. Would you have a moment to answer them?

Catherine: Yes, sure.

Presenter: Great! First we have Emily from Manchester. Are you there, Emily?

Emily: Can I choose the members of my team?

Catherine: Good question. And yes, you can choose up to three other people to join your team. However, each person will need to make a separate application.

Presenter: And Peter's in Bristol.

Peter: Hi Catherine. I've got a question for you. Do we need to pay anything to take part?

Catherine: Oh? Did I forget to mention the cost? Yes, there's a fee of €5 per person. This is to show us that you're really interested in the event.

Presenter: Now, here's Connor from Belfast.

Connor: Hi! This all sounds brilliant. How do we register for the competition?

Catherine: It's easy. As I said before, you can do it all online. Go to our website and fill in the application form.

Presenter: And now Samir in London.

Samir: Hi! What do we do if we have technical problems?

Catherine: Interesting point. If you have problems with applying for the event, please get in touch with us. If you have problems on the day, our team will be available. However, it is up to you to make sure that your laptop is working well before the day of the event.

Presenter: And finally Charlotte in Oxford sent us her question by text. I'll read it out: 'What are the prizes?'

Catherine: Full details of the prizes are on our website …

3 Elicit the rules for reported speech that students can remember, i.e. change the pronoun where necessary, change the time or place, change the tense. Put the students into pairs to discuss the rules for reported questions and then discuss them with the class.

Answers
a changes **b** changes **c** never **d** isn't **e** don't use

4 When the students have listened to the recording, allow them to discuss the answers in pairs or small groups. Elicit the answer and reasons.

Suggested answer
It's an organiser app which creates a work or study plan, reminds you when to take breaks, what to eat and get enough sleep. You can also share information with friends, for example, notes and ideas, or ask for help.

Track 65

Cindy: What does the app do, Emily?

Emily: Good question, Cindy. It's an organiser app. You put in what you have to do and by when and the app organises the week for you. For example, if you have to give a presentation or hand in a piece of work, you can put in how much time you'll need to do it with the date it's due and the app will create a work plan for you. You can do the same with exams; you put in what you need to study and by when and the app will create a study plan.

Harry: That could save some time. Does it do anything else?

Emily: Yes Harry, it tells you when to take a break and have something to eat too. It also recommends different types of exercise and the alarm reminds you to get enough sleep. It's a bit like one of those fitness watches but for work.

Phil: Can I use it to share work with friends and colleagues?

Emily: Yeah and that's the most useful thing, I think, Phil. You can make groups so that you can ask questions, share notes, tips and ideas and generally help each other.

Diana: Fantastic! Where did you get the idea from?

Emily: Thanks, Diana. One of the competition challenges was called 'efficient work through communication' and I thought of this idea. I never thought we would win though!

Lily: That's amazing, Emily! But will the app do my work for me?

Emily: That would be unfair, Lily!

5 Look at the first question with the class and elicit the reported form: *Cindy asked Emily what the app did.* Students then work in pairs to do the rest of the exercise. Monitor and help where necessary. Elicit answers from different groups and correct or elicit corrections if necessary. Point out that we still use *any* rather than *some* for reported questions.

Answers
1 what the app did **2** if it did anything else
3 if he could use it to share work with his colleagues
4 where she got the idea from
5 if the app would do her work for her

Students could do Grammar reference: Reported questions, Exercise 1 and 2, page 140 for homework.

▶ **Workbook page 50**

Vocabulary SB page 111
Negative prefixes

Lead-in
Tell students you are going to say three adjectives. They should write them down and give an example of something or someone they could describe. Say: *comfortable, expensive, possible.* Students work in pairs and write their ideas.

1 Elicit some of the negative adjectives that students looked at in Unit 8, e.g. *unpleasant, impatient, dishonest, unreliable*. Students do the exercise in pairs. Elicit the answers and that if an adjective begins with the letter *p*, it might take the prefix *im-* but it could also take the prefix *un-* (*unpleasant*).

Answers
1 un **2** in **3** im

2 Some of the adjectives here were introduced in Exercise 1. For the words that weren't, students should guess. Elicit the answers.

Answers
2 unhealthy **3** impatient **4** unsociable **5** inexpensive **6** impossible

3 Ask the first question to the class. Elicit reasons why it would be a good idea (less stressful) and why it would be a bad idea (some people may lose their jobs if apps could do the work). Set a time limit of five minutes for students to discuss the questions. At the end of the activity, elicit ideas from different students.

Extension idea
Remind students of the ideas they had in the lead-in. Now ask them to do the same but with the negative forms of the adjectives. Students work in the same pairs as for the lead-in. Set a time limit of one minute and elicit ideas for different adjectives.

▶ **Workbook page 49**

Speaking Part 1 SB page 112

Lead-in
Put students into small groups and ask them to think of three questions that they might be asked in the Speaking Part 1 on the topic of communication. Students then work in pairs with a student from a different group and ask and answer their questions. Elicit some of the questions the students thought of.

1 When they have listened and completed the table, allow them to compare their answers in pairs. Don't elicit the answers yet.

Answers

	Anton	Eleni	Victoria
1	✗	✓	✓
2	✗	✓	✓
3	✗	*	✓

*Although Eleni uses a range of vocabulary, her grammar is limited – she only uses 'is' and 'like'.

Track 66
1
Examiner: Anton, how do you get to school every day?
Anton: 8 o'clock.
Examiner: Do you walk to school every day?
Anton: Bus.
Examiner: Thank you.
2
Examiner: Eleni, tell us about a good friend.
Eleni: Her name is Maria. She's tall. Her hair is long and straight. She is very nice. I like her.
Examiner: Thank you.
3
Examiner: Victoria, how often do you use the internet?
Victoria: I'm sorry, could you say that again, please?
Examiner: Do you often use the internet?
Victoria: The internet? I use it every day. When I wake up, I check Facebook on my phone to see what my friends have been doing. I often go on the internet to look for information. I use it to buy bus tickets and tickets for the cinema or concerts. I also use the internet to listen to music and to watch films. I couldn't live without it.
Examiner: Thank you.

2 Elicit students' opinions and ask students to justify them by referring to the table in Exercise 1 (Anton's answers are one word and don't match the questions. Eleni is accurate but doesn't use much variety of language and her sentences are very short).

Suggested answers
1 I work about 8 km from here, so I go to work by bus at 8 o'clock every day. My flatmate sometimes gives me a lift when I'm late.
2 Her name is Maria and she's tall with long straight hair. I get on with her because she's very nice and easy-going. Everyone likes her.

3 Tell the students to work in pairs. Set a time limit of one minute and then elicit advice they would give to Anton and Eleni. Invite students to answer the questions as if they were doing the exam.

Answers
1 your name **2** do you live, do you come **3** you work **4** What do you, What do you **5** Do you often **6** Tell us about

Track 67
Examiner: Good morning. Can I have your mark sheets, please?
Eleni and Victoria: Of course. Here you are.
Examiner: I'm Janine Rodgers and this is Michelle Johns. She is just going to listen to us. Now, what's your name?
Victoria: My name's Victoria.
Examiner: Thank you. And what's your name?

Eleni: Eleni.
Examiner: Thank you. Eleni, where do you live?
Eleni: I live in Athens which is the capital of Greece.
Examiner: Do you work or are you a student?
Eleni: I'm a student.
Examiner: What do you study?
Eleni: I'm doing a degree in engineering at the university.
Examiner: Thank you. And Victoria, where do you live?
Victoria: I live in Montpellier, which is a city in France.
Examiner: Do you work or are you a student?
Victoria: I work.
Examiner: What do you do?
Victoria: I'm a teacher in a primary school. My pupils are nine and ten years old.
Examiner: Thank you. Victoria, how often do you use the internet?
Victoria: I'm sorry, I didn't catch that. Could you say that again, please?
Examiner: Do you often use the internet?
Victoria: The internet? I use it every day. When I wake up, I check Facebook on my phone to see what my friends have been doing. I often go on the internet to look for information. I use it to buy bus tickets and tickets for the cinema or concerts. I also use the internet to listen to music and to watch films. I couldn't live without it.
Examiner: Thank you. Eleni, tell us about a good friend.
Eleni: Her name is Maria. She's tall. Her hair is long and straight. She is very nice. I like her.
Examiner: Thank you. Now I'd like each of you …

Speaking Part 1 (general questions)
Elicit that the first two points ensure that you answer correctly and show your knowledge of English. The third point ensures that the interviewer can hear you. If you look down, it can be difficult to understand what you are saying.

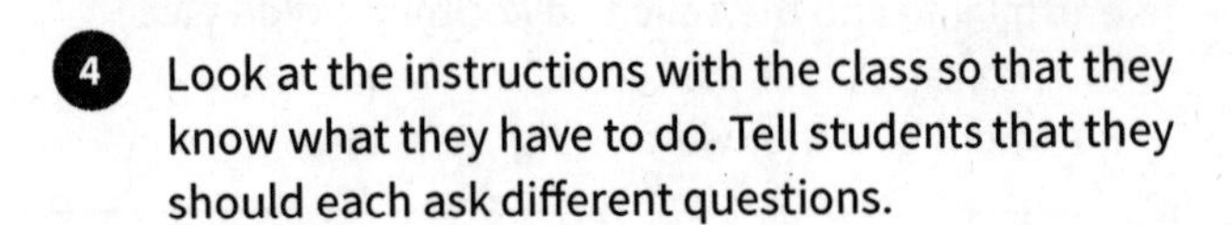

4 Look at the instructions with the class so that they know what they have to do. Tell students that they should each ask different questions.

▶ **Speaking bank page 152: Speaking Part 1**

Grammar SB page 112
Indirect questions

1 Put students in groups. Set a time limit of three minutes. When they have finished, elicit ideas from each group.

2 Elicit the answers from the students and ask how similar or different his answers were to their own.

Suggested answers
1 He uses Instagram and Snapchat. He uses Instagram to see what people are doing and for following famous people. He uses Snapchat to send photos to friends.
2 He talks about using a strong password for his social media accounts.

Track 68
Journalist: Good afternoon. I'm a journalist for Channel Thirteen and we're doing some research into communication for a TV programme. I was wondering if I could ask you some questions about how you use social media.
Bradley: Sure. What would you like to know?
Journalist: Firstly, could you tell me what your name is, please?
Bradley: Yes, it's Bradley Jones.
Journalist: Thanks, Bradley. I'd like to know how many different kinds of social media you use.
Bradley: I don't use as many as most of my friends or my sister even. I suppose I mainly use Instagram and Snapchat.
Journalist: Really? Could I ask you what you use each one for?
Bradley: Yes, I use Instagram to see what people are up to. It's also great for following famous people. Snapchat is good when you're out somewhere and you want to send a photo to your friends.
Journalist: And now for the last question. We're also interested in whether people are worried about others getting into their social media accounts. Do you have any idea if your accounts are safe?
Bradley: I think so. I always try to make sure that I use a strong password and I try to use a different password for each account but I know this is a big problem.
Journalist: Thanks for your answers Bradley. They're all very useful for our research.

3 Before the students listen again, look at the example with them and ask if they can define what an indirect question is, e.g. *It is where the question becomes part of a longer sentence.*

Answers
2 your name is **3** you use **4** what you use
5 your accounts are

4 Allow the students to work in pairs or small groups. Elicit the rules for indirect questions and that if the additional words used to form the indirect question are themselves a question, we need to use a question mark, e.g. *Could you tell me …?, Do you know … ?, Could I ask you …?*

Answers
1 yes **2** no **3** yes **4** yes **5** no

Students could do Grammar reference: Indirect questions, Exercise 1, page 140, at this point or for homework.

/P/ Intonation in direct and indirect questions

5 Play the recording. Elicit the answers and then drill each question with the class.

Answer
As a general rule, in questions with question words, the voice goes down and with *yes/no* questions, the voice goes up.

Track 69
1
Journalist: Could I ask you some questions?
2
Journalist: What's your name, please?
3
Journalist: How many different kinds of social media do you use?
4
Journalist: What do you use each one for?
5
Journalist: Are your social media accounts safe?

6 Again, play the recording and elicit the answers, then use the recording to drill each question.

Answers
As a general rule, where the indirect question is a statement (*I was wondering …*), the voice stays fairly flat and goes down slightly at the end.

Track 70
1
Journalist: I was wondering if I could ask you some questions.
2
Journalist: Could you tell me what your name is, please?
3
Journalist: I'd like to know how many different kinds of social media you use.
4
Journalist: Could I ask you what you use each one for?
5
Journalist: Do you have any idea if your accounts are safe?

7 Set a time limit of three minutes for students to write their questions. Monitor and help where necessary.

8 Encourage students answering the questions to give extended answers and to look at the students asking the questions.

▶ **Grammar reference page 140: Indirect questions**
▶ **Workbook page 51**

Writing Part 2 SB page 113

1 Set a time limit of one minute for each picture. Elicit ways of agreeing and disagreeing with each other and for making suggestions (e.g. *Yes, great idea. No, I don't think that's very likely. What about …?*). Elicit ideas from each group.

2 Elicit the answers and ask how the second question might affect their writing, e.g. a teacher may be more interested in vocabulary and grammar than in a funny or interesting story.

Answers
1 a story **2** your English teacher

3 Elicit the answers to the questions and ask the students what they liked or disliked about the story, e.g. it was good because it had a surprise ending.

Suggested answer
1 Task 2: Because the phone belonged to the teacher and she took her bag with her when she left the classroom.

4 Set a time limit of two minutes for the students to discuss the questions and find examples of 5 and 6 in the story. Elicit the answers and look at them in detail with the class.

Answer
They are all true.

Writing Part 2
It may be useful to look at the exam advice before the students do the task. Ask why the advice is useful. The first point is useful because it makes the story more interesting. The final point is just to show that the lesson isn't the same as the exam exactly.

Exam advice

5 Set a time limit of 15 minutes for the writing and two or three minutes for students to check their work. When they have finished, put them into groups to read out their stories.

> **Model answer**
> The message began, 'Congratulations! You've won first prize!'
> 'Look, this is the sort of email I was telling you about,' I said to my parents. They looked at my computer screen nervously, as if it might bite them! 'Don't worry,' I said. 'I can delete it and it won't do the computer any harm.' With one click it was in the bin, another and it was gone forever.
> Just then my sister came in. 'Alex,' she said, 'I forgot to tell you that I entered a photography competition but used your email address. Have you had any messages about the competition? My photo was amazing. I think I might win!'

- ▶ **Speaking bank pages 152–153: Part 1**
- ▶ **Writing bank pages 150–151: A story**
- ▶ **Workbook page 51**
- ▶ **Complete Preliminary new edition Test Generator Unit 12**
- ▶ **Complete Preliminary new edition Test Generator Term Test Units 9–12**
- ▶ **Complete Preliminary new edition Final test**

Vocabulary

Collocations: using your phone

call friends
check the time and weather
listen to music
play games
read the news headlines
set an alarm
share photos and videos
take selfies

ask, ask for, say, speak, talk, tell

ask
ask for
say
speak (a language)
talk
tell
tell a joke / a lie / the truth

Negative prefixes

impatient
impolite
impossible
incomplete
incorrect
inexpensive
unbelievable
uncomfortable
unfair
unfriendly
unhealthy
unsociable

Vocabulary activity 1

Put students into small teams. Write the three negative prefixes on the board: *im-* on the left, *un-* in the middle and *in-* on the right. Choose one student from each group to come to the board and stand in a line facing the middle of the board. Tell them you are going to read out a word and they have to jump left or right or stay where they are depending on which negative prefix they think it goes with. They can only jump once. Anyone in front of the wrong suffix is out. The rest win a point for their team. Students then sit down and you repeat the process with a different student from each group.

Vocabulary activity 2

Put students into pairs. Each pair chooses a three-word collocation from the Vocabulary list and writes each word on a separate piece of paper, e.g. *listen / to / music*. They then close their books and put the bits face down on the table. Pairs join with a second pair and choose one of the bits of paper from the other pair. Pairs take turns to guess each other's collocation from the word. This may be easy, e.g. if they picked the word *listen*, or it may be difficult, e.g. if they picked the word *to*. The first pair to guess wins a point. If they can't guess, they pick a second word. They can then repeat the activity with a different pair.

Vocabulary and grammar review Unit 11

1 **2** was built **3** seems **4** is rising **5** are washing **6** reaches **7** was completely flooded **8** disappeared **9** is done **10** know **11** were saved **12** was put up

2 **2** more quickly **3** (the) best **4** more frequently **5** harder **6** (the) worst **7** more heavily **8** more carefully

3 **2** invitation **3** celebration **4** completion **5** improvement **6** examinations **7** development **8** disappointment

4 **Across: 1** team **6** landscape **7** bee **8** penguin
Down: 2 exploration **3** mountain **4** movement **5** discussion **7** bear

Vocabulary and grammar review Unit 12

1 **2** said **3** asked **4** telling **5** ask/asked **6** ask for **7** tell **8** talking **9** speak **10** talked

2 **2** inexpensive **3** unfair **4** unhealthy **5** impatient **6** impolite

3 **2** A friend asked me what was my dog **my dog was** called.
3 Marta asked me why didn't I go **why I hadn't gone / didn't go** to the party.
4 My sister asked me why was I **why I was** crying.
5 Nicky asked me what was I going I was going to do.
6 Danny asked me what new sport should he he **should** take up.
7 I imagine you are wondering when am I **when I am** going to visit.

4 **2** they were looking forward **3** she had just bought **4** she was going to invite **5** they had won **6** she was sure they would have

5 **2** if/whether **3** told **4** the **5** was **6** to

Grammar reference answer key

Unit 1

Prepositions of time

1

1 on 2 in 3 at 4 on 5 in 6 on

Frequency adverbs

1

1 I go to the gym twice a week.
2 I hardly ever spend more than an hour there.
3 I sometimes run for half an hour.
4 I usually listen to music while I'm running.
5 When I get home, I'm always exhausted.
6 I go out with my friends every Friday.

Present simple and present continuous

1

1 are taking up 2 helps 3 use up 4 walk 5 go 6 I'm training
7 I'm spending

State verbs

1

1 do (you) weigh; prefer 2 helps 3 smell 4 is having 5 costs; think
6 owns; wants

Countable and uncountable nouns

1

As well as giving us energy, sugar in our diet makes our food taste better. Sometimes we add sugar to our breakfast cereals. Sugar is also used in biscuits, ice cream, chocolate and many other things we eat. It is also in fruit and vegetables and even in a glass of milk.

2

1 We haven't got **much** time.
2 I drink a little **water** when I wake up.
3 There are **a** lot of / **lots** of things we need to talk about.
4 Can you help? I need some **information** about train times.
5 How **many** friends do you have online?
6 We have a lot of **furniture** in our house.

Prepositions of place

1

1 on, in 2 at 3 in, on 4 at

Unit 2

Past simple and past continuous

1

1 was watching 2 often phoned 3 realised
4 was shining; were singing 5 won

2

1 was tidying; found 2 was leaving; realised
3 was watching; was cooking 4 heard; stopped; were doing; walked
5 crashed; was updating

used to

1

1 I didn't use to like hot weather (but I do now).
2 My brother used to play football (until he broke his leg).
3 I used to have blond hair / My hair used to be blond (but now it's brown).
4 Did you use to go on holiday with your friends (when you were a child)?
5 When I was younger, I didn't use to get up late.

So (do) I* and *Nor/Neither (do) I

1

1 So did I. 2 Nor/Neither did I. 3 So do I. 4 Nor/Neither do I.
5 So have I. / So do I.

Unit 3

Verbs followed by *to* or *-ing*

1

1 going 2 to have 3 going 4 to go 5 doing 6 living 7 to have
8 spending

2

1 ✓ 2 ✓
3 ✗ (In A, Ben stopped what he was doing in order to phone. In B, Ben no longer phones his parents.)
4 ✓ 5 ✓
6 ✗ (In A, the next thing they told us about was their holiday. In B, they didn't stop telling us about their holiday.)

Phrasal verbs

1

1 What should you do if your TV breaks down? c
2 Which of your parents do you take after? d
3 Do you like to dress up when you go to a party? a
4 Who do you really look up to? e
5 Do you ever have to look after anyone? f
6 What do you think about people who show off? b

2

1 I get on (well) with everyone in my family.
2 I've signed up for an English course.
3 I'm looking forward to seeing my friend again.
4 My father has given up eating sugar.
5 My brother's just taken up basketball.

Unit 4

Comparative and superlative adjectives

1

1 the thinnest 2 nicer 3 lazy 4 more comfortable 5 the best
6 worse 7 far

2

1 the wettest 2 the most beautiful 3 heavier 4 better 5 worse
6 further/farther

3

1 Josh isn't as tall as Roman.
2 My new phone is/was much more expensive than my old phone.
3 Fruit is a lot healthier than burgers.
4 Spain is a bit smaller than France.
5 The new shopping centre is far nicer than the old one.

Gradable and non-gradable adjectives

1

1f 2g 3e 4c 5b 6a 7d

2

1 delighted; surprised 2 cold 3 exhausted 4 bad; tired
5 excellent 6 huge

Unit 5

Modal verbs: *can, could, might* and *may* (ability and possibility)

1

1 can't 2 could 3 may/might/could 4 might/may/could 5 can
6 couldn't

2

1 d may 2 c can 3 a may 4 e could 5 b can

Modal verbs: *should, shouldn't, must, mustn't, have to, don't have to* (obligation and prohibition)

1

1 mustn't/can't 2 can/must; can't 3 can 4 can't 5 mustn't/can't

2

1 didn't have to 2 could 3 had to 4 had to 5 could 6 couldn't

Adjectives with *-ed* and *-ing* endings

1

1 interesting; interested 2 relaxed; relaxing 3 annoying; annoyed
4 excited; exciting

Unit 6

Present perfect

1

1 just 2 already 3 already 4 yet 5 yet

2

1 for 2 since 3 since 4 for 5 since

3
A: Have you heard? My oldest sister's getting married.
B: Who to?
A: A guy called Elliot.
B: Really! How long ~~did she know~~ **has she known** him?
A: Only six months. Apparently ~~they've met~~ **they met** at work.
B: Have you met Elliot ~~already~~ **yet**?
A: No, not yet, but my sister's told me a lot about him.
B: When ~~have you seen~~ **did you see** her?
A: ~~I've seen~~ **I saw** her last week. She drove me to work one day.

4
1 went; have just woken up 2 arrived; haven't seen her yet
3 have already seen; saw 4 have ever bought; cost; have never spent
5 Have you ever done; have never done
6 did you go; went; have never visited

Unit 7

Adverbs of degree

1
1 I was really cold because I had forgotten my coat.
2 Mia is fairly sure she will pass her exam.
3 The traffic is moving very slowly.
4 Be extremely careful when you cross busy roads.
5 That was a rather difficult question.

2
1 too ill 2 too good 3 big enough 4 enough hours
5 enough money; rich enough

Future forms

1
1 We're going to see 2 I'll be 3 I'm going to go 4 leaves 5 I'll go

Prepositions of movement

1
1 on 2 by; by 3 on/onto 4 out of 5 by 6 into

Unit 8

Conditional sentences

1
1 d 2 g 3 a 4 h 5 c 6 b 7 e 8 f

2
2 she spoke English, she could study in Canada.
3 I had enough free time, I'd learn to play a musical instrument.
4 I had enough money, I'd buy a laptop.

Conjunctions: *when, if, unless* + present, future

3
1 Unless 2 unless 3 If 4 if 5 unless 6 If/When 7 If 8 when

Unit 9

Defining and non-defining relative clauses with *which, that, who, whose, when, where*

1
1 whose 2 that/which 3 who 4 that/which 5 that/which
6 where 7 that/which 8 when

2
4, 7

3
1 The music which Gisela was playing last night was by Mozart.
2 The violin that Gisela was playing in the concert was not hers.
3 James, whose violin Gisela borrowed, is also a music teacher.
4 We've just listened to Gisela's latest recording, which is number 1 in the classical charts.
5 Gisela's mother, who was in the audience tonight, is very proud of her.
6 Tomorrow, Gisela is going back to Vienna, where she plays in an orchestra.

Past perfect

1
1 had rained; had stopped; was 2 had planned; had to
3 had been; started 4 could not / couldn't; had made 5 went; had seen

Unit 10

Commands and instructions

1
1 Do not eat; drink 2 Turn 3 Do not use 4 Be

Have something done

1
1 Have you had your hair cut? 2 I might have my bedroom painted blue.
3 Has Michael had his bike fixed yet?
4 I get my teeth polished every six months.
5 You should have your computer checked for viruses.

2
1 He has had his hair cut and his beard shaved off.
2 She had her car washed yesterday.
3 He's had his shoes cleaned.
4 They're having their house painted.
5 He had his tooth taken out this morning.
6 She'll have her eyes tested tomorrow.

Unit 11

The passive: present simple and past simple

1
1 was played; was watched
2 are taken; are driven
3 was written; were predicted

2
1 Our cat is seen twice a year by a vet.
2 The roads were closed (by the police) because of the storm.
3 The book was written by a famous author.
4 Cricket is played in Australia.
5 I was taught how to sing by my father.

Comparative and superlative adverbs

1
1 more clearly 2 the best 3 faster 4 harder
5 more seriously; better 6 the quickest

2
1 dances more beautifully 2 writes the best of all
3 the most patiently 4 work harder 5 earlier than you did last night
6 runs faster than me

Unit 12

Reported speech and commands

1
2 'I'm sorry but I can't lend you any more money.'
3 'I still feel ill.' 4 'I'm older than you.'
5 'We'll come and see you later.' 6 'I left yesterday.'
7 'Stop worrying!'

2
1 He said (that) he was leaving university at the end of the following year.
2 She said (that) she'd got a surprise for me.
3 She told him to shut the door.
4 They said (that) they'd all passed their English exam.
5 He said (that) it was his birthday the next day.
6 She said (that) I was the only person she knew who liked/likes classical music.
7 He told Max not to drink any more coffee.
8 They said (that) they'd gone to / been to Morocco for their holiday the previous year / the year before.

Reported questions

1
2 'Are you enjoying your new course?'
3 'Has anyone / Have you found my keys?'
4 'What did you do yesterday?'
5 'Can you come to my party this evening / tonight?'
6 'Can you tell us where the station is?' / 'Where's the station?'
7 'Who's your favourite actor?'
8 'Did you try to phone me?' / 'Have you tried to phone me?'

2
1 My colleague asked (me) why I was wearing my best clothes.
2 My colleague asked (me) where I was going.
3 My colleague asked (me) what I was going to do there.
4 My boss asked (me) if/whether I was going with anyone/someone.
5 My colleague asked (me) if/whether he knew who I was going with.
6 My boss asked (me) what time I'd be back.
7 My colleague asked (me) how I would get back.
8 My boss asked (me) what I would do if I missed the last train.

Indirect questions
1
1 where you live?
2 if you are doing anything at the weekend.
3 what they did last weekend?
4 what you thought of the film.
5 if/whether my seat number is on this ticket?

Phrasal verb builder answer key

Relationships
1
1 bring up 2 get on with 3 get together 4 go out with
5 look after 6 split up with
2
1 get together 2 get on 3 brought up 4 look after 5 split up
3
Students' own answers.

Travel
1
1 break down 2 check in 3 get back 4 set off 5 take off 6 turn up
2
1 set off 2 broke down; turned up 3 checked in 4 took off 5 got back
3
Students' own answers.

Communication
1
1 call someone back 2 fill in something 3 hang up
4 ring up someone 5 switch something off
2
1 switched it off 2 rang up 3 hung up 4 called back 5 fill in
3
Students' own answers.

Daily routines
1
1 get up 2 pick someone up 3 put something on 4 tidy up
5 wake someone up
2
1 get up 2 picks me up 3 wake up 4 put on 5 tidies up
3
Students' own answers.

Writing bank answer key

Making your writing more interesting
1
b7 c1 d5 e2 f4 g6 h8
2

adjectives	adverbs	linking words	time expressions
beautiful delicious modern wonderful	completely easily loudly quickly	and because but so	later that day the next day this morning yesterday

3 (other possible answers in brackets)
1 suddenly (finally) 2 but
3 early the next morning (the next day; later that day)
4 large (delicious; small) 5 really (very; extremely)
4
2 I was very tired, so I went straight to bed.
3 We all went to the party, and everyone had a great time.
4 Paul wanted to come with us, but he couldn't.
5 We all laughed because it was so funny.

Writing Part 1: An email

1
You have to respond to the news, say which month you can go, say which sport you would like to see, and suggest something you should buy as a souvenir.
2
1dR 2aS 3bO 4cP
3
1 **I'm** afraid I won't be able to come to your party.
2 Guess **where** I'm going next week?
3 I'm sorry, **but** Dan won't be here when you visit.
4 You'll be pleased **to** hear that I've now finished all my exams!
4
1 so 2 also 3 but 4 because 5 and
5
You should respond to the idea of a barbecue, say which day you'd like to come, suggest some ideas for food and explain what sport would be best.
6
Students' own answers.
7 (Sample answer)
Hi Logan,
I think a barbecue sounds like a great idea, and I'd love to come! It will be lovely, especially if the weather's going to be warm and sunny.
Why don't we have some salads and potatoes to go with the meat? Also, make sure you remember that some people in our class are vegetarians, so you'll need some special dishes for them.
I agree that sports are fun after a barbecue. We could play badminton. It's a very easy sport, so everyone can play.
See you on Saturday!
Eva
8
Students' own answers.

Writing Part 2: An article

1
The article is about your favourite city. You should say what the city is, why you like it and what makes it so special. You should then explain which city you would love to travel to in the future.
2
1 There are many benefits to keeping fit.
2 The internet has changed people's lives in many ways.
3 Teaching is a very difficult job.

3

clothes	films	food	countryside	weather
old-fashioned tight *fashionable* *expensive*	amusing frightening *exciting* *boring* *horror*	delicious tasty *spicy* *salty* *sweet*	peaceful quiet *beautiful* *wild* *empty*	freezing stormy *hot* *wet* *cool*

4

The article is about your perfect job. You should say what makes a job perfect for you. Then give your opinion about how important it is to earn a lot of money in your job.

5

Students' own answers.

6 Sample answer

For me, an architect is the perfect job because it is interesting, creative and very challenging.

For an architect, every day is different. You might design a modern house, then a new classroom for a school, then change an old factory into flats. So this job is never boring, because every building you work on is different. I think it would also be very satisfying to create beautiful buildings for people to live or work in.

I would say it is important to earn enough money so you don't have to worry about it. But if you enjoy your job, you don't have to be rich to be happy.

7

Students' own answers.

Writing Part 2: A story

1

2 is the best because it talks about what was in the letter, and suggests that something is going to happen in the story.

2

1 called 2 was waiting 3 had passed / 'd passed
4 was walking 5 had forgotten / 'd forgotten 6 closed

3

1 First 2 Then 3 Next 4 An hour later 5 Finally

4

1 curly 2 smart 3 spicy 4 entertaining 5 messy 6 disappointed

5

Students' own answers.

6 Sample answer

A day at the zoo.

The day at the zoo began quite well. I was there with some friends, and the sun was shining.

First, we saw some baby elephants. Then we watched some very funny penguins. By midday, we were getting hungry, so we decided to go for lunch. As we were walking towards the café, we suddenly heard people shouting. A tiger had escaped! We immediately ran to the cafe and shut the door behind us. It was quite scary, but fortunately the tiger was caught quickly and no one was hurt.

Finally, the café offered a free meal to everyone, so the day ended very well.

7

Students' own answers.

Speaking bank answer key and audioscripts

Speaking Part 1

1

Yes, she does.

Track 71

Examiner: What's your name?
Maria: My name's Maria.
Examiner: What's your surname?
Maria: It's Moretti.
Examiner: Where do you come from?
Maria: I come from Rome, in Italy.
Examiner: Do you work, or are you a student?
Maria: I'm a student.

2

Track 72

Examiner: What did you do yesterday evening?

Maria: Yesterday evening I went to the cinema with some friends. I often watch films with my friends because we all enjoy the same kinds of films.

Examiner: Do you think that English will be useful to you in the future?

Maria: Yes, I think it will be very useful. I want to work for an international company, so I hope I'll travel to different countries with my job, and I'm sure I will need English.

Examiner: Tell us about a place you would like to visit in the future.

Maria: I'd love to go to New York one day because it looks such an exciting city. Actually, my uncle lives there, so I hope I can go and visit him soon.

Examiner: Can you describe your house or flat?

Maria: My flat is quite small, because I just share it with one friend. The kitchen is very small, but the living room is quite big. Also, it's got a balcony, and I really like sitting there in the evening.

Examiner: What do you enjoy doing in your free time?

Maria: Well, I'm quite into sport, so I do quite a lot of sport in my free time. For example, I sometimes go running in the evenings and I often play tennis at the weekend. I also like spending time with friends. My friends are very important to me.

3

1 often 2 and 3 because 4 Actually 5 but 6 Also 7 so
8 For example

4

present simple	past simple	*be going to*
always sometimes usually	last night last weekend when I was younger	next weekend tomorrow tonight

5

1 b + i 2 d + h 3 a + f 4 e + j 5 c + g

6

1 because 2 for example 3 which 4 but 5 Unfortunately

Track 73

Examiner: Tell us about your English teacher.

Pablo: My English teacher is called Mr Adams, and he's from Manchester. He's really funny, and I like him because he always makes our lessons interesting. I think he's a really good teacher.

Examiner: Would you like to live in a different country?

Pablo: I'd like to visit different countries, for example the United States or maybe Australia, to get some experience of what life is like there. But I wouldn't like to for long, because I'd miss my family and friends at home.

Examiner: Can you tell us about your home town?
Pablo: My home town is Barcelona, in the north-east of Spain. It's a big city, and there are lots of beautiful buildings which are very famous. I like it because it's very friendly, and there are lots of cafés where you can meet your friends. Also, it's on the coast, so you can go to the beach in the summer.
Examiner: How do you usually travel to university or work?
Pablo: I usually catch the bus to work. It takes about half an hour for me to get there. I'd prefer to walk, but it's too far for me to walk every day.
Examiner: What did you do last weekend?
Pablo: On Saturday I played football for my team. We usually have a match every Saturday. Unfortunately, we didn't win last week. Then on Sunday I met my friends, and we went to the beach because it was very hot.

Speaking Part 2

1
They might be in a car park. They are probably friends.

Track 74

Pablo: The picture shows two teenagers playing basketball outdoors. I think they might be in a car park or something like that. It isn't a very attractive place, because there are no flowers, and there isn't any grass. It's a cloudy day, and it doesn't look very warm because one of the boys is wearing long sleeves. The two boys are at the front of the photo, in the middle, and at the back we can see a basketball net, and some buildings. They look like garages or sheds, something like that. On the left, you can see some houses in the background. The boys aren't actually playing a game, but they're practising. One of the boys is wearing a stripy top, with a hood, and he's holding the ball above his head. He seems to be aiming for the net, which is quite a long way away. The other boy, who's short and has dark hair, is running forwards. I think maybe he's going to catch the ball. I guess the two boys are probably friends because they don't look like brothers.

2
1 at the front 2 right 3 left 4 behind 5 In the background

3
1 are travelling 2 're smiling 3 is showing 4 is looking; is thinking
5 standing; is talking

Track 75

Pablo: The picture shows some people who are travelling by bus. There are two women at the front of the picture, on the left. They're smiling, and one woman is showing the other one something on her phone. On the right, there's an older man. He's looking forwards. I'm not sure what he's looking at, but maybe he's thinking about where to get off the bus. In the background, at the back of the bus, there's a man. He's standing up and I think he's talking to another passenger.

4
1 probably 2 might 3 looks 4 seem 5 guess

5

Track 76

Maria: The photo shows two people sitting in a living room in a house, a teenager and an older man. I think they're probably father and son. The teenager, who's on the right, is wearing a pullover and jeans, and the older man is wearing a blue shirt and jeans. He's got grey hair. The sitting room looks quite modern, and the sofa looks very comfortable. In the background, on the left, you can see some photos on a table. On the right, you can see some books. They might be watching TV because you can see that they're looking at something, and there is a remote control, or something like that, on the sofa on the right. They're eating something from a box, some kind of takeaway. It looks like pizza. They seem to be quite relaxed. I guess they're probably having a relaxing evening at home.

6
Students' own answers.

Speaking Part 3

1
Yes, they do. They agree on two cinema tickets.

2
1 think 2 sure 3 agree 4 opinion 5 idea 6 so 7 OK 8 go

Track 77

Maria: So, shall we start with the book? What do you think about that idea?
Pablo: I'm not sure. Some people enjoy reading, but a lot of people don't like it. And it's difficult to choose a book for someone else.
Maria: I agree with you. And I don't think flowers are a good idea because they're a bit boring, in my opinion.
Pablo: That's true. In my opinion, people buy flowers if they can't think of any other ideas. Would a T-shirt be a good idea? Most people wear T-shirts.
Maria: Well, I don't really like it when people buy me clothes, because I prefer to choose them myself.
Pablo: OK, so not a T-shirt. Would a concert ticket be a good idea?
Maria: Yes, I think that's a great idea. Everyone loves listening to live music.
Pablo: No, I disagree. There's only one ticket, and I don't think it would be fun to go to a concert on your own.
Maria: Yes, you're right. But there are two cinema tickets, so maybe they might be a better choice.
Pablo: Yes, I agree they would be a good choice. So, what else is there? I think a mug is boring, and chocolates seem quite a cheap present. What do you think?
Maria: Yes, I agree. And I'm sure she'd love to get a necklace, so that's a possibility.
Pablo: OK. So, it's time to decide. What do you think?
Maria: Well, I would say either the cinema tickets or the necklace. Do you agree?
Pablo: Yes, but the necklace might be too expensive, so maybe we should choose the cinema tickets. Are you OK with that?
Maria: Yes, good idea. We'll go for that one, then.

3
1 d 2 f 3 a 4 b 5 c 6 e

4

Track 78

Pablo: So, shall we talk about the barbecue first? I think it's a good idea. A barbecue is relaxing, and everyone can enjoy it. What do you think?
Maria: Yes, I agree with you. The only problem is that someone has to organise everything, like buying the food and cooking it, so it's quite a lot of work. In my opinion, eating in a restaurant would be better, because no one would have to cook.
Pablo: Yes, that's a good point. But a meal in a restaurant might be too expensive for some people. What do you think about going to watch a football match?
Maria: Well, it would be perfect for me, because I'm a football fan, but I don't think it's a good idea for a class celebration, because not everyone likes football.
Pablo: That's true. So, would the beach be a good idea? Everyone likes going to the beach. Do you agree?
Maria: I'm not sure. What if the weather's bad?
Pablo: Yes, you're right. The beach is great if the weather's good, but it's really boring if it's raining. So, what else is there? I don't think hiking is a good idea, because some people might not be fit enough to enjoy it.
Maria: Yes, I agree. What about going to a theme park? I'm sure people would enjoy that.
Pablo: Yes, that's a good idea. There are different rides, too, so not everyone has to go on the really scary ones. It's definitely more fun than a boat trip. That would be really boring, in my opinion.
Maria: I agree, because on a boat you're just sitting there for a few hours, but I prefer to be active.
Pablo: What about the zoo? That could be fun. And there are things to do indoors if it's wet.

Maria: Yes, that's true. And everyone loves animals.
Pablo: So, it's time to decide. I would choose the theme park or the zoo because I think everyone would enjoy them.
Maria: Yes. I think the theme park would be more fun, so I would choose that.
Pablo: OK. We'll go for that one, then.

Speaking Part 4

1
They give reasons, ask for each other's opinions, and use an expression to allow time to think about the answer.

Track 79

Examiner: Who do you most enjoy buying presents for?
Maria: Let me see. I would say my cousins. One is 14 years old, and the other is 12. I love buying presents for them because there are so many fun things that you can choose for children, like toys or games. What do you think?
Pablo: Yes, I agree with you, and it's also fun buying presents for children because they're always so excited when they open them. I've got a cousin who's ten, and I really enjoy buying things for him. He's really into football so it's easy to find things he likes. It's great.
Examiner: Which people in your family are the most difficult to choose presents for?
Pablo: That's an interesting question. My dad is definitely the most difficult to choose presents for. He never seems to want anything, and he doesn't have any hobbies, so I usually end up buying him something really boring, like socks. Do you agree that it's difficult to buy things for your parents?
Maria: Yes, I completely agree. It's much easier to buy things for people your own age, because you know what they like and what they're interested in.
Examiner: Do you like receiving money instead of presents?
Maria: Hmm, that's a difficult question. It's sometimes nice to receive money, because then you can buy something you really want, or you can save up to buy something bigger, like a new tablet. What do you think?
Pablo: Hmm, I'm not sure about that. When it's my birthday, I usually get money from three or four relatives, and it's good because I can use the money to buy something more expensive for myself. But in my opinion it's a bit boring if you don't get any presents on your birthday, just money. Do you agree?
Maria: Yes, I do. I love getting presents, but I think when it's relatives who don't know you very well it's better to get money, because sometimes they can give you things you don't really want.
Pablo: That's true. I prefer to get money from people who don't know me very well, but it's nice to get presents from people who know what I like.

2
1 buying 2 is sometimes 3 usually get 4 to get 5 getting

3
1 Do you agree? 2 That's true. 3 What do you think?
4 That's an interesting question.

4
Students' own answers

5

Track 80

Examiner: Would you like to have more social events with your English class?
Pablo: Yes, I think that more social events would be great, because it would be an opportunity to get to know other students in the class better. I would like some trips to the cinema, or maybe visits to other towns and cities. What do you think?
Maria: Yes, I agree. I think it would be fun to have more social events, and in my opinion it would also help us to study, because it's easier to study when you're with people that you know, because you're more relaxed. I agree with you that trips to the cinema would be fun, because then we could talk about the films together.
Examiner: Do you think watching sports events can be more fun than taking part?
Maria: I'm not sure about that. I love sport, and in my opinion it's always more fun to take part than to watch. When you play a game like tennis or football, for example, you really want to win, so it's very exciting and it encourages you to make an effort and do your best. Do you agree?
Pablo: Yes, I do. I'm really into sport, too, and I agree that it's exciting when you play a match and you really want to win. But when I watch my favourite football team I also want them to win, so that's exciting too. I also love watching really good players, who are much better than me!
Maria: Yes, that's true. It's exciting to watch good players, but I would still prefer to take part.
Examiner: Do you prefer cooking a meal for friends or eating out in a restaurant?
Pablo: I think it depends. I enjoy cooking, and I often cook meals for a few friends. But if I want to have a big meal with a lot of friends, I prefer to go to a restaurant. What do you think?
Maria: Yes, I think you're right. It would be very stressful to cook a meal for 15 or 20 people. But cooking for a few friends is fun, and it's nice because you're at home and you're relaxed.
Pablo: Yes, I agree with you. The only problem is that you have to do the washing up.
Maria: That's true. I think it's only fun if you have a dishwasher!

Photocopiable audioscripts

Unit 1, Student's Book p. 9, Listening Part 2, Exercises 2 and 3

Track 2

Narrator: Part 2. For each question, choose the correct answer. One. You will hear two friends talking about the kind of flat they would like to live in.

Man: Wouldn't it be great to live right at the top of that block of flats, with views across the city?

Woman: Nice views are fine but I'm not very keen on lifts. I think I'd rather be on the ground floor. It'd be good to live in a building that's not far from a bus stop, too.

Man: Or an underground station.

Woman: Right. But the most important thing for me would be to have my own room, so it'd have to be a three-bedroom apartment.

Man: I don't mind sharing, so two would be enough for me.

Narrator: Two. You will hear a man telling his friend about changing job.

Woman: I haven't seen you for a long time. How do you feel now about your new job?

Man: Well, before I moved at the beginning of January, I thought it'd be difficult to make friends with people in my new office, but they've given me a really warm welcome. Of course I'm a bit sad that I don't see anyone from my previous company, but there's nothing I can do about that. My work seems to be going better than I'd expected, too, so making the change hasn't been too hard, really.

Narrator: Three. You will hear a woman talking about a trip to the beach.

Man: How was your day out?

Woman: Great! The bus left early on Saturday so I had to get up at 5 a.m., but that meant we got to the beach really early.

Man: Did you go for a swim?

Woman: Yes, I thought I would enjoy that but it was a bit cold so we hired a little boat instead and sailed round the bay. That was fun, too, but not as much as having a game of volleyball. We're going there again in July when it'll be too hot for beach sports, but swimming in the sea will be wonderful!

Narrator: Four. You will hear two friends talking about the town where they live.

Woman: It's quite a good place to live, isn't it? Although I sometimes think it would be nice if more people lived here.

Man: Well, it might be livelier, but I think the size is about right, actually. In bigger places there are problems like street crime, especially at night, but here you feel safe anywhere, really.

Woman: That's true, although everywhere you go the roads are really busy, and it's the same here. All that noise and pollution is horrible early in the morning.

Man: I know. I wish people would walk or go by bike instead.

Narrator: Five. You will hear a man talking to a friend about shops.

Woman: I don't really know this part of town. Where's the best place to do a bit of shopping?

Man: The little shop on the corner isn't bad. The range of things there is a bit limited but just about everything is amazingly good value, especially if you compare it to the local supermarket.

Woman: The one opposite the station?

Man: Yes, you can find almost anything you want there but it always seems to be really crowded, with lots of people waiting to pay because it's short of staff.

Woman: Thanks – I'll definitely avoid that one.

Narrator: Six. You will hear two friends talking about their homes.

Man: I like my room, though I haven't got much space for my things.

Woman: Mine's about the right size really, but I know what you mean. My cupboards and shelves are far too small.

Man: At least mine's got big windows, so I get plenty of sunshine.

Woman: I do too, though it's a pity I can't turn the central heating up in winter.

Man: Does it get noisy? It can do at my place, especially in the morning rush hour.

Woman: My flatmate complains about traffic noise waking her up too! But I'm on the inside of the building so I hardly notice it.

Unit 2, Student's Book p. 21, Listening Part 1, Exercise 3

Track 10

Narrator: Part 1. For each question, choose the correct answer. One. What do the people need to bring for the cycling trip?

Woman: Just before you leave. Ssh! Listen carefully. Don't forget it's our annual day out tomorrow and the office will be closed. For those of you on the cycling trip, we're meeting outside the train station. Lunch will be provided so you don't have to bring any food but don't forget a water bottle. It may be hot. Please don't bring any large items like heavy bags or cameras as you won't be able to carry them.

Narrator: Two. What time does Stuart need to be at work?

Woman: Stuart! It's ten past nine.

Stuart: I know, I'm late again. You see, I left my mobile at home so I went back for it. Then I missed the bus and the next one was at half past eight. There was a terrible traffic jam so I got off the bus and ran the rest of the way.

Woman: Yes but the shop opens at nine. I can't manage everything on my own. You should really be here by ten to nine.

Stuart: I'm sorry.

Narrator: Three. Where does Jack live?

Jack: Hi it's Jack. Do you still fancy going to the swimming pool later? George lives near the pool so he might want to come too. Shall we meet outside the cinema? You know, the one where I used to live. And if you like, we can get a take-away afterwards and have it at my house. They've opened a great pizza place next door to us. Let me know what you think. Bye!

Narrator: Four. Where did the man find his football boots?

Man: Have you seen my football boots anywhere? I brought them home from training yesterday. They were wet so I left them in the kitchen to dry and now I can't find them.

Katie: We were tidying up this morning. Have you looked in the cupboard in the hall?

Man: Yes, but they weren't there. Wait a minute. What's in that bag over there? Oh, they must be my boots.

Narrator: Five. What did Julia eat before she came home?

Man: Hi Julia. How was your day? I'm just having a cheese sandwich. Would you like one?

Julia: No thanks. I'm not hungry. You know Nigel at work, don't you? It was his birthday today and he brought in a homemade chocolate cake. It was delicious.

Man: I guess you don't want dinner then.

Julia: Oh yes, I do! What are you making?

Man: It's my special burgers tonight. They should be ready by about eight.

Narrator: Six. What are the two friends going to buy Paul for his birthday?

Man: It's Paul's birthday next weekend. We should get him something. We got him a book about his favourite band last year.

Woman: Oh yeah, that's right but his sister had bought him the same one so he took it back to the shop. He got a book about surfing instead, didn't he?

Man: Yes, that's right. I know! My brother's reading a new spy thriller. It's set in Italy and he says it's really exciting. Let's get him that.

Woman: OK.

Narrator: Seven. What is the weather forecast for tomorrow?

Joe: Best of luck with the tennis competition, Vicki! It's tomorrow, isn't it?

Vicki: Thanks, Joe! They might have to cancel it. It hasn't stopped raining all day today and we're playing outdoors.

Joe: Have you looked it up on the internet? It says on this page that it's going to be cloudy but dry. It won't be sunny though.

Vicki: That's OK – I don't like playing when it's hot but I'll take my sun cream just in case.

Unit 3, Student's Book p. 27, Listening Part 4, Exercise 3

Track 13

Narrator: Part 4. For each question, choose the correct answer. You will hear a radio interview with the Instagram photographer Marc Pasqual.

Interviewer: Today I'm talking to photographer Marc Pasqual, who posts all his pictures on Instagram. Marc, what made you want to do that full-time?

Marc: I was an international tour guide, visiting some amazing countries. I was also doing wedding photos as a hobby, but I was finding that pretty boring and was keen to try something more creative, even though I felt it unlikely I'd earn much money from it. I noticed my favourite people on Instagram, like the chef Lauren Bath, had given up interesting careers to concentrate on photography, so I decided to make the change, too.

Interviewer: How did you become such a good photographer? With a good teacher?

Marc: I did have some lessons with an experienced photographer. He encouraged me to think about how I wanted my photographs to look before I actually took them. That works for some people but not others, and personally, whenever I arrive somewhere new I start taking photos, such as drops of rain on a flower, or the sun shining through a small window. Not everyone notices these little things and it can really improve your pictures.

Interviewer: Did you make any mistakes?

Marc: Well, some beginners can't help posting lots of selfies on Instagram, but I avoided doing that. However, only uploading weekly, as I did at first, means people soon forget you. I saw those ads for expensive apps that promise to make you an Instagram star in a week, but fortunately I ignored them.

Interviewer: What's the best thing about your work?

Marc: I love getting messages on Instagram and replying to them, or working with other photographers because I get lonely if I'm by myself. But nothing gives me quite as much pleasure as having the memories of all the fantastic places I've travelled to. Taking photos means I'll never forget them.

Interviewer: What do you most want to do next?

Marc: I've thought of studying photography at university and that would be great, but it'd probably be more useful for someone aiming to start a career in a large organization. I'd rather read lots about it since its invention in the 19th century, and still be able to work on my own.

Interviewer: What would you say to new Instagram photographers?

Marc: Make sure people on Instagram notice your work. Research shows that it doesn't really matter whether you post on weekdays or weekends, so do so whenever you like. Some photographers say you shouldn't add any text, but I disagree. I tell the story of each picture, saying why and how I took it and people like that. Also add a link to your blog or Facebook page and upload some of your photos there, though keep your best ones for Instagram.

Unit 4, Student's Book p. 40, Listening Part 3, Exercise 3

Track 22

Narrator: Part 3. For each question, write the correct answer in the gap. Write one or two words or a number or a date or time. You will hear a woman talking to a group of people about the bushcraft courses she organises.

Justyna: I'm here to tell you about our bushcraft courses. Since 2007, we've been teaching people the necessary skills to stay alive in the wild by using the things around them.

So what are weekend courses like? On Saturday morning, your guide will pick you up for your adventure in front of the station and drive you to our main office. There, you'll need to repack your backpack with just the essential equipment and then it's time to walk to the forest camp.

The first lesson is how to use the equipment, for example you'll learn how to use a knife properly so that you don't hurt yourself or others. The next job is building your own hut. It doesn't need to be beautiful but it will be your place to spend the night as it will get cold. But don't worry, your guide will have an emergency tent for the group to sleep in if necessary.

You'll learn how to catch a rabbit, although I can't promise you'll be lucky enough to get one. If you do, I'll show you how to prepare it and we'll have it for lunch. We'll also go fishing in the river but whatever we catch there, we will have to put back into the water. Those are the rules in this area.

Over the rest of the weekend you'll learn how to make drinking water, use the stars and moon to find your way and check the clouds for rain or a change in temperature.

Please visit our website for more details but if you have any questions, please email me on Justyna at bushcraftskills dot com, that's J-U-S-T-Y-N-A. Or if you prefer, you can telephone us. Our number is zero one, double seven, three, double four, double two, five, six. There's someone in our office from Monday to Friday from ten to five.

Unit 5, Student's Book p. 45, Listening Part 2, Exercise 3

Track 24

Narrator: Part 2. For each question, choose the correct answer. One. You will hear a woman talking about taking part in a singing contest.

Man: What did you think of the judges' scores?

Woman: Well, I thought I'd sung pretty well, certainly nothing to be ashamed of, but I must admit they were lower than I'd expected. I knew then that I had little chance of beating the others, but at least I'd done my best. For me that's the most important thing.

Man: Yes, definitely. So do you think you'll try again in next year's contest?

Woman: Yes, if I can. I might not win but I think I could do better than this year.

Narrator: Two. You will hear two friends talking about camping.

Woman: I'm going camping in the mountains on Friday.

Man: That'll be great fun, especially with the hot weather we're having right now, but the temperatures there can really drop at night, even in summer. You'd better put a jacket and a thick sweater in your backpack instead of lots of things to eat. You can always get a tasty meal in one of the local villages. Where exactly will you be going?

Woman: Up by the lake.

Man: It's beautiful there, isn't it? But perhaps it'd be best to put your tent up somewhere else. At this time of year the mosquitoes there are awful. They never stop biting!

Narrator: Three. You will hear a student talking to his friend about a literature exam.

Woman: You've got that literature exam next week, haven't you? How's the revision going?

Man: I thought I'd be tired of it by now, but your suggestion that I should watch films of the books we have to study has made it more interesting and I understand the stories better. Usually just before an important exam like this one I feel really worried about what could go wrong on the day, but this time it's quite different.

Woman: That's great to hear. I'm sure you'll do really well on Monday morning. Good luck!

Narrator: Four. You will hear a young woman telling a friend about studying abroad.

Man: Did you enjoy your month abroad?

Woman: Yes, I was in a small town in the countryside. The lessons were good even though the rest of the class were younger than me and we didn't have much in common. I had a lovely room in the house where I was staying with a couple. They were kind to me but they had a busy social life and I hardly saw them. So I went to the main square where all the shops and cafés are and made friends there. We had a great time hanging out and chatting.

Narrator: Five. You will hear a man telling his friend about how he travels to work.

Woman: I see you're using your bike every day now, instead of coming to work in your friend's car.

Man: Yes, I've been doing that for a couple of months. Actually he still goes right past our office on his way to work, so it's not about protecting the environment, spending less on petrol or anything like that. It's just that I realised I was spending nearly all my time sitting down, in the office and at home, and I thought I'd better do something about it.

Woman: That's a good idea. Maybe I should do the same.

Narrator: Six. You will hear a woman talking to a friend about going shopping.

Man: So how was your shopping trip yesterday? I imagine the city centre's pretty crowded on a Saturday morning at this time of the year.

Woman: Yes, there were lots of people walking in the streets and the department store was full of customers, too. I don't mind that, but I wasn't happy about having shop assistants trying to sell me stuff when all I wanted to do was look at things. I noticed they were bothering other customers, too. If they carry on like that, their shop won't be full much longer.

Unit 6, Student's Book p. 57, Listening Part 1, Exercise 3

Track 30

Narrator: Part 1. For each question, choose the correct answer. One. What would the woman like to try on?

Woman: Excuse me. Could I try on one of the jumpers in the window please?

Shop assistant: Sure. Do you mean one of the striped ones? They'd look good on you.

Woman: I was actually thinking of a plain one. Have you got it in a small?

Shop assistant: I think so. I'll check. Did you want it with a V neck?

Woman: I'd rather have a round one.

Shop assistant: OK. I'll just get it for you to try on.

Narrator: Two. Where has Matt left his keys?

Matt: Ava, I think I've lost my keys, have you seen them? I put them in my jeans' pocket a minute ago but they're not there now.

Ava: Not again! You were wearing your coat just now. Have you checked all the pockets? You usually leave your keys there.

Matt: I've looked in all the pockets. Was I carrying my backpack when I came in?

Ava: I think so. I bet they're in there.

Matt: You're right again, Ava!

Narrator: Three. What did Karen buy last weekend?

Man: Did you have a good weekend, Karen?

Karen: Yes, I did, thanks. On Saturday I went to the new shopping centre with my aunt. She wanted to get a dress for the summer.

Man: Did she buy one?

Karen: They were all the wrong size. Then she tried on loads of tops.

Man: What about the red one you're wearing?

Karen: Isn't it lovely! She didn't like the colour so I got it instead.

Man: So, she didn't buy anything but you did!

Karen: That's right! It'll look good with that skirt I got for my birthday.

Narrator: Four. Which one is Sarah's cousin?

Man: Sarah, did you manage to get your cousin something for her birthday?

Sarah: Don't ask! We got her some earrings in the end but then we found out that she never wears jewellery.

Man: Oh no! I thought that girl over there with long hair and huge earrings was your cousin.

Sarah: That's my sister, but they look alike, don't they? They even used to have the same length hair.

Man: Has she had it cut?

Sarah: Yeah but she says she's going to grow it long again.

Narrator: Five. Where did the man get the trainers he's wearing now?

Woman: Nice trainers! Have you just been to that new sports shop?

Man: Yeah! It's a great store with some amazing bargains. I bought some trainers there last week, but they weren't the right size so I had to take them back. Then one of my friends suggested looking in the market, so I did and found these. They fit perfectly.

Woman: My flatmate keeps telling me to look on the web. She buys everything there.

Man: She's right! You know the boots I wore to the party? I got them online.

Woman: They're really cool! Were they expensive?

Narrator: Six. What's the latest time visitors can buy a ticket today?

Man: You have reached Lansdown Art Museum. We're sorry that there's no one to take your call right now. If you are interested in seeing the Photographer of the Year exhibition, the ticket office is open from nine a.m. to half past five. You need to leave the museum at quarter to seven but remember that last admission to the gallery is at quarter to six. Thank you for calling.

Narrator: Seven. What sorts of TV programmes does the woman like watching?

Connor: You look tired. Did you go to bed late last night after the football?

Laura: I think my flatmate was watching the match in his bedroom. I don't even care who won it, to be honest! I watched this comedy instead, about two men who get lost in a department store.

Connor: I saw that! I haven't laughed so much for years. Wasn't the ending good?

Laura: Well, I'd kind of lost interest by then. I'd much rather watch a wildlife documentary.

Connor: Oh? I didn't think you liked those sorts of programmes.

Unit 7, Student's Book p. 62, Listening Part 4, Exercise 2

Track 33

Narrator: Part 4. For each question, choose the correct answer. You will hear an interview with a woman called Olivia talking about her experience of travelling through a snow-storm with her friend Grace.

Interviewer: Today I'm talking to Olivia Richardson, who was with a friend on a skiing holiday in central Italy when over two metres of snow fell in 24 hours. Where were you, Olivia, when that happened?

Olivia: Grace and I were near Capracotta, in the mountains. There'd already been some light snow and we stopped for a quick meal before carrying on to a crossroads, but there we took a wrong turning and got completely lost. Then, while we were trying to decide how to return to the main road, some really heavy snow started coming down.

Interviewer: Was that frightening?

Olivia: At first I was quite certain it wouldn't last long. It was March in Italy so I wasn't worried. Of course, it was rather annoying we'd gone the wrong way, but I couldn't blame Grace because it'd been my idea. And we were still moving, but not very fast.

Interviewer: When did you have to stop?

Olivia: Well, it was getting quite difficult to see and we nearly crashed into a parked car. There was more and more snow on the road, so when we tried to go up a steep hill the wheels started going round really fast but it was so deep the car just wouldn't move forwards. It looked as if we'd be stuck there, but we didn't have much petrol left so we switched off the engine. Grace tried to phone for help but couldn't get through.

Interviewer: How did you stay warm? With the car heater?

Olivia: That meant having the engine on so we only used it a bit. Instead we got all our jumpers, trousers and socks from our suitcases and wore them all night. We were still frozen, though, and wished we had some coffee or tea with us.

Interviewer: So you spent the whole night inside the car?

Olivia: Yes, I'd at last managed to contact the emergency services. They knew our location from my phone and they advised us to 'stay in our vehicle until help could be sent the next day'. That's what we did, but by then the snow was starting to cover the car completely so we cleared a space next to the doors in case we needed to get out.

Interviewer: How did you get moving again?

Olivia: The rescue vehicles didn't get there until the afternoon. They'd called to ask if we needed an ambulance and luckily we didn't, so they just cleared the snow and led us along the road to the nearest village. There we stopped for an enormous hot meal of roast fish and pasta with cheese, the most delicious I've ever tasted!

Unit 8, Student's Book p. 74, Listening Part 3, Exercise 3

Track 41

Narrator: Part 3. For each question, write the correct answer in the gap. Write one or two words or a date or a number or a time. You will hear a man called Ben Richards talking about how to get famous on YouTube.

Presenter: Hi! Ben Richards here. About a billion people around the world use YouTube. While some people just watch videos, others upload around 300 hours of them a minute. That means that by the time I finish this introduction there'll be 500 hours of new videos on YouTube. Have you ever dreamt of becoming a famous YouTuber? Here's my advice to help you get started.

Do your research! Find out what kind of videos people are into right now by searching for 'Popular on YouTube' and then choose your style. Everyone loves watching animals doing funny things – in fact, the first ever video on YouTube was a visit to a zoo but the ones with the most likes are often music videos.

Next, think about how you can make something bigger, better and different, something that you and the people you know would like to watch. Your audience will also want to get to know you, so avoid being a clown or a film star, just act like yourself.

Practise making very short high-quality videos first. Tell your friends about your videos and ask them for their opinion. However, aim to upload at least 10 good ones before letting them know about your channel. You'll need to create a video for this which attracts attention.

Make sure you upload new videos with new information at least once a week. Choose a day and let the people who follow you know. To increase the number of people watching your videos, each one should have an unforgettable title and a clear description, but once again, try to be a bit different.

Many people give up after two or three months because nobody's watching but attracting a large audience takes time, often two or three years. It's hard work, but definitely worth it!

Unit 9, Student's Book p. 81, Listening Part 2, Exercise 2

Track 44

Narrator: Part 2. For each question, choose the correct answer. One. You will hear a woman telling her friend about running in a 20-kilometre race. Why did she decide to run in the race?

Man: Why did you run in that 20-kilometre race over the weekend? To get fit?

Woman: Well, as you know, I do a lot of athletics training most weeks so a single race wouldn't really make any difference. But my friend Julia, who keeps fit by running in other races like this, told me the winner gets £500. I thought if I could somehow manage to come first, I'd be able to give that to a good charity, so I went online, found the website and registered for it straight away.

Man: Did you win?

Woman: I came second. But I still made £200 for charity.

Narrator: Two. You will hear two friends talking about a film they have just watched.

Woman: So what did you think of the film?

Man: It was pretty good, I thought. It was quite long but it was certainly more interesting than the last one we watched here.

Woman: Well, I found it rather slow and a bit hard to follow in places. And I noticed a lot of people in the seats around us left before it ended.

Man: Yes they did, and it was a shame because they missed the best bit in the last few minutes. I really didn't expect it to finish like that.

Woman: That was quite a shock, wasn't it?

Narrator: Three. You will hear a student telling his friend about his bicycle.

Female student: I think I've just seen an ad on the notice board for your bike. Are you really selling it?

Male student: Yes, it's in great condition and I should get a good price for it. Then I can get a brand-new phone.

Female student: I'm really surprised. I often see you riding it when I'm going to university, even on cold winter mornings.

Male student: Yes, I know I'll miss it but I can't afford to replace it with a new one as well as buy a phone. The screen on the one I've got is just too small and it's damaged, too.

Narrator: Four. You will hear a young man telling his friend about a concert he went to.

Woman: I heard you went to the concert in the park on Saturday night. How was it?

Man: Well, I know normally you'd pay a lot of money to see a top band like that so it was good in that way, but it was still a bit of a disappointment. They didn't play any of their big hits, just a load of new songs from their latest album and they seemed to go on for hours. Like a lot of other people there, I went home quite a while before the end because it wasn't interesting. The only good thing really was that the concert was free.

Narrator: Five. You will hear a man telling his friend about his illness.

Woman: I saw you were off work at the end of last week and someone said you were ill. What was the matter?

Man: Yes, I had a nasty cough, a sore throat and a stomach ache, but fortunately that's gone now.

Woman: So do you feel better today?

Man: I've still got a bit of a headache and I don't have any energy at all, maybe because I wasn't eating properly until today. But at least I've got rid of the fever I had.

Woman: Good. Remember to keep warm and have plenty of drinks, especially hot ones.

Narrator: Six. You will hear two friends talking about their local sports centre.

Male student: There are definitely lots of things to do at that new sports centre next to the park.

Female student: If you like team sports or racket sports, yes, but they need things like athletics and gymnastics, too.

Male student: Their swimming pool's a really good size, though, and there's a reduced admission fee for students.

Female student: That's true. Actually, I should go more often because it's only about ten minutes by bus from my place.

Male student: And even less from mine. Actually, I could walk there instead and save a bit of money.

Female student: If we have enough time, let's go next weekend!

Unit 10, Student's Book p. 91, Listening Part 1, Exercise 5

Track 50

Narrator: Part 1. For each question, choose the correct answer. Two. What did the woman take to the party?

Man: Hi Katy! How was the party? Did everyone like the biscuits you made?

Woman: I didn't make them in the end. I baked a cake instead. But then, I phoned Mark to see what time his party was and he mentioned that he had already made a huge chocolate one. I didn't know what to do. So I bought a couple of pizzas on the way and we ate those at the party.

Man: What a shame! Perhaps we can have it for dessert today.

Narrator: Three. What food will the man try?

Presenter: And I've just got a few minutes left to tell you about a new programme where we send our presenters around the world to try local dishes. Today, Paul's in Milan, Italy where his favourite food, *fritto misto de pesce*, is on the menu. This is a plate of mixed fried fish, and will make a change from his usual favourite of steak and chips! Then next week his sister's going to Granada, Spain to try *gazpacho*, a cold soup made with tomatoes, peppers and cucumber.

Narrator: Four. Where did the woman go yesterday?

Man: Hi. Are you doing anything later? We're going to the early-afternoon performance of that new spy film. The reviews are incredible. Do you want to come?

Woman: Oh! I saw it yesterday with my cousin. He wanted to see a play but I didn't fancy it. I heard it was very long with no interval.

Man: Would you recommend the film, then?

Woman: Oh yes! It's brilliant, but I don't think I want to see it again. Are you going to the concert tomorrow? It's going to be amazing.

Narrator: Five. What do they need to bring for training tomorrow?

Trainer: Shh! Great work today guys! Now listen carefully, because as you know, tomorrow we're going to train at the sports centre on their indoor climbing wall. Remember to wear comfortable clothes. A tracksuit is much better than shorts. The sports centre will provide you with a helmet and a pair of climbing shoes. Your hands may get a bit sore, I'm afraid, but it isn't really a good idea to wear gloves because you might slip on the wall.

Narrator: Six. What activity did the man do for the first time on holiday?

Woman: You're looking well. How was your trip to Egypt?

Man: Great, we've just got back. We had an amazing time. We went diving on the first day and we took some beautiful underwater photos.

Woman: But you've done that before, haven't you?

Man: Yeah, that's right! Then my friend persuaded me to try waterskiing. I'd never done that before and by the end I was quite good at it. It was fun but my favourite watersport is still windsurfing. Do you remember when we both tried that for the first time at university?

Narrator: Seven. Where has the woman been?

Woman: Sorry I'm late. I've been trying to find a present for Mum. I was on my way to the bookshop, but then I remembered it's closed today.

Man: What did you get her in the end?

Woman: Well, I went to the art gallery to see if they had a nice picture in a frame for her but I didn't really like any of them and they were quite expensive. I'm going tomorrow to get her some earrings or a necklace from that new jewellery shop on the corner.

Unit 11, Student's Book p. 99, Listening Part 4, Exercise 2

Track 56

Narrator: Part 4. For each question, choose the correct answer. You will hear a young woman called Ellie talking about a trip to southern Spain to see the Iberian lynx.

Interviewer: With me today is Ellie Johnson, who went to Spain with her university friend Marta to see the beautiful Iberian lynx, one of the world's rarest wildcats. So, Ellie, which location did you choose, and why?

Ellie: A place with a stream next to the forest, with plenty of rabbits. The huge fall in the number of rabbits is the main reason why the lynx is so rare, because an adult lynx needs to eat three rabbits a day. Marta knew the area but I didn't until I saw on TV photos of a lynx taken there a few days before.

Interviewer: How easy was it to get there?

Ellie: Well, it was summer and temperatures were really high during the daytime, so it made sense to set off really early – at five a.m. in fact, when it was still cool. The moon was bright, and we were pleased about that because it's easy to go in the wrong direction in the dark. The track was really challenging in places – it went up and down a lot. We didn't actually find it too exhausting, but it did mean we got to the stream later than we'd expected. Once we were there, we looked for somewhere to hide.

Interviewer: Where did you hide?

Ellie: There was an empty hut nearby but it was locked, so it looked like the best place was behind some large rocks. There was no shade there, though, so instead we lay down just inside the forest and waited. In fact, we waited there for ages. I was going to suggest leaving, when suddenly we heard something running through the bushes.

Interviewer: What was it?

Ellie: Well of course we hoped it'd be a lynx and we both grabbed our cameras, but it was just a frightened-looking little rabbit. Just then, though, another creature appeared, running after it. It was grey and brown, about the size of a small cat: it was a young lynx!

Interviewer: I can imagine your excitement! What did it do?

Ellie: Well, by then the rabbit was far away and the lynx's chance of catching it had gone so it stopped and looked around, though it didn't notice us. We were so busy taking photos of that cute little animal that we didn't see a much larger one approaching. It was an adult female, and clearly the little one was hers. That was why it had stopped.

Interviewer: How long did you stay there?

Ellie: The sun had almost set but we stayed another hour, taking photos of them until we couldn't see anything. Marta wanted to stay overnight to see them again at sunrise, but we didn't have a tent, so we set off, reaching the hostel just before midnight.

Unit 12, Student's Book p. 110, Listening Part 3, Exercise 4

Track 63

Narrator: Part 3. For each question, write the correct answer in the gap. Write one or two words or a number or a date or a time. You will hear a woman called Catherine Bryant talking about a competition on the radio.

Catherine: Let me tell you about an app design competition which will take place in Lisbon, Portugal from the sixth to the seventh of June. All you need to do is fill in an online form by the first of June. If your application is accepted, you should hear from us before the fourth of June.

On the day, you can take part alone or join one of the teams. You'll need to choose one of the challenges from a list of four and create an app which solves a problem. Last year's challenges were connected to the environment. For example, one of the challenge winners created an app which finds the nearest recycling bin for the rubbish you want to throw away. All I can say about this year is that the challenges have something to do with communication. The rest is a secret!

The competition judge is blogger Fran Maddison, that's M-A-D-D-I-S-O-N. She presents the 'Apps Programme' on Channel Seven. Her latest book *Apps are me* will be on sale soon.

There are some amazing prizes. There's €1,000 and a tablet for the best app for each challenge. The four winners will then compete in the final for the first prize which is an unbelievable trip to California.

You won't be able to bring your own food into the event, but reasonably priced refreshments will be available. You mustn't forget your laptop, but you'll be able to hire headphones and chargers there.

And finally, if you can't make the Conference Centre in Lisbon in June, consider the Grand Hotel in Prague in October. There'll be more information about this event on our website at the end of August.

Now, any questions?

Workbook Answer key with audioscripts Units 1–12

Unit 1

Vocabulary

1
1 duvet **2** pillow **3** sink **4** fridge
5 microwave **6** towel **7** mirror **8** tap

2
1 at **2** in **3** on **4** in **5** in **6** at **7** on **8** on

3
Countable: beach, bus, cooker, day, floor, friend, game, hall, house, tap, time (for occasions, eg *four times*)
Uncountable: electricity, food, furniture, homework, make-up, money, rain, shampoo, space, time (period of time)

Reading Part 5

1 C **2** A **3** D **4** B **5** C **6** B

Listening Part 2

1 B **2** A **3** C **4** B **5** C **6** C

Track 2
Narrator: For each question, choose the correct answer.

1
Narrator: You will hear a mother and her son talking about his old school books.
Boy: Mum, where should I put my old school books? I've hardly got any space, so I need to get rid of some.
Woman: Well, they are sometimes useful when you want to check something, but Aunt Sylvia asked me if we could let your cousin Harry have them this year.
Boy: That's not a bad idea. I can always borrow one back if I ever need it.
Woman: All right, just put them in the cupboard in the hall for the moment and I'll tell Sylvia to pick them up.
Boy: OK, Mum.

2
Narrator: You will hear a boy telling his friend about helping at home.
Girl: Hi, Luke. Shall we go into town this morning?
Boy: I'd love to, but my mum wants me to help her move stuff. She's clearing out the garage, and she can't do it by herself. We're going to look through all the old boxes of photos and toys. I'm actually looking forward to seeing what's there. It would be quicker if Jack helped, but he has to study for a university exam at a friend's house.
Girl: Yeah, my brother's always got an excuse too!
Boy: I think it's true this time! We can meet tomorrow, OK?

3
Narrator: You will hear two college students talking about a trip.
Woman: Hey Pete, are you coming on the trip to the mountains tomorrow?
Man: Well, I signed up for it and I even bought some new walking boots. Actually, I think they're a bit small, so I'll have to change them. But that's not important, because in the end I can't go.
Woman: Why not?
Man: I promised to take my girlfriend to see her parents. I got the wrong day when I told her about the trip and now I can't change anything.
Woman: That's a pity. But you've got those boots for the next time!
Man: I have!

4
Narrator: You will hear two friends talking about a TV series.
Man: I saw that new series last night. It was amazing!
Woman: I know, it's really interesting, isn't it? The things that happen seem so true to life – in fact, they're a bit like my family sometimes!
Man: You're not serious! They have too many problems to be true, but I agree the brother and sister play their parts really well.
Woman: Yeah, I think they're convincing. I'm looking forward to the next episode. I want to know what happens in the end to their friend who disappeared.
Man: I reckon the sister knows where he is.
Woman: We'll see if you're right next week!

5
Narrator: You will hear a woman talking to a friend about a house.
Man: So, how's your new house?
Woman: Well, it's OK. The kids have got their own rooms and my husband has put a gym in the garage. You know, with an exercise bike and other machines.
Man: Wow! That's great!
Woman: Yeah, but I prefer going out to the gym. It also means we have to leave the car outside. I don't really like leaving it on the street, especially because we live on a busy main road. I have to park it round the corner. But at least I can walk to the office.
Man: That's better than when you had to take the train every day!

6
Narrator: You will hear two friends talking about a shopping centre.
Woman: Have you been to the new shopping centre yet?
Man: Yes, I went yesterday. It's got loads of great shops, hasn't it?
Woman: Well, if you like clothes, but there isn't much else there. I think our area needs more places to eat and I expected a cinema or something for entertainment.
Man: You're right, but anyway, it's easy to get to on the bus and there's a car park.
Woman: True. It only took me ten minutes last Saturday, but I won't be going much. I prefer the local shops on the High Street.

Grammar

1
1 They occasionally eat in a restaurant.
2 I go skiing once a year.
3 He hardly ever takes photos on holiday.
4 I eat a good breakfast every day.
5 She doesn't often go on holiday abroad. / She doesn't often go abroad on holiday.
6 Some people read the newspaper almost every day.
7 I take my dog to the park most days.
8 They are never at home in the mornings.

2
1 b **2** c **3** c **4** c **5** b **6** a **7** a **8** a

3
1 is snowing **2** know **3** opens
4 hates **5** misses **6** wear
7 are growing **8** is learning **9** is getting
10 watch

4
1 am ('m) spending **2** feel **3** have
4 go **5** start **6** finish
7 attend **8** am ('m) not studying **9** am ('m) sitting
10 don't have **11** are ('re) doing **12** means
13 am ('m) taking **14** are you doing **15** Do you want

Writing Part 1

1
1 d **2** c **3** a **4** b

2
Inviting: Would you like to come to my party? Do you want to go to the theatre tonight?
Suggesting: Shall we go to the exhibition? Why don't we have a barbecue?
Asking for information: Which is the best place to visit? What kind of films do you like?

3 (*Sample answer*)

Dear Robin,

Thanks for your email and your invitation. Jack is very kind! I'd love to go on holiday with you to the coast.

I think the second week is better for me, if you don't mind. My father's birthday is on the 5th August and I want to be at home for that.

I don't often go to the beach, so I'd like to sunbathe and swim in the sea. We could also try some of the local food. You know I love going to restaurants.

Shall we get him some plates for the kitchen? My local shop sells some really nice ones.

I'm looking forward to seeing you.

Love,

Unit 2
Vocabulary

1
1 take, pass **2** fail **3** work, study, teach, learn
4 lose **5** set off, miss

2
1 ~~wins~~ → earns **2** ~~do~~ → make **3** ~~earn~~ → spend **4** ~~made~~ → did
5 ~~do~~ → spend **6** ~~spent~~ → took **7** ~~makes~~ → takes **8** ~~earned~~ → won

Reading Part 6

1 of **2** for **3** have (/) 've **4** the **5** but **6** me

Grammar

1
1 spent, took, Did (you) go, didn't have
2 got / did, Did (she) earn / make, had
3 went, Did (you) make, met
4 didn't do, made, didn't spend, had

2
1 used to enjoy **2** was giving, stopped **3** Did you spend
4 was raining, came **5** was talking, received **6** didn't use to let
7 was concentrating, didn't realise **8** decided, were shopping

3
1 set off **2** was shining **3** looked / was looking
4 arrived **5** was running **6** felt
7 stopped **8** noticed **9** were coming
10 didn't walk **11** began **12** was still raining
13 didn't matter **14** had **15** felt / were feeling

Listening Part 1

1 B **2** A **3** C **4** B **5** A **6** B **7** C

Track 3

Narrator: For each question, choose the correct answer.

1

Narrator: What job does the student want to do after university?

Man: It's really hard to decide what to do after university. As a kid I wanted to be a pilot. I thought engineering was good for that, but you need to train a lot after university, so now I'm not so keen. I like design but most jobs involve sitting in front of a computer all day, and I don't want to do that the rest of my life. I'm interested in helping others to learn, so I think I'll try to stay on where I am.

2

Narrator: Where are the woman's glasses?

Woman: Have you seen my glasses? I think I left them on the kitchen table last night, but they're not there now.

Man: You usually leave them in the bathroom when you're doing your make-up. Where did you have them yesterday?

Woman: I was on the computer after lunch, but in the evening I decided to read on the sofa downstairs for a while.

Man: Look, they're just where you were sitting yesterday evening!

3

Narrator: When do the students have to give their final presentation?

Girl: Hi Danny. I'm just phoning you because I was ill yesterday, and I missed the meeting about our final presentation. Did the teacher say when the presentation is?

Boy: Yes, she wanted us to do it next Tuesday but a lot of us have an exam that day, so she changed it to the end of the week.

Girl:	Oh, that's great. If it's on Friday, we'll have more time to prepare.
Boy:	Don't forget we've got to do our project work for Thursday morning as well.
Girl:	Oh no!

4

Narrator:	Which activity does the man recommend?
Woman:	What activity do you think I should do at the sports centre this year?
Man:	Well, last year I played badminton. It was a friendly group, but a lot of the adults stopped going, so there may be too many children.
Woman:	Hmm, that's not so good. I'd like to meet people as well as get some exercise.
Man:	In that case, kick-boxing is popular, especially with women.
Woman:	That sounds difficult.
Man:	Not really, and it helps reduce stress! You'll meet more people there than if you only do something like swimming on your own.

5

Narrator:	What did they do when it started to rain?
Man:	How was your trip to the mountains, Jenny?
Woman:	It was great at first. It was really hot, and we found a fantastic place to have lunch under some trees. But in the afternoon the weather changed, and it began to rain really hard. It was a long way to the car, but we found a cave where we waited for it to stop. The sun came out again on the way back, so we didn't get wet at all.

6

Narrator:	What was the first prize in the competition?
Woman:	Now, we have good news. The winner of our nature photography competition this year is Mark Young from Bristol University photography club. His photo of sunlight on the trees in the park means that the club will get a video camera. The second prize is cinema tickets for four people. This went to Jenny Jackson from Bath University for her photo of a snail. Thanks to all the university clubs that took part. They will all receive a certificate.

7

Narrator:	Why did the man go to bed late?
Woman:	You look tired, Sam. Did you go to bed late last night?
Man:	Yeah, I was watching that TV series about detectives in New York when my brother phoned.
Woman:	The one who lives in Australia?
Man:	That's right. He didn't remember that it was late for us, but anyway we were talking until after midnight.
Woman:	Is he OK?
Man:	He's having a great time although he's working hard in a restaurant every evening.

Writing Part 2 (An article)

1
What makes a good university or college, teachers, facilities, something else and the social activities a university or college should offer.

2
Tick 1, 3, 4, 5, 7 and 8

3
Students' own answers

4
1 opinion **2** sure **3** think / agree **4** agree

5 *Sample answer*

A good university

There are several reasons why a university or college is a good place to study. I think that the lectures are very important, but there are other things that make the experience special. For example, if you are studying science, it's good to have laboratories and equipment to do practical work.

However, in my opinion I think that one of the most important experiences at university is meeting other people, so the social activities it has are vital. Some people like sport, others like dancing. There should be activities for all kinds of people so that they can have fun after studying and make friends. (108)

Unit 3

Reading Part 3

1 C **2** D **3** B **4** A **5** B

Vocabulary

1

1 in front of	**2** above	**3** on / to	**4** behind
5 under	**6** between	**7** inside	**8** in

2

1 ran out of	**2** sign up	**3** hang on	**4** join in
5 give up	**6** set off	**7** go on	**8** look after

3
1 rides – cyclist **2** plays – (chess) player
3 takes – photographer **4** goes – diver **5** plays - musician

Listening Part 4

1 A **2** B **3** C **4** B **5** C **6** A

Track 4

Narrator:	For each question, choose the correct answer. You will hear a radio interview with a young magician called Megan.
Interviewer:	Today we're going to talk to a young woman with a very exciting hobby. During the day she works in an office, but in her spare time she's a very talented magician. Tell me, Megan. How did you become interested in magic?
Megan:	Well, my interest in magic began when I was only five years old and I got a magic game as a present. Then after seeing a magician at a birthday party when I was eight I knew that this was what I wanted to do. My friends used to call me Magic Megs and I became a member of a magician's club to learn more.
Interviewer:	What did you learn in the club?
Megan:	Of course, I learnt lots of new tricks. I also realised that not many girls did magic because everyone else there was a boy! I was amazed! I used to practise for hours every day, and I entered the Young Magician of the Year competition when I was 16. No girl had ever won this competition at the time, so I was really proud when I came second.
Interviewer:	So, do you work as a magician now?

Megan: Not often, it's not easy to earn enough money working as a magician, and I do have other interests apart from performing. I studied animal conservation at university, and during the day I work in an office helping with environmental projects. I can't do many shows because it takes me ages to prepare and practise for each one.

Interviewer: What do you think has been your greatest achievement?

Megan: I love my work helping animals and I got good qualifications from university, but I was so pleased and amazed when I was chosen to be the secretary of The Magic Circle, one of the most important magicians' clubs in the world. I was the first woman to be elected in an organisation that has traditionally been run by men.

Interviewer: What style of magic do you do?

Megan: Well, I like to combine magic with another of my hobbies, dancing. I've loved this since I was a child as well. Some magicians talk a lot when they're doing magic, but I prefer to perform with music and I like wearing fantastic costumes and make-up.

Interviewer: So, are you happy with your life now?

Megan: Well, … I'll worry about the future when it comes. I won't ever give up magic, but I love my job too. There's something magical about nature, perhaps more than any trick I could do. In both cases I feel I'm doing something good, making people happy when they see me perform and helping protect the world we live in when I'm at work.

Grammar

1
1 being **2** to meet **3** to go **4** to drive **5** doing
6 reading **7** seeing **8** speaking **9** to come

2
1 a **2** b **3** b **4** a

3
1 meeting **2** taking **3** to eat **4** to ask
5 to bring **6** to put **7** going **8** dancing

Writing Part 2 (A story)

1
Students' own answers

2
Example A is better. It answers the questions in Exercise 1. In example B, the second sentence does not follow on logically from the given sentence because it doesn't talk about anything amazing but rather it describes a normal situation.

3–5 *Sample answer*

I walked into the room and everyone stopped talking. All my family were there in the living room and they looked at me in surprise. I didn't know why.

I sat down and said, 'What's the matter?' My mother said, 'James, what happened to your hair?' I went out to the hall and looked in the mirror. My hair was green! Then, I remembered washing my hair with a new shampoo the night before.

I went back into the room and saw my little sister laughing. She showed me a little green bottle and ran out of the living room. I ran after her, really angry.

Unit 4

Grammar

1
1 freezing **2** totally **3** absolutely
4 extremely **5** bad

2
1 best **2** quick **3** easiest
4 earlier **5** more important **6** worst

3
1 ~~more~~ **2** ~~that~~ → than **3** ~~larger~~ → largest
4 ~~longer~~ → long **5** ~~thing~~ → things

4
1 a lot / far / much smaller
2 as far … as
3 much / far / a lot more expensive than
4 as big as
5 a bit / a little / slightly longer … than
6 much / far / a lot later than
7 much / far / a lot nearer … than
8 a bit / a little / slightly cheaper than
9 as small as

Reading Part 1

1 C **2** A **3** B **4** A **5** C

Vocabulary

1
1 b **2** c **3** f **4** d **5** h **6** a **7** g **8** e

2 (*suggested answers*)

wildlife holiday	camping trip	city break	beach holiday
enjoy nature see animals	make a fire sleep in a tent	buy souvenirs go sightseeing	go snorkelling sunbathe

3
1 journey **2** trip **3** travel **4** travel
5 journey **6** trips

Listening Part 3

1 / one / an hour **2** music **3** tents
4 (fantastic) robots **5** Monday(s) **6** T-shirts

Track 5

Narrator: For each question, write the correct answer in the gap. Write one or two words or a number or a date or a time. You will hear a guide talking about tours of a film studio.

Guide: This week we have three different tours for you to try. They are all based on films made in these studios.
First, the *Robert the Bruce* tour, especially popular with fans of history. There's an hour-long tour in the morning at ten. You'll visit the palace built for the film and you can use headphones to hear actors' voices from different moments in the story. Afterwards, there's a 15-minute documentary about the different places

where the film is set, with fantastic scenes of mountains in Scotland and life in the old city of York, accompanied by music from the film.

Another exciting tour is to the Native American camp that was built for *The Totem Men* – the film about the history of Native Americans in the northwest USA. This tour takes 30 minutes and you go into tents where you watch actors cooking, making clothes and preparing to hunt, showing you how families lived at that time.

Finally, our most popular tour is the 45-minute visit to the science-fiction world of *Ricky Ranger*. You will love this tour because you can see inside Ricky's spaceship and meet some of the team that made the film. They'll explain how the fantastic robots in the film were created using the latest Japanese technology.

If you want to complete your day with a meal, visit our Oakwood cafeteria. We serve healthy salads and burgers every day except Mondays. On Wednesdays there's a special offer of two pizzas for one. Don't forget to visit our gift shop to pick up a free poster. We also sell a wide range of T-shirts for children and adults. Finally, you can collect the photos of your visit from the office by the entrance.

We look forward to welcoming you to the studio soon.

Writing Part 1

1
Tick 1, 2, 4, 6 and 7

2
1 pretty **2** amazing **3** excellent / amazing
4 delicious **5** clean / warm **6** long
7 historic / pretty / amazing / fascinating

3
1 ~~absolutely~~ → extremely **2** fasinating → fascinating
3 ~~amazed~~ → amazing **4** ~~historical~~ → historic
5 ~~beatiful~~ → beautiful **6** ~~a bit~~

4 *Sample answer*

Dear Toni,

It's fantastic you are going to visit my country as it's an amazing place and there are a lot of exciting things to do. The only problem is that it's enormous, so you can't see it all!

I think the best place to go is the south coast. It has a lot of historic villages, with lovely white houses, and there are monuments from ancient times, which you can visit.

It also has some wonderful beaches where you can go swimming and diving, and you can go on a boat trip to the beautiful islands together.

I hope you enjoy it!

Love,

Unit 5

Vocabulary

1
1 disappointed **2** jealous **3** mean
4 afraid **5** embarrassed **6** fond
7 nervous **8** ashamed

2
1 angry with **2** afraid of **3** bored with/of
4 ashamed of **5** pleased with **6** depressed about
7 sure of/about **8** crazy about

3
1 generous **2** miserable **3** funny
4 complicated **5** fantastic **6** positive
7 relaxed **8** ordinary

4
1 a boring **b** bored **2 a** embarrassing **b** embarrassed
3 a relaxing **b** relaxed **4 a** excited **b** exciting
5 a amusing **b** amused

Reading Part 4

1
Yes, the writer enjoyed the experience.

2
1 G **2** D **3** H **4** A **5** B

Grammar

1
1 could, can't **2** can, might **3** can't, might
4 may, might **5** Can, can

2
1 shouldn't **2** mustn't **3** have to
4 ought to **5** don't have to **6** must

Listening Part 2

1 C **2** B **3** A **4** C **5** B **6** C

Track 6

Narrator: For each question, choose the correct answer.

1

Narrator: You will hear two friends talking about a basketball match.
Woman: Hi, Jake, did you go to the match yesterday?
Man: Yeah, but it was a bit disappointing.
Woman: Why, what happened?
Man: Well, it was quite exciting to begin with, but then Sam Turner fell and hurt his leg. He's going to be off playing for a month – just when we need him for the final next week. You know he's our star player.
Woman: Did your team win?
Man: Only by one point. They usually play much better than that.

2

Narrator: You will hear a woman talking to a friend about moving home.
Man: Hi Amelia. I haven't seen you for ages! Are you enjoying sharing a flat at university?
Woman: Well, it's not bad. The flat is nice and although the bedrooms are fairly small, mine's fine.
Man: Have you seen your friends much, now you're living in a different place?
Woman: You know, before I moved I thought that might be a problem, but we're right next to the station and there's a direct train back to my home town as well as buses to the city centre, so I needn't have worried. We all met up last weekend, which was fun.

3

Narrator: You will hear a student talking to a friend about a website.

Man: Hey Jasmin, you know that project on pollution in cities we have to do next week?

Woman: Yeah. I'm worried about where to get information. It's not easy to find what we need.

Man: Well, I think I've found the perfect place. It's a site for students, and it's got pictures we're allowed to download for university work.

Woman: Great! So we can use those for the presentation. What about the text we have to write?

Man: The website can help with that too because there are sections about nearly all the cities in our project.

Woman: So we only have to find a bit of information somewhere else.

Man: That's right.

4

Narrator: You will hear two friends talking about a party.

Man: The party at Leo's house was fun, wasn't it?

Woman: Yeah, I had a great time, good food, good music and you know I love dancing.

Man: I know! You didn't stop most of the evening. It was tiring just watching you!

Woman: Well, I did talk to people too. Did you chat to Lucy. She told me all about her trip to India last year. It was fascinating.

Man: No, but I met a boy from Germany who is here for a month staying with Kevin.

Woman: Oh, I could have practised speaking German with him.

Man: You were too busy dancing!

5

Narrator: You will hear a student telling a friend about a board game.

Girl: My cousins came over yesterday and brought that new board game. You know, the one everyone is crazy about.

Boy: Oh yeah, it's great. I played it at Ryan's house all afternoon last Sunday.

Girl: That's the problem. It takes *hours* to play it, so you can't do anything else, and people take ages to decide their next move while everyone else just waits. Still, they're all trying to distract each other by chatting about different things, which is quite funny. My cousins have been playing it for the last month, so they're real experts, but I had to really concentrate.

6

Narrator: You will hear two friends talking about a sports centre.

Man: I went to the new sports centre last week. Have you been?

Woman: Yes, I think it's amazing. There's lots to do and it's not too expensive.

Man: The classes aren't that cheap. I wanted to do Pilates, but I don't think I can afford it.

Woman: Still, there's lots on offer and the booking system is so efficient it's easy to sign up for whatever you want.

Man: That's true. I also met some of the trainers, who were very friendly.

Woman: But the receptionist is a bit rude, don't you think? She didn't smile once and ignored me when I asked for information.

Writing Part 2 (A story)

1

Place(s): at work / on holiday / at home / in a sports match
People: my husband / a teacher / a shop assistant / my family / a police officer / a friend / my wife
Problem(s): I lost something / I forgot something / I missed the bus/train / I broke something
Feelings: angry / miserable / sad / nervous / depressed / embarrassed / disappointed

2

1 E **2** A **3** D **4** B **5** C

3 *Suggested answers*

1 nervous **2** angry **3** embarrassed

4 *Sample answer*

I remember the day I met my hero. It was a beautiful day. My best friend and I wanted to climb the mountain behind my house, so we left early in the morning with sandwiches and water in our rucksacks.

At about 12 o'clock we were feeling hungry and tired, so we stopped to have a rest. Suddenly, we heard a voice singing. The sound was coming from the trees behind us. It was a wonderful sound. We stood up and went to see who it was.

What a surprise! It was my favourite singer. He was walking in the mountains, too. I was so excited because he's always been my hero.

Unit 6

Vocabulary

1

1 quiz show **2** the news **3** comedy series
4 cooking show **5** reality show **6** wildlife documentary
7 sports programme

2

1 perform **2** book **3** screen
4 subtitles **5** admission **6** stage
7 Refreshments **8** interval **9** live
10 tickets

3

1 known; met **2** got to know him **3** gone
4 been **5** been **6** found out

Reading Part 2

1 D **2** H **3** E **4** C **5** B

Grammar

1

1 for **2** already **3** just **4** since **5** yet
6 already **7** just **8** yet

2

1 have you known **2** took **3** haven't been
4 learnt/learned **5** have ('ve) told **6** went

3

1 ~~have had~~ → had **2** ~~He's bought the tickets yet~~ → He's already bought the tickets / He hasn't bought the tickets yet.
3 ~~gone~~ → been **4** ~~are~~ → have been **5** ~~know~~ → have / 've known
6 They **have** / **'ve** already seen the film.

Listening Part 1

1A 2C 3B 4A 5C 6B 7A

Track 7

Narrator: For each question, choose the correct answer.

1

Narrator: Which programme did the man enjoy?

Man: I saw a great programme on TV yesterday.

Woman: Was it that new comedy?

Man: Well, I started watching that, but it wasn't very funny, so I switched channels and saw something else. It was a competition between four people to see who could make the best cake, but at the same time they had to explain what they were doing.

Woman: So you learnt something useful as well?

Man: Yes, the winner could answer all the questions about how to do it well. It was good, so I might make one myself.

2

Narrator: How much did the ticket cost?

Woman: Did you get a ticket for the concert?

Man: Yes, I got it online. It was quite expensive. I didn't want to pay £30, but there were no cheaper tickets.

Woman: I thought they cost £20. That's what the advert said.

Man: That was the one I wanted to get, but there weren't any left. Actually, that was all the money I had, so my sister lent me some money. Now I have to give her £10 back when I get paid next week.

Woman: Never mind. It'll be worth it!

3

Narrator: Where does the woman want to watch the football match?

Man: Are you going to watch the match on Saturday? I've got tickets for the game.

Woman: I'm not keen on watching it live because you can't see so well and it's cold at the moment. Anyway, I've already told Ollie that I'm going to watch it at his house. He's got a big-screen TV, so we can see it really well there. Last time, I tried watching the final on my computer, but my internet connection isn't good, so I missed the second half.

Man: How annoying!

4

Narrator: Which shirt does the man buy?

Shop assistant: Can I help you?

Man: Yes, I'm looking for a present for my brother. I think he'd like a shirt.

Shop assistant: What about this one? We've got it in all sizes.

Man: Well ... he doesn't like stripes, and I think it's too formal. Have you got anything with short sleeves?

Shop assistant: There's this one that has two colours or this other plain one.

Man: Have you got the plain one in a small size?

Shop assistant: Oh, I'm sorry, we haven't. We may get some more soon.

Man: It's for tomorrow, so I'll take the other short-sleeved one then.

5

Narrator: Who is the man's tennis coach?

Man: Look over there, Sal. There's my new tennis coach.

Woman: Where? Is he the one with glasses and a black jacket?

Man: No, he's much older than that. Remember I told you he's been teaching at another club for years. He's the one with the beard and glasses.

Woman: Oh yes, he's talking on his phone.

Man: Yeah. He does that in our lessons as well! I'm not too happy about it.

Woman: Oh, that's a pity. It's hard to find good coaches, isn't it?

Man: Yeah!

6

Narrator: What has the girl forgotten?

Woman: Hi Mum, it's Laura. I'm on the coach with the rest of the team, but I've got a bit of a problem. The thing is I think I've left my swimming costume at home. I remember seeing it on the bed with my towel, but I don't remember putting it in my sports bag. I looked in my bag to check I'd got my ticket, and that was when I realised. Is there any chance you could bring it to the pool for me? *Please.* Can you call me as soon as possible?

7

Narrator: When did the concert finish?

Man: How was the concert yesterday?

Woman: It was good, but we didn't get home until really late, about midnight, I think.

Man: Oh, I thought it started quite early.

Woman: Yes, but they had a problem with the sound system at the concert, so it didn't end until 11, and then I had to wait half an hour for the bus. Luckily, I was with Hannah, so I didn't have to wait on my own.

Man: That's good, but you must be tired today.

Woman: Yes, I am!

Writing Part 2 (An article)

1

1 Have you ever seen a live basketball match?

2 Why do people like going to the cinema at the weekend?

3 Do you prefer going out or staying at home on a Saturday night? / Do you prefer staying at home or going out on a Saturday night?

2

A 3 **B** 2 **C** 1

3

1 TV and film (cinema) **2** He talks about watching a comedy show with his wife, and about why he enjoys going to the cinema.
3 a question at the beginning of the article

4 *Sample answer*

Do you like Saturday nights? I do, because there is always something fun to do.

A great way to spend the evening is going to watch sport. In my town there is always a football or basketball match at the sports centre. The atmosphere is exciting and I can meet my friends there.

If you want to watch a film, I think it is better to go to the cinema. You can go with family or friends, it doesn't matter. Don't you like eating popcorn and watching a romantic film? The big screen is amazing and much better than sitting at home alone.

Going out on Saturday night is fantastic!

Unit 7

Reading Part 1

1 C **2** A **3** B **4** A **5** C

Vocabulary

1

1 frost **2** showers **3** foggy **4** ice
5 freezing **6** thunderstorms **7** rainy **8** sunshine
9 windy **10** snowy

2

1 sunny **2** temperature **3** thunderstorm
4 freezing **5** weather **6** raining
7 foggy **8** lightning

3

1 signpost; crossroads **2** sightseeing; guidebook; suitcases
3 overnight; campsite; backpack

Listening Part 4

1 A **2** B **3** A **4** C **5** A **6** C

Track 8

Narrator: For each question, choose the correct answer. You will hear an interview with a student called Adam, who is going on a trip to the desert this summer.

Interviewer: Good morning. Today we're going to talk to Adam Gill, who has come to tell us about his plans for this summer. Adam, I've heard that you're going to the desert.

Adam: Yes, I'm going to spend two weeks in the Sahara Desert in Morocco with a group from university. We're all medical students, and we'd like to learn how the people there manage their health in difficult conditions. There are plans to build a new medical centre there because the current building is rather old and not big enough for all the patients.

Interviewer: And what's your job going to be?

Adam: Well, I'm the official photographer! My plan is to take photos and make a video there. We want to show people back home what's happening and try to raise money for the medical centre. I'll start from when we get off the plane, although the longest part of the journey will be overnight in a lorry, so I don't suppose I'll be able to do much then.

Interviewer: And will you need a lot of equipment?

Adam: Not really. A friend has lent me a video camera – it works better than my phone – and I've got a great digital camera that my parents gave me. I'll have to be careful though, because it might be hard to charge the batteries. I think the power is only on for a few hours in the evening.

Interviewer: Will you need anything else? If it's hot, you won't need heavy clothes.

Adam: Well, it does get quite cold at night, so I'll have to take a warm jacket, but I won't take many clothes. It's more the heat of the day that worries me because we have to wear long-sleeved shirts to protect ourselves from the sun.

Interviewer: What about food?

Adam: I've heard that Moroccan food is delicious, but the desert area is very dry and not much grows there. Most of our food will come with us in the lorry, so we don't use what little food the local people have there.

Interviewer: So, are you excited about the trip?

Adam: Of course! But I'm a bit nervous as well. I'm really not sure what it'll be like. It'll be my first time abroad, in fact, but a friend who went last year has told me the people are really friendly, even though he couldn't speak their language. He said if you don't mind not having a comfortable bed, then it's an amazing experience.

Grammar

1

1 too hot **2** old enough **3** too far
4 clever enough **5** too dark **6** warm enough
7 too small **8** too many

2

1 fairly **2** really **3** quite **4** really

3

1 into **2** out of **3** by **4** on **5** on **6** off

4

1 I'll bring **2** starts **3** I'm playing **4** is going to get
5 does your train arrive **6** I'll see

5

1 am ('m) going to see **2** will ('ll) get **3** am ('m) going to visit
4 will ('ll) help **5** will ('ll) call **6** will ('ll) have

Writing Part 1

1

1 to **2** sunny **3** for **4** sunglasses
5 will ('ll) be / would be / could be **6** saw
7 in **8** will ('ll) buy

2 *Sample answer*

Hi Alex,

It was great to hear from you. Thanks for reminding me about Lucy's birthday! I like your ideas, but it's better to go to your house because I think the restaurant will be too expensive for some people. I'm going to the cinema on Sunday afternoon, but I'm free on Saturday. Is that a good day for you?

I'm not sure what we can give Lucy. I know she likes music. Maybe we can buy her an Ed Sheeran CD because he's her favourite singer. I can go to the music shop tomorrow. Do you want to come with me?

Lots of love,

Unit 8

Vocabulary

1

1 make up **2** brought up **3** grew up **4** ran out of
5 got on **6** found out **7** took up **8** set up

2
1 strict **2** lazy **3** clever **4** quiet
5 generous **6** rude **7** anxious **8** confident

3
1 cheerful **2** unreliable **3** helpless **4** beautiful
5 unpleasant **6** dishonest **7** successful **8** helpful
9 impatient **10** unfriendly

4
1 long, straight, dark **2** short, curly, broad **3** blonde, pale
4 wavy, grey, beard **5** bald, moustache

Reading Part 6

1 how **2** If **3** has **4** them **5** than **6** at

Grammar

1
1 gets (1) **2** would ('d) tell (2) **3** go (1)
4 Would you travel (2) **5** will give (1) **6** wakes up (0)
7 wouldn't do (2) **8** find (0)

2
1 If **2** unless **3** if **4** when
5 unless **6** when **7** when **8** unless

3
1 g – if **2** f – unless **3** d – unless **4** c – if / when
5 b – when **6** e – if / when **7** a – unless **8** h – unless

4
1 ~~came~~ → come **2** ~~Did~~ → Would **3** ~~Unless~~ → If / ~~has~~ – hasn't
4 ~~doesn't~~ → didn't / ~~she'd~~ → she'll **5** ~~will~~ → would / ~~won~~ → wins
6 ~~When~~ → If

Listening Part 3

1 Wales **2** shape **3** chemicals
4 (five-litre) boxes **5** 25,000 **6** supermarkets

Track 9

Narrator: For each question, write the correct answer in the gap. Write one or two words or a number or a date or a time. You will hear a lecturer talking to a group of students about a young couple who have set up a fruit juice business.

Lecturer: Maciek and Karina are two young entrepreneurs who are running a fruit juice business. Although they are originally from Poland and Lithuania, they studied for their degrees in Wales. Then they decided to stay there and start their own company because the business opportunities were better than back home.

The idea for their business began when they realised that a lot of fruit was being wasted because it's too small, too big or it isn't the right shape for sale in shops. This fruit tastes fine and gives the juice its natural colour, but farmers can't sell it directly to supermarkets and greengrocers. This means they often have to throw away a lot of their produce.

So the young couple decided to use this fruit to make juice. This has helped the farmers and provides a healthy fruit drink made from apples or strawberries. The company only uses natural ingredients and the juices are free of chemicals.

Maciek and Karina are also concerned about other environmental issues, such as the containers the juice comes in, so the juices are delivered in glass bottles that can be recycled. When they set up the business, in 2016, they sold juice in five-litre boxes, but then they changed to glass to reduce plastic waste.

They started the business by asking for help online and they received £2,500 in gifts from people who liked their idea. Later, they won £5,000 prize money for a business competition. After this, they were successful in getting a loan of £25,000 from a government organisation so the business could really begin to grow.

At the moment most of their customers are restaurants and catering companies, but they hope to expand to supermarkets in the future. They also support food charities because the aim of the company is to make not only money but also a better world.

Writing Part 2 (An article)

1
Spelling: 1 ~~ofen~~ → often **2** ~~funn~~ → fun **3** ~~Fisics~~ → Physics
4 ~~habilities~~ → abilities **5** ~~freind~~ → friend
Punctuation: 1 ~~dont~~ → don't **2** ~~england~~ → England
3 ~~holiday's~~ → holidays **4** *habilities → habilities,* **5** ~~Hes~~ – He's

2 *Sample answer*

I am lucky because I have lots of friends. A good friend is kind and helpful when you have problems. A good friend can be smarter than you or not as clever as you, but he or she always has time to listen. Sometimes, I just need someone to talk to.

I think you can relax with a good friend. You can just be together and have fun. It doesn't matter where or when. My friends don't all have the same hobbies. I like people that are different from me, who can give me new ideas or show me a new activity.

Unit 9

Listening Part 2

1 A **2** B **3** A **4** B **5** C **6** A

Track 10

Narrator: For each question, choose the correct answer.

1

Narrator: You will hear a man talking to a friend about their exercise class.

Woman: Hi Josh. What happened to you last Monday? You didn't come to the yoga class.

Man: Yeah, I'd had flu the weekend before, but because I was feeling better that day I thought I'd go. Then I got a message from my son to say his car had broken down, so I had to go and pick him up. I took me longer than I expected, and it was too late to go by the time I got home.

Woman: Oh no! Are you coming tonight? I can give you a lift if you want.

Man: That would be great, thanks.

2

Narrator: You will hear two friends talking about a table tennis competition.

Man: You know there's a table tennis competition next Saturday. Do you want to be my partner?

Woman: I'm not sure. You're much better than me.

Man: Oh, come on. Anyway, it's not about winning. We'll all play a few games and there's food and drink. Everyone from the club will be there.

Woman: I haven't seen some of them for ages, so that'll be fun.

Man: Yeah, I usually spend Saturday mornings cleaning the house, so it'll be good for me to do something different too.

3

Narrator: You will hear a woman telling her friend about a football match she went to.

Man: Hi Lizzie, how was the match on Saturday?

Woman: Well, it was OK, but I was a bit disappointed.

Man: Why? What happened? Did your team lose?

Woman: Yes, but that wasn't the problem. It was raining the whole match too, but luckily we had seats under cover so we kept dry. The thing is my brother had invited one of his friends to come with us and he spent the whole match shouting in my ear. I couldn't concentrate on the game and nearly missed the goal our team scored.

Man: What do you expect at a football match? Maybe you should watch it on television next time!

4

Narrator: You will hear two friends talking about a trip to an art gallery.

Man: So what did you think of the art gallery?

Woman: Well, I had a good time in the end. But I thought the summer exhibition of modern art would be better. I've seen a few of the pictures in other shows.

Man: Oh, I missed it last year, so I thought the art was pretty unusual. That guide gave us some useful information, she told us more than just the name of the artist and the date. But I didn't think the pictures were organised very well.

Woman: True. It wasn't always easy to see with those lights, but she did make it more entertaining.

5

Narrator: You will hear a boy talking to his mother.

Man: Hi, Mum. I'm home!

Woman: Where have you been? I was getting worried.

Man: I'm really sorry. I had a problem with my phone. I put it in my coat pocket and left it in the locker in the changing room when we went to play badminton. Harry's brother gave me a lift to the station and we were halfway there when I remembered my coat. By then it was too late to go back because the sports centre had closed. Plus the train was late and no one would let me use their phone to call you.

6

Narrator: You will hear two friends talking about going skiing.

Man: Hi Alicia, guess what! I'm going skiing this weekend! What do I need to take?

Woman: Well, warm clothes, especially gloves and a hat. I don't think you need to get any expensive equipment until you know if you like it or not. You can rent skis quite cheaply.

Man: I'm scared I might break a leg, or crash into someone and hurt them.

Woman: Don't worry. If you don't mind falling sometimes – beginners always do – and just relax, you won't hurt yourself. As for other people, if they can ski better than you, then they have to move out of your way.

Vocabulary

1

1 beat, football **2** drew, athletics **3** bat, baseball
4 gloves, skiing **5** racket, tennis **6** score, volleyball

2

1 bike **2** rollerblading **3** skateboard
4 surfers **5** exercise **6** Mountain biking
7 breath **8** exhausted

3

1 b **2** d **3** c **4** g **5** h **6** a **7** e **8** f

Reading Part 3

1 C **2** D **3** C **4** B **5** D

Grammar

1

1 who/that **2** whose **3** when **4** who
5 where **6** which

2

1 who/that lives in the flat next door.
2 whose mother was my nurse in hospital.
3 when our team won the cup.
4 where my parents got married.
5 who is a pilot

3

1 ~~which~~ → who / that **2** students **who** / **that** use
3 ~~there~~ **4** ~~her~~ **5** ~~who's~~ → whose

4

1 had('d) had **2** had('d) finished / finished
3 did you go **4** had seen **5** got **6** had('d) hurt

Writing Part 2 (A story)

1

1 when **2** then **3** Luckily **4** after
5 Suddenly **6** finally

2 *Sample answer*

Sam was both anxious and excited when he left the house. He and his brother got into the car and drove to the mountains because today was the first time he was going to compete in a snowboarding competition.

When they arrived, he put on his helmet and gloves and went to the start of the race. He heard the bell and went down the mountain. He was snowboarding very well, and he was feeling confident, when suddenly he fell. His leg really hurt, and he couldn't move. A doctor came and said, 'I think you've broken a bone.' She called a helicopter, which took him to hospital. Poor Sam! He couldn't walk for six weeks.

Unit 10

Reading Part 2

1 E **2** H **3** D **4** A **5** F

Vocabulary

1
1 meal **2** main **3** courses **4** dish **5** food
6 dessert **7** products **8** light

2
1 library **2** garage **3** bakery / baker's
4 chemist's / pharmacy **5** bookstore / bookshop
6 hairdresser's **7** dentist's **8** dry cleaner's

3
1 borrow **2** book **3** make **4** buy **5** complain

Grammar

1
1 have my car cleaned
2 have their kitchen painted
3 has her shopping brought
4 are having their wedding cake made
5 have a photo of the family taken
6 have her meals prepared

2
1 think **2** Don't invite **3** accept **4** Send
5 Buy **6** Make **7** don't forget

Listening Part 1

1 C **2** A **3** B **4** C **5** A **6** B **7** C

Track 11

Narrator: For each question, choose the correct answer.

1

Narrator: What was the man unhappy with at the restaurant?
Man: You know, I don't think I'll go back to that new restaurant again.
Woman: Why's that? I heard it was quite good.
Man: Well, actually the food wasn't bad. We had some delicious chicken and chips, but the service wasn't great. They took ages to bring our meal, and when we complained, the waiter said he was very busy. When we finally got the bill it wasn't too expensive, but we'd been there for *two hours*.

2

Narrator: Where is the girl going?
Girl: Hi Dad, I'm just calling you to let you know my plans. You know I wanted to go to the concert this evening? Well, it's been cancelled, so Lily and I thought we'd go shopping. There's a new music shop in the shopping centre, not far from the hairdresser's where Mum goes. I want to get something for Richard's birthday. The thing is, it's raining a lot now. Can you pick me up outside the shopping centre at 8.30? Please!

3

Narrator: What did the man forget?
Man: I didn't think it would be so hot today. I'm boiling.
Woman: You really should wear something on your head. The sun is very strong.
Man: I know, I put my cap out next to my rucksack this morning, but now I can't find it.
Woman: Have you looked in the side pocket where you've got your water bottle?
Man: Ah yes, it's here. But my sunglasses aren't.
Woman: Well, the cap will protect your eyes a bit anyway.
Man: I suppose so, but it's annoying I left them at home.

4

Narrator: What does the man want to borrow?
Man: Hi Zoe. How's things?
Woman: Fine. What a surprise!
Man: Well, er, I'm calling to ask you a favour.
Woman: Yeah sure, what is it?
Man: Have you got a sleeping bag I could use? I'm going on a camping trip. My sister's lent me her cooking equipment, so I've got everything else.
Woman: I suppose so, but you will give it back, won't you? I think you've still got the torch I lent you two months ago.
Man: Oh dear, I'm sorry. I'll give both things back after the trip, I promise.

5

Narrator: How much will the woman pay for the meal?
Woman: That was an amazing meal! Let's get the bill, shall we?
Man: OK. ... Excuse me, could we have the bill, please?
Waiter: Here you are, sir. That'll be £45.40.
Woman: Right, so we'll pay half each. Let me do the maths. That's umm £22.70, then.
Man: I had a dessert, so I'll put in £5 more. Your share is £17.70.
Woman: That seems fair. It isn't expensive at all here, is it?

6

Narrator: Where does the man need to go first this afternoon?
Woman: Do you want to meet for a coffee this afternoon? I haven't seen you for ages.
Man: I'd love to, but I've got lots to do. I've got to meet my younger brother straight after he finishes school and take him to have his hair cut, and we have to go to the shopping centre before that to get him some new trainers.
Woman: What about later on then? We could have a pizza instead?
Man: That sounds like a good plan.

7

Narrator: Which film does the reviewer recommend?

Reviewer: There are three new films on at the Central cinema this week. *West Texas* is a classic cowboy movie, but I was disappointed by the story, which had no new ideas. If you're a fan of science fiction, as I am, then you'll love *The Time Traveller* with its adventures of a boy who finds himself living on the moon. The film *Happy Day* follows the life of a footballer, which some people might enjoy – I found it rather long.

Writing Part 2 (An article)

1

1 c **2** a, f, i **3** e **4** d, g **5** b, h

2

No, he didn't answer about the amount of sleep.

3 *Sample answer*

Everyone knows it is important to have a healthy lifestyle because then you have a better life and enjoy yourself.

If you sleep well for enough time, you wake up feeling good. Exercise is essential as well. You should walk everywhere if you can and doing a sport is good for your mind and body.

I think the most important way to be healthy is to eat the right food. You should have a diet that includes different types of food and drink lots of water.

If you can eat well sleep enough and have fun doing exercise, you will be healthy and happy.

Unit 11
Listening Part 4

1

1 C **2** B **3** A **4** B **5** A **6** B

Track 12

Narrator: For each question, choose the correct answer. You will hear an interview with a young man from Bermuda called Magnus, who helps protect the oceans and the wildlife in them.

Interviewer: Today we're talking to Magnus Henneberger, who lives on Bermuda, an island in the Mid-Atlantic. So Magnus, when did you first become interested in the sea and marine wildlife?

Magnus: Well, we'd been reading about it in class at school. Then someone from an environmental organisation came and gave a presentation about the amount of plastic in the ocean and what they're trying to do about it. I was really impressed and registered to become a member.

Interviewer: What was the first thing you did after you joined the organisation?

Magnus: We had to go out on a paddle board – that's like a surfboard – on a lake. We attached a kind of net to the board and collected plants and pieces of plastic. These went to a laboratory to be tested in order to find out which things were contaminating the water.

Interviewer: What did you learn from this?

Magnus: We found very small pieces of plastic called microbeads that are used in everyday things like toothpaste and skin-care products. These aren't thrown away. We use them on ourselves and they get into water when we wash. We think these won't hurt anything because we use them on our bodies, but the plastic gets into rivers and is washed out to sea. This is very dangerous because marine animals, especially fish, eat them and sometimes die, and if humans eat contaminated animals they can become ill as well.

Interviewer: What advice would you give people about helping to protect marine life?

Magnus: I've actually started a campaign to tell people not to buy some beauty products. When you buy creams and liquids, check on the label that they are not made with microbeads. It's better to have less smooth skin than end up with no life in the sea.

Interviewer: So, what has been your greatest achievement so far?

Magnus: We have regular beach-cleaning days, and I think we're beginning to make a difference, but I felt most proud when our local aquarium decided to display my sculpture. I'd made it from objects that I'd collected on the beach. Now all the tourists that visit can see how we're polluting our planet.

Interviewer: And what do you want to do next?

Magnus: Well, there are some charities which have some great environmental projects that I would love to take part in. But before that, of course, I need to get a degree in environmental science. Afterwards, I would love to come back to the island and carry on my work here.

Interviewer: Thank you, Magnus, and good luck!

Grammar

1

1 was stolen **2** aren't used **3** were woken up
4 are often hunted **5** was watched **6** was created
7 wasn't blown down **8** are protected

2

1 When was the aquarium built?
2 When was the environmental organisation set up?
3 Where is the rubbish taken for recycling? / Where is the rubbish for recycling taken?
4 When were the results given to the students?
5 What are the machines used for?
6 How are the animals captured?
7 Were you brought up in the countryside?
8 Are the animals well looked after / looked after well in the zoo? / Are the animals in the zoo well looked after / looked after well?

3

1 is ('s) used **2** is ('s) not protected **3** were cut down
4 was built **5** was set up **6** were picked up
7 are not / aren't prevented **8** is ('s) read

4

1 When was **that photograph taken**? **2** ~~paint~~ → painted **3** ~~was~~
4 ~~been~~ **5** ~~writen~~ → written **6** garden **is** / **was** surrounded

5

1 the fastest **2** better **3** more quietly
4 more carefully **5** more slowly **6** more easily
7 the hardest **8** the worst

Vocabulary

1

								K
	P	E	N	G	U	I	N	A
T		C			O			N
I		A			S			G
G		M	B		T			A
E		E	E		R			R
R	F	L	A	M	I	N	G	O
			R		C			O
	E	L	E	P	H	A	N	T

1 elephant **2** camel **3** flamingo **4** tiger
5 ostrich **6** penguin **7** bear **8** kangaroo

2
1 confirmation **2** discussion **3** invitation
4 Pollution **5** replacement **6** translation
7 excitement **8** development **9** reservation
10 exploration

3
1 announcement **2** education **3** completion
4 inventions **5** disappointment **6** entertainment

Reading Part 5

1 D **2** A **3** C **4** A **5** B **6** C

Writing Part 1

1
1 that I have a few days off
2 accept the invitation; which activity you prefer; why I don't need boots; a suggestion about something else to do

2
1 I'd love **2** haven't had **3** did **4** have already grown
5 love **6** is **7** I'll be

3
No, he forgot to mention the boots.

4 *Sample answer*

Hi Freddie,

Thanks for your invitation for this weekend. It's a brilliant idea! It will be great to see you after so long.

I'd like to do both activities with the environmental club, but it might be more fun to work in the river because we can see more wildlife there. Are there any fish? I don't need to borrow boots since I've got special ones that I use for fishing.

On Saturday night we could go out to eat. I'd like to invite you to a good dinner! There's an excellent Italian restaurant near your house, isn't there?

See you soon!

Cheers,

Unit 12

Listening Part 3

1 (TV) studio **2** May **3** beauty
4 clothes **5** show **6** using lights

Track 13

Narrator: For each question, write the correct answer in the gap. Write one or two words or a number or a date or a time. You will hear a woman called Jemma talking about a video-making course she went on last year.

Woman: It all began when I met someone at a party who invited me to go to see him at work in a TV studio. While I was there, the camera operator let me try filming and it was amazing, so the next day I went to the camera shop as soon as I got up to buy a cheap video camera.

I wanted to learn more, so I decided to sign up for a film course at the weekends. The course was every Saturday morning from 10 till 2. It lasted from September to May with a break in December, and then we had some extra sessions in the afternoon when we reached the final month of the course.

We worked in groups. I was with some really nice people and we created all kinds of productions, like giving beauty tips, teaching dance routines and writing and performing our own comic plays or short dramas.

We didn't need any experience or equipment – they had enough computers for us to share and cameras for each group. The only thing we had to bring was any special clothes we needed. I remember I borrowed several things from my elderly aunt!

At the end of the course, I got a certificate to show I had learnt basic video production skills, and we did a show for friends and relatives, so they could see the work we'd been doing. That was probably the best moment, when I could see how people enjoyed what we had created.

I'd really recommend this course to anyone who wants to find out about making great video clips. I wasn't very good at dancing or speaking in front of the camera, but I'd like to improve my skills at using lights, so I'm sure I'll do another course soon.

Vocabulary

1
1 check / see / look at **2** call / phone **3** play **4** take
5 go **6** share **7** text **8** play / listen to

2
1 tell **2** speak **3** said **4** talk **5** ask for
6 say **7** tell **8** talk

3
1 impolite **2** incomplete **3** impatient
4 unbelievable **5** incorrect **6** impossible
7 uncomfortable **8** inexpensive **9** unfriendly

Reading Part 4

1 C **2** H **3** A **4** E **5** F

Grammar

1
1 (that) we couldn't leave
2 (that) he didn't want
3 (that) they were leaving
4 (that) Zoe would come
5 (that) Harry had lived
6 (that) she had ('d) enjoyed

2
1 Are you going to China?
2 When will you give me a day off?
3 How many people has Mia invited to the party?
4 Do you want to go to the beach?
5 Why can't you stay longer?
6 Where did you buy that dress?

3
1 to write clearly
2 not to use a pen
3 to be careful with spelling
4 not to worry about understanding every word
5 to guess the meaning
6 not to forget to bring an identification document

4
1 ~~said~~ → told **2** ~~can~~ → could **3** ~~to~~ **4** ~~told~~ → asked
5 ~~don't~~ → not to **6** **had** found

5
1 what time it is
2 I can/could take a photo
3 where the IT department is
4 how often you look at your phone
5 where Thomas lives

Writing Part 2 (A story)

1
C A B

2
1 Lucas said, 'I've hurt my leg.'
2 The police officer asked, 'When did you arrive home?'
3 Marina announced, 'I'm going to America.'
4 Charlie replied, 'I don't know.'

3
1 Lucas said (that) he had hurt his leg.
2 The police officer asked when I/we had arrived home.
3 Marina announced (that) she was going to America.
4 Charlie replied (that) he didn't know.

4 *Sample answer*

I slowly opened the box and looked inside. There was nothing there! I felt disappointed because I had expected a present for my birthday.

My wife was watching me. She smiled and told me to look more carefully. Then I saw a tiny envelope. I quickly opened it and read the note inside. It said 'Look outside.' I immediately ran to the window and looked out.

At the front of the house I saw a brand-new black motorbike. I was amazed. I hugged my wife and said, 'Thank you. This is the best present ever! Let's go for a ride.'

Vocabulary extra

Unit 1

1
Across: 1 armchair **5** hall **9** cupboard **11** kitchen **14** sofa **15** garage **16** toilet
Down: 2 cushion **3** blanket **4** balcony **6** wardrobe **7** cooker **8** bath **10** stairs **12** chest **13** bedroom

2
1 cupboard **2** furniture **3** mirror **4** dining
5 drawers **6** kitchen

3
1 on **2** at **3** at **4** on **5** at **6** in

Unit 2

1
Across: 2 staff **4** quit **7** employee **9** retire **11** gap **12** experience
Down: 1 business **3** accommodation **5** apply **6** degree **8** form **10** career

2
1 failed **2** learned / learnt **3** passed **4** took
5 missed **6** set off **7** studied **8** taught

3
1 took, passed **2** set off, missed **3** studied, failed
4 taught, learned / learnt

4
1 ~~do~~ → make **2** ~~make~~ → / have **3** ~~pass~~ → spend
4 ~~learned~~ → taught **5** ~~made~~ → took **6** ~~lose~~ → miss

5
A 1, 4, 7, 8 **B** 3, 5, 9 **C** 2, 6

Unit 3

1
1 chain, helmet **2** bake, recipe **3** brush, watercolours
4 fire, sleeping bag **5** digital, cameras **6** practise, performance
7 queen, board **8** water, wetsuit

2
A**4** B**8** C**6** D**5** E**7** F**2** G**1** H**3**

3
1 feel like / fancy, look forward to **2** suggest
3 take, afford **4** remember, promise **5** run out of, finish
6 fancy / feel like, go off **7** put down, enjoy

Unit 4

1
1 good time **2** dry **3** hire
4 snorkelling **5** peace and quiet **6** trip
7 sightseeing **8** market **9** souvenirs
10 original **11** journey **12** hang

2
Across: 3 palace **5** hall **8** monument **9** youth **10** camping
Down: 1 sports **2** department **4** gallery **6** factory **7** fountain

Unit 5

1
1 miserable **2** cheerful **3** annoyed
4 confused **5** surprised **6** embarrassed
7 frightened **8** jealous

2
Positive: brave, cute, funny, generous, grateful, pleased, satisfied
Negative: afraid, angry, ashamed, bored, depressed, disappointed, guilty

3 *Suggested answers*
1 boring **2** cute **3** angry
4 guilty **5** generous **6** grateful
7 brave **8** satisfying

4
1 tiring **2** surprised **3** frightening **4** relaxing
5 amazed **6** confusing

5
1 about **2** of **3** about **4** with **5** by **6** of

Unit 6

1
Across: **1** fair **7** interval **9** screen **11** director
12 entertainment
Down: **2** audience **3** admission **4** stage **5** review **6** series
8 book **10** row

2
1 opera **2** live **3** chat **4** crowd
5 scenery **6** ballet

3
1 found out **2** gone **3** met **4** known
5 got to know **6** been

Unit 7

1
1 roundabout **2** railway **3** underground
4 car park **5** thunderstorm **6** traffic jam

2
1 roundabout **2** underground **3** railway
4 thunderstorms **5** car park **6** traffic jam

3
1 B **2** D **3** E **4** A **5** C

Unit 8

1
1 f **2** e **3** a **4** c **5** d **6** b

2
1 noisy **2** cheerful **3** modern **4** lazy
5 old-fashioned **6** polite **7** miserable **8** rude

3
1 confident **2** generous **3** selfish **4** quiet
5 anxious **6** kind **7** shy
word in grey: friends

4
1 Danny **2** short, dark, curly **3** Jamie **4** Jamie
5 long, dark **6** straight/short, blonde **7** Sara, Danny
8 Jamie

5
1 made up **2** grew up **3** get on **4** ran out of

Unit 9

1
1 cut **2** high temperature **3** operation
4 medicine **5** plaster cast **6** bandage

2
1 go **2** track **3** scored **4** court
5 went **6** hit **7** do **8** gym
9 pitch **10** beat

3 *Suggested answers*
1 helmet – cycling, ice hockey, American football
2 bat – table tennis, cricket, baseball
3 kit – Most sports have their own 'kit'.
4 net – tennis, badminton, volleyball
5 trainers – athletics, running
6 swimsuit – swimming, beach volleyball, diving
7 racket – tennis, badminton, squash
8 gloves – skiing, snowboarding, football (goalkeeper)

Unit 10

1
Across
2 customer **4** teeth **5** library **7** bakery / baker's
10 hairdresser **11** bill **12** chef
Down
1 bargain **3** vegetarian **6** butcher **8** chemist **9** garage

2
1 mended **2** borrow **3** complained **4** made **5** book

3 *Suggested answers*
Proteins: beef, cheese, chicken, eggs, peanuts, steak, tuna
Carbohydrates: bread, cake, chips, pasta, rice
Fruit & vegetables: apple, cucumber, grapes, lettuce, mushrooms, pear, spinach
Milk & dairy products: butter, cheese, yoghurt
Fats & sugars: butter, cake, chocolate, sweets

4
1 jug **2** fork **3** spoon **4** frying pan
5 knife **6** glass **7** chopsticks **8** plate

Unit 11

1
1 cliff **2** hill **3** beach
4 island **5** rock **6** wood
7 lake **8** valley **9** stream
10 waterfall

2
1 pollution **2** solar **3** wild
4 waste **5** protect **6** danger
7 save **8** aims

3
1 announcement **2** discussion **3** creation
4 excitement **5** enjoyment **6** invitation
7 education **8** reduction

Unit 12

1
1 lies **2** an email **3** your manager
4 speak **5** meaning **6** slang **7** say **8** ask

2
1 c **2** f **3** g **4** d **5** h **6** a **7** b **8** e

3
1 unhealthy **2** patient **3** unfair **4** polite
5 expensive **6** unsuccessful **7** perfect **8** incomplete

Acknowledgements

Photography

Front cover photography by Silke Woweries/Corbis/Getty Images; Yagi Studio/Taxi Japan/Getty Images

Page make up

emc design ltd